Inn Aff the Bar

*This book is dedicated
to footballers and drinkers
past and present.
And
of course those
East Kilbride Wags
Irene and Kate*

*(Special thanks to Ian Baillie for his help with
editing our attempts at English)*

Inn Aff the Bar

Craig Stevenson and John Mackay

Cheapwayround Publishers

East Kilbride

Copyright © 2013 Craig Stevenson and John Mackay

First Published in 2013 by
Cheapwayround Publishers

ISBN No. 978-0-9570252-3-3

Typeset in East Kilbride by
Cheapwayround Publishers

Printed and Bound by
Bell and Bain Ltd.
Burnfield Road, Thornliebank,
Glasgow, G46 7UQ

Cheapwayround Publishers
22 Balfour Terrace, East Kilbride, G75 0JQ

cheapwayroundpub@yahoo.co.uk

Contents

Introduction

This is our fourth book. The first three books were about our wanderings around Scotland using our Bus Passes, keeping our spending to a minimum on all but the absolute necessities; drink. Our mission was to report on the quality of the service in the pubs we visited in the towns and villages the bus took us to. The bus did not always take us to the places we had planned to visit. But to be honest, who cares where we land as long as there is a wee place where we can fill up with beer. Some of readers may think it's not a very noble or inspiring thing to do, if that's the case you have probably bought the wrong book.

In this book, we have completely changed what we are doing. All right, we may be using the Bus Pass to get about, just like our first three books. We may be taking pieces, just like our first three books and we may be reporting on the quality of service in the pubs we visit, just like our first three books, but that's where the similarity ends, sort of.

In this, our fourth outing, we have given ourselves the Herculean task of visiting every Football Club in the four divisions in Scotland, and report on the quality of the bars in their area, and the bar inside the ground, if there is one, and they let us in.

Why are we doing this? Well apart from another great excuse to get away from the wives for the day and have a few pints, the real reason we are producing this book, which we are sure will become an encyclopedia for football fans who enjoy a small refreshment, is that it has never been done before. The quality of the grounds themselves, the pies that are sold at grounds and other unimportant things have been catalogued till the cows come home, but never the quality of the bars around, as well as inside the grounds.

We also tell you at the end of each visit how to get to the ground by bus from Glasgow. We feel this is very important, especially for the over 60's supporters. From Glasgow (or wherever you live) you can see your favourite team's away matches for the price of the admission, and remember, us oldies usually get a good discount. What we are saying is this; +travel by bus, take pieces and enjoy the glory of Scotland as well as a match.

If the thought of the match is too much for you, remember, the pubs stay open and rarely is a good drinking session abandoned because of bad weather. In this encyclopedia we travel from East Kilbride and describe our adventures from there, but we felt that as Glasgow is fairly central to a huge proportion of Scotland's league teams, it would be better to give you the travel details from there.

The importance of this book to Scottish Football fans, as well as the literary world in general cannot be overstated. Anyway, we believe that between us we have created a book that is of some use to a great percentage of the travelling Scottish Public.

For this book we have decided to ditch the old Russell Standard which saw us awarding pint glass logos on a scale of one to five to depict the standard of service we received in any given pub. Every pub bar man/woman would be compared to our favourite barman Russell. Who, in his own mind, is the best barman in Scotland. Although he is still our favourite: times change.

The standard has proved too complicated, mainly because neither of us could ever agree on which figure to award each pub. To that end we have come up with something we can both understand.

From now on each pub will get a logo depicting either a 'Thumbs Up' symbol, ⬆ 'Thumbs Down' symbol, ⬇ or a rather strange looking symbol, ▥ suggesting a midpoint.

Suffice it to say that getting the Thumbs Down is a fairly good indication that the offending pub will, in all likelihood, cease trading very soon.

In the interests of fairness we welcome your comments and suggestions. Simply write them down on the back of a tenner and send them to us care of The Lum, East Kilbride.

Craig and John

Queen of the South

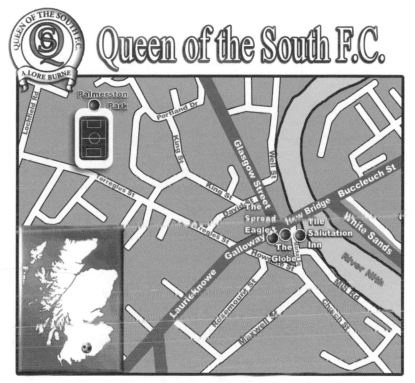

Palmerston Park
Ground opened - 1919

John: Although alphabetically we are getting toward the last of the teams, Queen of the South was the very first visit we made. The reason for this decision was that at the time we were planning to start our trips, we got an e-mail from Dumfries requesting some books. Now as most of you who have read our previous books will know, we usually have to deliver the books ourselves. If we posted them or used a carrier, the small profit we make on the books would disappear. Remember, we've got to pay the printer, and Waterstones take a tiny amount, aye right!

As usual, I had checked the 'Scottish Football Ground Guide' web page to find out the pubs near, or in the actual ground. With this information to hand we left East Kilbride on a lovely January morning. Lovely means it was not pouring down and blowing a gale. The weather recently had been bogging.

I had tried to book us tickets for the bus, but the Stagecoach web site is absolutely hopeless. It is impossible to buy a ticket from one place to another. On the other hand, if you want a four-monthly pass for a left handed French man who only speaks Welsh, no problem, but don't try to buy a simple ticket to Dumfries, no chance. By the way, the Citylink site is great. Stick that in your pipe Stagecoach.

We had just enough time in Hamilton Bus Station to nick into the wee shop which sells everything and get snashters for the bus. I didn't want to get a drink as it was a one hour and forty minute journey and I didn't know if there would be a toilet. There was! The bus was nearly empty and we sat a couple of rows behind the driver which allowed us to hear a conversation between the driver and a wee old man (our age) who wanted to talk to the driver continually. One great thing we heard was the driver telling this wee man not to worry about the seat belts. I quote 'If it's your time to go, it's your time to go'. Normally you get a 10 minute health and safety lecture. I think I prefer his outlook.

The run down to Dumfries was very nice and after a wee sleep we arrived in the border town about one o'clock.

The first job at hand was to deliver our books to Waterstones. This completed, we wandered back down through the town to the bus station to check the time of our return trip. I had checked on the 'Traveline' web site the night before, but it's not to be trusted. Neither are the employees you ask, as the guy we spoke to for the return journey

10

times told us what turned out to be a load of crap, and he was the driver! Never mind, we got home ok.

Craig; We spent a lot of time trying to decide in what order we should visit the football clubs. John got vocally excited about all the lovely spreadsheets he could make up for this project. I actually felt a wee bit guilty when I ruined his best laid plans by suggesting that we find out which shops needed books delivered and chose one that had a team playing a home game on a day that suited us.

That's how we ended up in Dumfries for our first chapter and what a good start it was. I had actually delivered books to Dumfries before so I knew exactly where we were going. John, on the other hand took every opportunity to head off in the wrong direction.

John; We walked the short journey up to the ground, the legendary 'Palmerston Park', home of the 'Doonhamers', a great nickname. This is an old and traditional ground, which means it's in a run down state and needs a bit of money spent on it, money nobody has. But it's the supporters that count, and what a great crowd of nut cases the ones we met were.

The first thing we had to do was find the bar attached to the ground. I had checked the Queen of the South web page and found out it was in the West Stand. When we got up to the ground Craig smiled and asked me if I knew where West was. I didn't want to give him the satisfaction of me admitting I had no idea, so to cut a long story short, we walked right round three sides of the blasted ground before finding the bar in the West Stand.

My excuse to Craig was that the sun was behind a cloud so I couldn't tell which direction was West. His reply is not worth repeating in a classy book like what this is!

The sign outside said Queen of the South lounge bar. So in we went, and glad we were that we did. It was a great wee bar with memorabilia all over the walls. Most of the guys in the bar were wearing the colours and the atmosphere in the place was great.

We introduced ourselves to some of the guys at the bar and told them what we were doing. They took us into their company right away and regaled us with stories of people and games that have made the club one of the legends in Scottish Football.

11

Derek, Rab, Maradona and loads of other guys we met do a great job raising money for the youth team in the club through their 'Barflies' supporters club.

Apart from raffles and other normal things, one of the more unusual ideas they tried was a tasteful, but slightly risky, almost naked calendar. This was well before the Calendar Girls came on the scene, but the manageress in the bar at that time was a little bit stuck up and would not allow the club lounge bar to be used for excess flesh to be shown. She probably had too much herself. Don't know if I'm allowed to say that!

That being said, one photo was taken of the shy and retiring Frankie Kirk wearing only a club scarf tied round his waist and hanging down between his legs. I commented on the length of the scarf being almost to his knees. Without any embarrassment, he assured me that it was taken on a cold December day, or the scarf would have been well below his knees. These guys are certainly not Queens of the South!

We also met Jim Thomson, captain of the Scottish Cup Final team who went so close to beating Rangers in a great Hampden final.

Jim Thomson meets a couple of Barflies

Another great sportsman was in the bar, David Bogie, one of Scotlands' greatest ever Rally Champions.

The club chairman was also in the bar enjoying a drink. The place has a great atmosphere and is one of the most welcoming bars I have ever visited.

One of the things I like to find out is local popular drinks. In Dumfries it's a 'Caribbean', which is Morgan Spice with Coke, and a dash of Guinness. I think I asked Derek what size of dash was allowed; he said he wasn't sure but they all got theirs in a pint glass. Sounds great to me!

Time was marching on and we had at least another couple of bars to visit, so with a heavy heart and light wallet (Jim talked me into buying a couple of raffle tickets), we said our goodbyes, wished the boys all the best for today and the rest of the season and headed down towards our next bar.

On the way, we went via the wall behind one of the terraces on which some of the clubs history is depicted on a series of Murals which are brilliantly painted on four panels of the wall. I have forgotten the name of the lady who did them, but she is brilliant. They are well worth a trip to have a look.

Craig; We decided to head over to Queen of the South's stadium as John had found out that there was a supporters club there. Now his only problem was finding it. Apparently the club was at the back of the West Stand, so obviously John turned due East and wandered off. Eventually I managed to get him round to the club and we had our first pint of the day.

John's direction-finding improved immediately and he found the bar easily. I would have to admit that he has become very proficient at this ever since we adopted the 'kitty system' a few years back. Whether this is just a coincidence or a serious character flaw I would not like to comment, but I have my suspicions.

It was still quite early and there was plenty of room at the bar. Actually the place is called 'The Palmerston Lounge Bar'.

We were served quickly and efficiently by a friendly barman so we immediately felt at home. I decided to take a photo of the bar just to remind myself of the layout of the place. As ever, as soon as my camera cleared its case John started posing outrageously directly in front of me.

I just thank god there wasn't a microphone lying about the room or it would have been sing-along-a-John time for a good half hour.

Despite not getting to sing in the spotlight, he was soon the centre of attention. I did try to explain to the guys standing at the bar that I was only taking a snap-shot of their lounge, but I was ignored as they crowded round John, who was still posing like a big haddie in the middle of the lounge.

Somehow or other, between the time it took me to focus the cameras and press the button, he managed to produce a copy of our last book and was flashing it around like 'Del Boy' on steroids. Personally I think he must have a shoulder holster for it. Definitely a bit of a fast draw!

I would imagine that he would tell a different story. Probably making out that it takes me so long to take a picture that he could have written half a chapter of the book before I had the focusing done.

Anyway, the lads at the bar wanted to have a look at John's copy of 'Goin' Roon the Edge' and made a nice fuss about it. Maybe they were just humouring the two old strange geezers who had wandered into their club, but I like to think they were genuinely interested.

I don't actually remember how many pints we had in there, but it was a few and they were good. The patter was good as well. We got to know a bit about the history of Queen of the South and enjoyed a few good tales of the things only football supporters get up to.

Frankie's story had the potential to get an X certificate. He showed us a picture of himself at a recent birthday party which had been held in the club. I took a photo of it as, to be honest, it defies description.

If this was a Channel four television programme, someone would now be saying something like, 'viewers are warned that the following programme contains scenes which are likely to put you off your tea'.

Personally, and obviously, I can't speak for John here, but I don't like pictures of naked men, even if they have kept themselves in good shape and are in no way scary looking. Unfortunately for anyone unlucky enough to have caught a glimpse of Frankie's photo, he doesn't actually fit into these two categories. He barely fits into anything.

Looking on the bright side, it is only a photo; most of us were lucky enough not to be there when he was strutting his stuff.

14

I'm only kidding, Frankie is a great guy and up for a laugh. He told us that he had suggested a calendar shoot for charity. Legend has it that it was only called off when the committee found out that Frankie wanted the team's female support to strip off along with him.

Frankie gets his kit off

That might have been a wee bit seedy but you have to give him ten out of ten for effort, depraved effort perhaps, but he's definitely a trier.

The other guys in the supporters club, 'The Barflies', were also good for a laugh and we thoroughly enjoyed our stay. It was almost a pity that the football had to spoil our day. We couldn't stay to watch the game.

John; The next pub we ventured into was the 'Spread Eagle Inn'. It was getting onto three o'clock and the pub was a bit quiet. There were a few guys in the bar and I asked the barmaid why they were not at the game, only to be told that they were Celtic and Rangers supporters in for a few pints and to watch the racing. They should have been up the road supporting their local team if you ask me, although I didn't mention it to them. They looked a bit fierce. It was a nice bar and worth a visit if you are in town.

15

Because of time restraints, we only had one pint, then wandered round the corner and into 'The Globe Inn'. This was a great bar. As I always say, it's the guy (or girl) behind the bar, and the regulars that make a bar great.

Although the game had started and the bar was quiet, the owner Tom Nisbet was terrific company. He introduced us to a regular, David Blackie, who is Belgian. Although he has lived in Dumfries for over 30 years, I think, he had no trace of a Belgian accent, although I've no idea what it would sound like anyway. He told us that he has split up from his wife, who was Scottish. She now lives in Belgium and he lives in Dumfries. That's how a marriage should work.

'The Globe' is the home of 'The Barflies', so as well as being a great bar, it is carrying out a first class service for the town, I think.

Although we were having a great time, and we had already decided to go for a later bus, if there was one, Tom said we must take time to visit the pub across the road called 'The Salutation Inn'. So we did, and it was another smashing pub with a great barman, I've forgotten his name, and great regulars. We enjoyed a couple of pints, but before we left Dumfries, we felt we had to go back over to 'The Globe' to have another one, or was it two, and say farewell to the home of the 'Barflies'.

One of the great things about the day was that 'The Doonhamers' had an excellent result. After losing an early goal and having a man sent off, they rallied and ran out 5-1 winners against Arbroath. They are now well clear at the top of the league.

Although it is the hospitality, and not the football, that is important to us, it was good to know that 'The Barflies' would sleep happily, and pissed, tonight.

Craig; *When we were planning this day out we had both, independently, looked at the internet to find pubs in or near the ground, and of course we had both come up with exactly the same list so there were no surprises.*

The next nearest pub was 'The Spread Eagle' just down at the crossroads near the park. I love that name, it has such a good mental image for me. Not being an ornithologist, I obviously see the image of a well spent day out rather than Scotland's national bird in majestic flight.

Back in my youth, in my old home town of Auchinleck, we might also have called the art of getting spread eagled, as getting starfished! Happy days.

16

What a disappointment it was then to enter this Dumfries pub. It wasn't empty exactly, it just lacked any atmosphere whatsoever. I'm thinking, bus shelter with central heating. It was probably much livelier earlier on, before kick off at 3.00pm, but I'm not so sure. It seemed like one of these racing pubs. Back in the bad old days there would probably be a bookies runner hovering around waiting to take bets along to the nearest Turf Accountant.

Actually, that was always what really wasted my Saturday morning pub session. I hated, with a passion, listening to the horse racing on pub tellies. This pub brought all that back.

To be honest, the girl who served us was pleasant enough and the beer was really good, but the atmosphere just wasn't right. It gave me the idea that perhaps we were in for a bit of a let down after 'The Palmerston'. After all, most guys would be round at the park watching the game.

When we moved just around the corner to 'The Globe', my pessimistic mood didn't change. Going in to this pub increased the bar population by 66% if you didn't count the barman. Then again you would be making a big mistake if you didn't count the barman! Not for the first time we learned the lesson, it's not the pub, it's the people!

I've been in really busy pubs where you might as well be in there alone, bu, thankfully we had wandered into a pub with only one customer and a barman, where we were treated as friends immediately.

Although we didn't actually meet very many pub regulars - they were at the game, where they should have been -we really got the feel of the place, and what a great place!

If for whatever reason you find that you have to move to Dumfries, be it work related or perhaps witness relocation, you could do a hell of a lot worse than choose 'The Globe' as your new local.

I might be a wee bit biased of course as our host Tom Nisbet turned out to be a former pupil at my old school in Kilmarnock. Although the place was almost empty we were entertained by some great stories about the pub and its clientele.

Tom told us that his regulars were always up for a laugh. On one occasion he got back from holiday to find that some of his regulars had disposed of the pub's piano. Since it was completely out of tune he suspected that it might have been a gang of music lovers. It has long

17

since been replaced by an electronic keyboard. Apparently the customers are as tuneless as they've always been.

John having a ball in 'The Globe'

You would imagine that the landlord might be a bit wary of going off on holiday again, but not Tom. When he returned from his next break he discovered that the whole pub had been redecorated. I didn't fall into the trap of saying what a bloody mess they made of it, just in case it had been done up again since then. To be honest 'The Globe' is a nice tidy pub and when it's customers are not off watching 'The Doonhamers', I am sure it's a lively, friendly place to spend a few hours. It would be very easy just to stay where we were and enjoy the beer and the patter, but we forced ourselves to move on. Actually we only moved about 30 feet. 'The Salutation Inn' was much busier than 'The Globe'. I put this down to the fact that there were very few supporters in 'The Globe'. There seemed to be an even mixture of men and women in the bar, which, let's be honest, doesn't tend to make for outrageous fun days out.

Don't get me wrong, 'The Salutation' was a nice friendly pub where we had a great time talking to the customers. It just wasn't what us two old reprobates enjoy, when we are allowed to.

Rather than go to the bother of finding another pub to visit, we simply tottered back across the road to 'The Globe' for a final drink or two and a few more laughs.

18

We get a cheery greeting in the Salutation Inn

John; I think we got the six o'clock bus. The journey home, and my sleep, was interrupted on more than one occasion by two men, who both had dogs, arguing with each other. I think it almost ended up with fisticuffs. Thankfully, one of the arscholes got off at Moffat, and after five further minutes of the wee self - important driver shouting god knows what to god knows who, we headed back to Hamilton without further dog loving loudmouths making arses of themselves.

We were anticipating getting the old 201 up to East Kilbride, but got a surprise when we stopped next to an X16. The X16 takes 15 minutes less than the 201 to get to EK. We had 10 minutes to spare, so we went back into the wee shop that sells everything you want to eat, if you're drunk that is. I had Chicken Pakora, with the red sauce and everything. It was great.

Craig is a very nervous eater, and was worried about the ability of one wee woman to be able to supply food from a menu with about 100 items without the quality being impaired. I was starving and didn't care. It was great.

We got back to EK with me eating the Pakora on the bus. The smell was driving Craig mad, but he wouldn't admit it.

We both got a bag of chips at the EK bus station and ate them walking up to 'The Lum' for a final nightcap and to review our day visiting the fabulous 'Doonhamers'.

I think I spent about £40 today. Now I know many people will say 'what a drunk', or words to that effect, and many people will wonder how I can drink about 10 or so pints with my bladder condition. The answer is that today I went onto Vodkas and Soda after about four pints. A glass of Vodka has only a third of the alcohol of a pint of lager, if you don't have doubles!

Craig; Apart from a minor shouting match between passengers and the less than helpful intervention of the driver, the journey home was uneventful.

Our visit to the land of 'The Doonhamers' was a great success, three of the drinking establishments we sampled being well above average. The fourth one is probably best forgotten, which to drinkers of our capacity and age will be easily done.

Pubs we visited:

Q of the S Lounge;

Spread Eagle Inn;

The Globe Inn;

The Salutation Inn;

How to get there by bus:

X74 from Buchanan St. Bus station to Dumfries.

Dunfermline

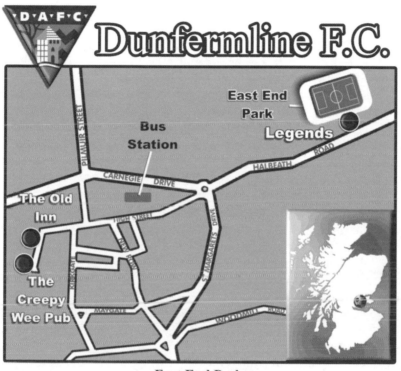

East End Park
Ground opened - 1885

John; 'The Pars'. A great nickname. We travelled East to visit Dunfermline on the 12th January, 2013. Thought I'd mention this as within a few weeks I will have no idea of when the trip was made. I don't think it matters when we do the visits as long as we enjoy ourselves, drink is consumed, and most importantly, the service is great. We also try to meet a few of the supporters.

As you know by now, if there is a Waterstones in the town we are visiting, we give them a phone to see if they need any of the books.

This helps to cover the cost of the trip; well it would if they wanted about 100 books, which they never do.

Today was slightly complicated. Kirkcaldy had e-mailed us to say they wanted three of each of the titles, nine books in all. The profit on nine books would cover a couple of rounds if we were lucky.

Not to be put off, I checked to see if Raith Rovers were at home, they weren't. What a bummer. Then I had a great idea. Dunfermline is on the bus route to Kirkcaldy, so I checked and found out that they were at home. I chanced my luck and phoned the Waterstones store in Dunfermline and discovered they wanted 10 books.This was magic. A day away and a profit, well almost. Does life get any better than this?

Craig came up with what he said was a great idea. As the bus would stop in Dunfermline on the way to Kirkcaldy, where we were only going to deliver books then get back on a bus to Dunfermline, he suggested that he would get off in Dunfermline, deliver the books and check the place out in time for my arrival back about an hour and a half later. This, he claimed would save us a lot of time for more drinks.

I couldn't fault the logic. I could fault the fact that he never suggested me getting the extra bevy time in Dunfermline. Never mind, I thought, he is really bad with the arthritis and these buses can be real bone shakers. What a guy I am, and modest with it.

We had a fairly early start, so the night before I packed up the books and made my pieces, my old favourite, Corned Beef with lashings of English Mustard.

So about quarter to nine on the Saturday morning I wandered down the well worn path to collect Craig and get the No. 18 into Glasgow. If I had a pound for every time we got that bus into Glasgow I would be able to give up writing this nonsense!

It was a quick run into Glasgow and we managed to get an earlier bus which left 20 minutes before our planned one. Craig was really pleased, it meant that I had no time to buy my ultra right wing Daily Mail and he reckoned the earlier bus would give him more time in Dunfermline for a few pints before I would arrive back. It didn't work out that way!

It was a cold and bright day for a change and we had a lovely run to Dunfermline. Craig got off with his load of books and a smile on his face at the thought of a few extra pints. I carried on to Kirkcaldy, delivered the books and then got a text from him telling me he had left his money and his plastic cards at home and couldn't even buy himself a coffee. If I had been sitting on a chair I would have fallen off it laughing.

Craig; Dunfermline is not a place I have spent much time. Until today's trip I reckon I couldn't have spent much more than 20 minutes in the place, and that was spent waiting for a bus to get me out of it. Today we would be visiting Dunfermline Athletic's stadium and a couple of the town's watering holes. As it turned out, because of a catastrophic piece of bad luck, and poor planning, I would be seeing quite a bit of the town.

The reason for choosing Dunfermline for today's little adventure was quite simple. The town had all the elements for a good day out. There was a senior football team playing at home; there were pubs open; and last but certainly not least, there was a branch of Waterstones which required fresh supplies of our books.

We like to pretend that we are doing something useful when we go away for the day. Not that anyone would be looking for excuses from us for taking off for a day on the bevy. It's really just ourselves we are kidding. The money we could get from all the books we were delivering wouldn't cover half of the expenses.

I really wish they had paid us cash in hand on this occasion as that would have saved me a lot of pain and embarrassment. When we were setting out for the day I had managed to convince John that he should stay on the bus and travel on to Kirkcaldy while I got off at Dunfermline. He had books to deliver there so it made sense to split it up. It certainly made sense to me at any rate. While he was bouncing along the road to Kirkcaldy I could be sitting sampling the beer in two or three of Dunfermline's finest ale houses. It was a great plan but unfortunately it was me who planned it, so naturally it was doomed.

I was really feeling pleased with myself as I delivered my parcel of books to the book store. It had proved very easy to find the shop, which surprised me as I usually manage, when faced with a choice of only two possible directions, to go for the wrong one. This time everything was working perfectly. Come to think of it that should have been my first warning. Out in the street I was spoiled for choice in the area of good looking pubs. In fact, I was so confident of finding a really good 'Howff' that I took some time out to photograph the famous Dunfermline Abbey.

On my way down to the Abbey, I noticed an odd wee pub that in my opinion warranted investigation. It was called 'The Creepy Wee Pub'.

Just before I pushed the door open I did my usual check. I always try to make sure that I don't take out all of my money at once when I go into a strange pub. As it turned out that wasn't going to be a problem today. I had no money whatsoever in any of my pockets. To say I was devastated just doesn't go far enough. Only my tough Auchinleck upbringing saved me from crying like a big wean. Although I have to admit that there was a fair amount of lip trembling going on.

John; After a call to Irene, she found all his money and cards in the washing machine. You couldn't make this up. Craig was raging at Irene, but not to her face. Luckily I had money and plastic as well as a begging Craig. Great start to the trip.

On the way out of Dunfermline the bus passed the ground not too far from the bus station, so I phoned Craig and told him to start walking to the ground and I would get off the bus and meet him there. Well that was the plan before my helpful driver put a spoke in the works. When the ground was in sight, I wandered up to ask him if I could get off at the ground. Now he could have told me politely that he was not allowed to stop till the bus station, which was the case. But no, this little Hitler gave me dog's abuse and told me to sit down. I know I've said it before, but a large proportion of the people in Scotland who are supposed to be helpful to the public are complete arseholes.

Before we got to the bus station the bus passed Craig who was by now walking the other way. I had texted him to tell him of my run - in with the driver, so he was good enough to give the driver the finger as we passed.

Craig; After a few minutes I regained my composure and texted Irene to get her to check if I'd left my money in the pocket of the shirt I had been going to wear before I changed my mind. Stupidly I had expected a certain amount of sympathy from her but for some reason she thought it was hilariously funny. The text I got back said that she had found my money when she had emptied the washing machine. I toyed with the idea of grassing her in for laundering money, but decided not to as my phone was running out of battery power. Thank god I hadn't left it in my shirt pocket!

I did have to let John know and he took it really well. In fact he sent me a rather amusing text, at least he thought it was amusing.

Eventually I made my way to the stadium and waited for 'money bags Mackay' to make an appearance. I had noticed a young man with a clipboard standing just inside the doorway to the supporters club bar. he checked off everyone's name as they came in. To my mind this suggested that entry was either by invitation or strictly members only, so I didn't bother asking. With the kind of luck I was having it was quite possible that they would set the dogs on me. Just then moneybags Mackay arrived. As I've said before, this man is missing the embarrassment gene. He produced a copy of one of our books and started giving the lad at the door his speech about us being semi-famous travel writers. It turned out the lad was a very nice guy and said it would be fine for us to go into the club.

John; By the time I caught up with Craig he was at the ground with the news that we were not allowed into 'Legends Bar' in the stand because the lad on the door told him we were not on the list. Charm has never been a strong point with Craig. I had a wee word with the lad, a lovely guy called Andy Aitken and explained to him why we were at the ground. He was a very helpful and intelligent young lad and allowed us in and hoped we would have a great day.

It is good to know that there are still some young people in Scotland who know how to behave, even when they have some power over the public, even if it's only on the door to the bar at East End Park.

It was a fantastic bar with plenty of supporters having a few pints before the game, which was against Airdrie, I think. As you know, the game is not the point of our visits.

We sat down beside a crowd of regulars and immediately were included in their company. When we told them what the reason for our visit was, they were only too happy to relate dozens of stories about the club and their part in it.

I have forgotten some of their names (through drink), but I'm sure Stevie, Kenny and Bruce were to the fore. They run a club within the club called 'Pars Alive'. They raise money doing crazy things. It is no exaggeration when I say that the money they raise is helping the club to stay in business. It is because of great guys like them that clubs like Dunfermline are managing to keep going, although from what we were told, this state of affairs can't go on for long.

They run a supporters club out of Kincardine, I think, and go to all the away games, doing daft things on the road. The one I remember them telling me was a Tapas trip, where everybody had to bring a different Tapas. God knows the state the coach must have been in when they got home.

Some of them are members of The Tartan Army, and follow Scotland everywhere. I didn't say they were sensible.

As supporters go this lot are well up to Par

They introduced us to a slightly older guy called 'Dennis the Pole'. He's called this because he is a Pole, from Poland. He has lived in Dunfermline since he was young and the guys told us a great story about him when he was a boy about 11 years old. Dumfermline had just won the Scottish Cup, in 1968 against Hearts, I think, and he was sitting on his father's shoulders in a pub in Dunfermline while his father celebrated the historic event. The word came that the bus with the victorious team was about to pass the pub, so Dennis's dad, in his excitement, forgot his son was on his shoulders and raced out the door to see the team. You can just picture it; wee Dennis nearly got decapitated. Days later when he recovered, the doctors said that he should be all right, but might be prone to some crazy habits. Dennis has supported Dunfermline since that day!

I started talking to two old guys, Gordon and Norrie. They were great company and Gordon told me he was in the RAF during the Second World War. Their patter was great and when they left to get their

26

regular seats, I told them how much I had enjoyed their company and meeting a man who had been a pilot in the war. Gordon looked at me and said, 'You didn't tell me you were a pilot in the war'. You can have great conversations with older guys, like me!

Pars regulars Ally & Joan

We gave the guys one of our books to raffle and will send them the other two when we get home, if they remember to e-mail us their address. If not I am just going to send them to the park.

They gave us the name of good pubs to visit in the town and then they left us to go to the match. It's these guys that are keeping Scottish football alive.

Craig; I'm really glad we did get in. What a good time we had. The bar was really nice, very modern and airy. We were served straight away and I have to admit it was a really good pint. So much for all my theories about young bar staff not being able to serve a decent pint!

Quite soon after getting our beers we got talking to a bunch of fairly young supporters. They were very interesting to talk to and even laughed at some of our attempts to be funny. That always earns extra points on our survey of good places to visit. It turns out that the guys run a supporters club called 'Pars Alive' and raise funds for the club. We had a great time talking and laughing with them. These boys are real fans, as in the original meaning of the word fanatics. I really enjoyed the contrast when we got talking to a couple of old boys. They maybe weren't as vocal as the young guys, but they were every bit as committed to their team.

27

Just before we left, Kenny told us about a couple of pubs we should visit when we made our way back into the town. Obviously, as soon as we hit the fresh air outside we made straight for them. You just can't beat a personal recommendation.

John; We were having a great day, so much so that we reckoned we would have to get a bus back along the road to the town centre. When we got off the bus, Craig was sure he knew exactly where the bars were, and he was right for a change.

The first thing I had to do was get to a 'Hole in the Wall' for some money as Craig had been spending mine all day. It was then into a great pub called 'The Old Inn', I think. Everything was becoming a blur at this stage. It was in this pub in 1885 that Dunfermline Athletic were formed and Ryan, the barman, and a couple of great blokes who were regulars told us the history of the club.

I feel I should apologise that I don't remember any of the interesting stuff they told me, but the reason for our trips is to find out if the pubs servicing the grounds are up to scratch, and this one definitely was. It was a brilliant pub and so were the barman and regulars. We had a great time. Dunfermline is really my kind of place.

Ryan told us that the pub next door was a really old pub as well and worth a visit. It was called 'The Scary Wee Bar' I think. I must be honest and say that by now I was struggling with talking, let alone remembering what I was talking about. The pub was nice and atmospheric, but Craig reckoned the barman was the scariest thing about the place. I'm sure we had a great time in it anyway.

Craig; *To be honest, I was a wee bit sceptical of their first choice. 'The Old Inn' doesn't have what you might call 'street presence'. It is ordinary looking to a great degree. I would have chosen the pub next door to it, the aforementioned 'Creepy Wee Pub' as the more interesting place to visit. However, by this time I had begun to realize that I was not on a winning streak that day, and opted to go with the guy's advice. That was the first smart thing I had done all day! I had no idea the pub was as old as it turned out to be. Inside you get the idea that this place has got some history behind it. The thick walls and the layout immediately let you know that this pub has been there for a long, long time. I suppose there had been a clue in the name of the place, but I've never been too quick on the uptake.*

28

Ryan chats to a couple of old guys in The Old Inn

We had a great time chatting to the staff and customers. Added to that, the beer was pretty good as well. 'The Old Inn' has a historic connection with Dunfermline Athletic FC. The club was formed in that very pub back in 1885. The owner, Mark, told us that the team was actually created by the cricket club as a way of keeping their players fit during the winter months. While we were at the bar I couldn't help noticing that our barman, Ryan, was dressed in the now standard uniform of the ned, i.e. tracksuit, trainers and all that nonsense. It was like a breath of fresh air when he mentioned he was a football coach working with the SFA. Usually wearing sports gear is an indication that you can't, or won't, walk the length of yourself. We got talking to some great guys up at the bar. They claimed to be rugby men by way of explaining why they weren't at the game.

Our stay in 'The Old Inn' was very pleasant and I would thoroughly recommend a visit. In fact the only thing I found to complain about was their suggestion that we should visit the pub next door.

Visiting 'The Scary Wee Bar' was in my considered opinion a big mistake. We should have stayed where we were. I got the impression that we were intruding on the barman's rest period. He seemed to be permanently parked in his seat up by the window. John seemed to remember things differently, but there is an obvious reason for that. So obvious in fact that I'm not even going to mention all the vodka he had been choking back all day.

29

John; So we must have left and got the bus, because the next thing I knew I was arriving at Buchanan Street Bus Station, refreshed and reasonably sober, but with a slight thirst.

'The Horseshoe' solved the thirst problem before we got on the train to EK. I phoned Kate to let her know we were on the train and were going to have one in 'The Monty'. She said she would pick us up after our one (or maybe two), I think she knew the state we were in. We met Jackie, my son Alasdair's wife's father and had an enjoyable end to the day.

Dunfermline supporters have got some great bars to visit in the town, as well as a great facility in the stand.

Sometimes I remember to tell you how much I spent, sometimes I forget. I'm not a real writer remember. Anyway, today I started off with £40 in my pocket and ended up with £60. Assuming I lifted £100 from the Hole in the Wall, that's £80. We'll have to shift a hell of a lot of books to cover that bar bill.

If Craig ever gives me the £40 he must owe me, I will only have spent £40 on drink. That's a hell of a lot of drink, and to be honest, I remember the guys at the bar in the ground buying us a drink as well. Ah well, what can you say?

Pubs we visited:

Dunfermline Lounge;

The Old Inn;

The Creepy Wee Pub;

How to get there by bus:

X27 Glasgow to St. Andrews stops at Dunfermline Bus Station.

30

Dumbarton

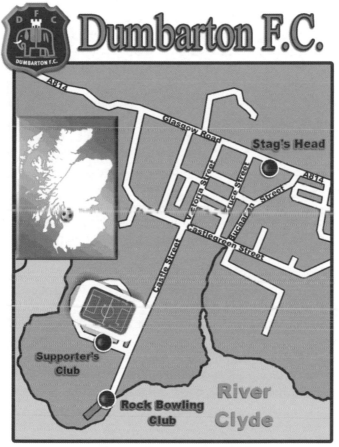

Ground opened - 2000

John; Dumbarton, 'The Sons', a good old nickname which dates back to somewhere. I assume, probably wrongly, that the new stadium is named after someone, which is usually a bad idea. But Bet Butler sounds like someone from 'Gone with the Wind', so it's ok with me.

Our trip was carried out on Saturday, 26th January, 2013. Today's game was against the Hamilton Accies. When I was young, in the politically incorrect days, this used to be a common rhyming slang name for our cousins from abroad who owned corner shops in Glasgow, and fine people they are. In these days, we did not mean any harm, it was just the way of the world, well, the Glasgow world. But back to today's politically correct times.

It is an easy trip, doon the watter to Dumbarton. The cheap train ticket into Glasgow Central, wander across Hope Street and then the Number One First Bus was the information given to me on my visit to the web. I was not, as I usually am, apprehensive about the information it spits out as I knew there were dozens of buses that go along Argyle Street on their way to Dumbarton and other places on the North shore of the Clyde.

This was our third trip in this book. The first two had gone very well, and we were getting into the hang of how to find the right people to talk to. This means getting to the bar in the ground a couple of hours before kick off to meet the older worthies for some great stories of the team, and more importantly, the bars in the area of the grounds.

When I checked on the web for ground information, I found out that it was a fairly new ground. I assume the old ground was in a good position and the land was worth a lot for re-development as a supermarket or houses and the club was given a new ground in a more out of the way place. I aim to find out the truth during today's visit, although, to be honest, I am more interested in the pubs in the new ground's surrounding area.

It was not too early a start and at about 11.00am I picked up Craig to get the old 201 along to Hairmyres Station to catch the 11.30am train into Glasgow Central. Although we have to pay £1.20 for an old folks return on the train, we prefer it to the hour journey the bus takes. We are long enough on buses and £1.20 wouldn't even buy you a half pint. My casual approach to spending money takes your breath away sometimes.

Today's slight inconvenience, or a nightmare for Craig, was caused by the fact that you can't get a concession ticket from the machine at Hairmyres station so you have to rely on the conductor selling you one on the train. In the old days, you were glad if you could get away without buying a ticket, but now they have put those barriers up in Glasgow Central, so you need a ticket to get off the platform. If any of you have been to the Central Station recently, you will have seen that the crazy thing is that there are more staff helping you to get through the barriers than they used to have to collect the tickets without all this crap new technology.

Anyway, because it was a Saturday morning and it was a big and busy train, the conductor didn't have time to get to everybody who wanted to buy a ticket, or to quote Craig, a lazy B!!

This means getting off the train as quickly as you can and queue up to buy one on the platform in Glasgow Central, so you can get off the same platform; is it just me or is the world daft? We were fairly near the front but the man in the ticket booth was useless. Eventually another man with a mobile ticket machine appeared and said 'next please' We were next, so Craig, who had the money, dived up to him, only to be told that the woman behind him was next. You couldn't make it up. I think it's the uniform that makes wee Glasgow men think they're important. We eventually got our tickets and Craig got out a hanky to dry his ears which had got soaked with all the steam coming out of them.

We went down the moving stairs and out of the station at the corner of Hope Street and Argyle Street. I reckoned we still had about five minutes till our bus was due, but there was one waiting at the lights, so we did our impersonation of two people trying to run for a bus. We got it no bother.

Craig; Today's trip was to Dumbarton FC's stadium. This actually came as a bit of a surprise as I didn't know Dumbarton had a football team. As a matter of fact, since I didn't see a ball kicked at any time while we were there, I couldn't swear to its existence.

Anyway, we set off on the road to Dumbarton at about 11.00am. We had decided to let the train take the strain, as far as Glasgow Central at least.

The train was very busy but I had no reason to worry as we got seats quite easily. What I failed to realise was that the ticket inspector had no chance whatsoever of reaching us before we got to Glasgow.

This meant that we would have to join the scrum at the ticket office on the platform. About a year ago Scotrail in their wisdom erected automatic barriers at the station. Like all the other passenger harassment schemes inflicted on us nowadays this is meant to be a cost cutting measure. It supposedly means that fewer people are needed to check the tickets of passengers leaving the train.

Of course now they need extra staff to sell tickets on the platform and even more staff to sort the barriers when they decide to chew up your ticket.

Far be it for me to tell them how to do a proper job of things, but it does occur to me that if they actually hired enough conductors for the trains in the first place they might save themselves some money. And as a by-product they might even make life a wee bit easier for the people who pay their wages.

Apart from a few queue - jumpers trying to push their way in we were relatively happy to wait our turn at the ticket office. Of course we had no way of knowing that Scotrail hadn't finished with us just yet.

The wee man on the portable ticket machine might have been having an off - day or, as I suspected, he was a bit of a nutter.

Being next in the queue, when he roared, 'Next!' I thought he meant that I should step forward and part with my cash. Not so. Apparently the person behind me was more worthy of his attention.

I turned my attention to the ticket booth and waited to be served. The guy sitting in the booth did not inspire confidence. He did his best to get me my ticket but to be honest it was like watching a chimp trying to reprogramme a computer. Every time his machine failed to spit out my ticket he would just shrug his shoulders and laugh. Personally I couldn't see the funny side of it but John seemed fairly amused.

John; It was a nice new and very comfortable bus and we enjoyed our free trip down to Dumbarton.

I know we complain about everything, including bus drivers, but today's guy gave us one of our best laughs ever. A wee woman rushed up to the front and told the driver he had gone past her stop. Quick as a flash he replied, 'I'm very sorry dear, but my course on mind reading is not till next week'; it went right over her head.

I ate my pieces on the bus. For some reason I was starving, and I don't think it was the munchies. Kate had made them, they were plain bread and sandwich spread. They tasted great even though it was Light Sandwich Spread.

Most foods you buy nowadays have a 'Light' version, and they usually taste crap, but this one was not too bad. We alighted (got off) under the bridge at Dumbarton East station and went into 'The Stag's Head'. I had read about this pub on the supporter's web page. To be fair to the guy who wrote the review, he only said it was handy for the ground. Inside it was a bit like a run down Wetherspoons. A new one is bad enough but this place was a bit tired looking, though the drink was great and very cheap. The couple of pints were only about £4.70. It's worth a visit if only for the prices.

Craig; *The bus journey up to Dumbarton passed without incident and we got off just down the road from our first pub of the day, The Stag's Head.*

This suited us fine as we were both ready for a pint. To be frank The Stag's Head was a bit of a disappointment.

It looked like the original version of a Wetherspoon's pub. Perhaps Mr Wetherspoon stopped in there for a quick pint one day and liked what he saw.

There seems to be a trend nowadays to cover the walls of even the smallest pub with large flat-screen televisions. I just don't get it. Maybe it wouldn't be so bad if they showed a western on one of them instead of wall to wall sport.

I got the impression that The Stag's Head was trying to achieve the best of both worlds in that it is kitted out like a lounge bar but tries to attract the clientele of an ordinary public bar.

Personally I thought there was far too much carpet in the place. I'm a traditionalist after all.

On the plus side, the barmaid was very nice and the beer was very good and reasonably priced. Actually as soon as I realised how much the beer cost I changed my mind about The Stag's Head. It's a great place to visit.

On the way round to the stadium John kept going on about the Bowling Green he claimed to have found on his Google search of the area. Apparently visiting fans gather there before games. I could see no sign of one and suggested that maybe John's skill with the computer was on a par with that of his timetable reading. He wasn't amused.

John; Our next port of call was the bar in the ground itself. The web page said it was for home supporters only. I find it funny in today's hard times that they are doing themselves out of the chance of selling a good few extra pints. I can't imagine the Hamilton Accies supporters running amok after a couple of pints.

We approached the main door in the centre of the stand and asked the two security girls just inside the door how we could get into the bar. One of the girls, who Craig reckoned was a member of the Hitler Youth, was very officious and said we had to go to the end of the stand, pay the £15 each to get in and then go into the bar. I explained that we were not actually going to watch the match and told them the reason for our visit. I showed them a book and everything. I might as well have been talking to the wall. There was no way she was letting us into the bar. This was going to ruin our day as there were no other decent bars near the ground, and the idea of £30 coming out of the kitty was not worth discussing with Craig. So I asked her, using all the persuasive techniques I had developed over 30 years selling Thomson Litho to the world, if there was anyone else in a position of power who would understand our plight. She eventually got tired of my pleading and pointed over to a counter with a girl behind it, but warned us it would be no good, we would not get in. I thanked her very much. My sarcasm went right over her head. Craig's ears were soaked again.

I explained the reason for our visit to the girl behind the counter, a lovely person called Antonia Kerr, who told us it would be a pleasure to welcome us to Dumbarton Football Club. So with our belief that the Nazi party had not completely taken over Dumbarton, in we went.

It is a fairly new ground so the lounge bar was big and featureless with a dozen or so big round tables. But none of that matters, as the important thing is how we feel about the place and the people in it, and they were great.

We made friends with a lot of the supporters, many of whom help to run The Sons Supporters Trust which, among other things, raises money to help bring youngsters through into the senior team. They have raised over £200,000 in the last couple of years. Most clubs in Scotland would be finished without these guys working in the background.

One old guy (my age) we met called Campbell Yule had great patter and kept us entertained with his stories. He has visited every club in Scotland following Dumbarton and offered to give us advice on the best pubs near all the grounds. I hope I don't lose his phone number. Also turns out he knows my pal David Rainey who is another Dumbarton worthy.

Two rather old 'Sons'(Campbell on the right)

The time just shot in and we said goodbye to everybody and wished them all the best for the match. They won 3-1. Craig had a huge smile on his face as we went out and passed the girl who had refused us entry.

Craig*; Round at the stadium itself I had deep reservations about our chances of getting into the supporters club. According to John it was for home supporters only. Given how much I know about football in general, never mind the Dumbarton variety of it, I didn't fancy my chances of bluffing my way in as a home supporter.*

I must say that given the dwindling attendances at games these days having a locals only policy for a social club seems a wee bit daft.

Anyway, when we got to the front door of the stadium we were stopped by a wee lassie dressed up as an SS officer. She certainly played the part very enthusiastically.

According to her there was no chance of us getting into the club unless we paid the £15 entry fee to the game first. She would not be persuaded otherwise.

Luckily she had never had to deal with anyone like John before. He just kept smiling and talking over the top of her objections. Eventually our little storm trooper gave up and told us to ask at the main desk.

Within a couple of minutes, with the help of the very friendly girl at the desk, we entered the supporters club.

We soon got talking to a few guys inside the club. Once again we found that the people who help run the club are a great bunch of guys.

They were keen to talk about all aspects of the club. It would probably have meant a lot more to me if I knew a wee bit more about senior football; perhaps that should read 'anything about senior football'.

Eventually we got talking to one of Dumbarton's most enthusiastic supporters. Campbell Yule was his name and I would be very surprised if anyone knows more about the club than he does.

John and Campbell got into discussing the state of Scottish football and I applied myself to sampling the beer. It was quite good! The service I experienced at the bar was efficient and friendly. So full marks there then.

Once my companions had finished sorting out everything that is wrong with our national game I started listening again.

It turns out that our new pal Campbell knows quite a bit about Scottish football grounds. He has visited every one of them during his years of following Dumbarton F.C. Fortunately, like us, he also has been known to take a drink now and then and will be able to help us find some interesting watering holes as we continue our journey, especially in the North of the country.

John; We had planned to visit The Rock Bowling Green which the supporters web page said was the place the visiting fans went to. I checked it out on Google Earth, and the map it produced showed it was halfway up the road to the Stadium. But it wasn't. Craig had been slagging me off all the way up the road about my lack of ability to do anything right on a computer. I told him I don't have a computer, it's a lap top. He just laughed at me. The funny thing was that when we left the Stadium, Craig immediately turned right towards the river and sure enough, the bowling club was there. I reckon he knew where it was all the time and just didn't let on.

The club was starting to empty as we were settling ourselves at the bar. I think Dumbarton could at least let the Hamilton Accies fans into their bar. They looked a very nice crowd and were even clearing up their own glasses as they left. Leslie and Lewis who were behind the bar were great company and Lewis even bought a book. We had two or three drinks and had a great time in a great wee bowling green right on the banks of the Clyde. It would be a lovely spot to enjoy a game of bowls and a pint in the summer, if we ever get one.

Feeling no pain, we said goodbye and wandered back up the road past the ground. It was very quiet as it was half-time. We decided to get the train back to Glasgow as my bladder was not to the fore at this stage. A train came right away and it took only half an hour to get to Queen Street. This was half the time the bus took. The toilet on the train was out of order, but I managed to hold on no bother.

Craig; I'm pretty sure that John only found Dumbarton's ground, and therefore this club, completely by accident so a little help with navigation would be welcome.

While I was chatting with one of the other supporters I asked him if there were any other pubs nearby which were used by fans on match days. He told me about the Bowling Green, saying that it was mainly used by opposition supporters.

Fortunately he told me exactly where to find it as I had told him about John's phantom Bowling Green from earlier on.

Somehow I managed to forget to tell John that I had been given instructions on how to find our next drinking venue. I just told him I had a hunch that we might find it if we took a wee walk down by the side of Dumbarton Rock.

We only had to walk a couple of hundred yards before we 'discovered' the Bowling Green. I think he was really impressed with my path finding skill. He didn't actually say so, but I could tell.

It will probably not surprise anyone to hear that bowling is yet another sport that I know nothing about. However, if I was ever thinking about taking it up this place would be my ideal spot. The views over the Clyde are fantastic.

There is of course no real danger of me ever becoming a member of the club but I quickly volunteered to become one of its customers.

Lewis and Leslie

When we arrived in the bar the place was still full of Hamilton Accies supporters. It has to be said that they seemed to be a very well behaved group of fans. In fact I think they would have fitted in quite well up at the club in the stadium without causing any major upset if only they were allowed in.

At the bar we quickly got talking to the staff, Leslie and Lewis. We asked them if there was ever any bother because of the football and were told that there was never any trouble. In fact quite a lot of Dumbarton fans also drink in the bowling green.

After we told them what we were up to Lewis bought one of our books. He was either very impressed or else he had joined the rest of the football fans in there and got himself a wee bit well oiled.

By this time we were in no condition to tell either way

The big story going around at this time was the horse meat scandal. Large amounts of horse meat had been discovered in supermarket beef burgers

We had a few good laughs about this before Leslie told us about something which had happened to her on the bus the other day.

Apparently she keeps horses and had been telling friends on the bus about what they were like . Before she realised what she was saying she told them, "My horses are fussy burgers".

This was the cue for a prolonged period of hysterical laughter from her friends on the bus, and from two new acquaintances she had just made in the bowling green.

John; Today was Australia Day, and as one of my sons, Campbell lives in Sydney with his wife and children, Kate and I usually do something to celebrate the day. I had got a text earlier from Andrew, who is Australian and has been living in Scotland for about six years. Andrew is a relative and great guy who is like a fourth son to me. Anyway he was going to be in 'Walkabout', a huge Australian bar in Glasgow, so that's where we headed when we got off the train.

After a visit to the toilet, we met up with Andrew, his partner Rhoda, and a few of his mates. As it is an Australian bar and I love the beers there, I had a few VB's and a great time.

We got the train back to EK, wandered up to 'The Monty' for a couple, then Irene picked us up and so ended our adventure in Dumbarton.

Craig; We had a couple more drinks and a few more laughs before it was time to leave.

John insisted that we get the train back into Glasgow and to be honest I was quite glad he did.

He had arranged for us to meet up with some friends in Walkabout, the Australian bar. It was Australia Day after all!

To cut a long story short, I now know why Australians are all as mad as hatters; they drink Touey's Beer. Anything which happened after seven o'clock is a matter which neither John nor I are in a position to comment on.

Pubs we visited:

Stags Head;

Bar at ground;

Rock Bowling Green;

How to get there by bus:

No18 Glasgow/Helensburgh First Bus.

Queens Park

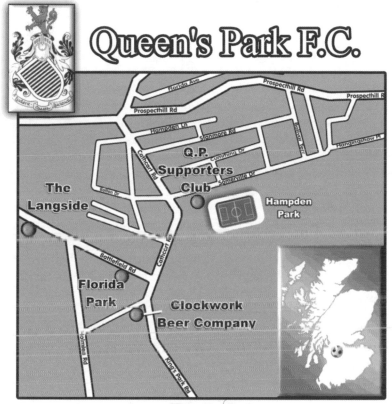

Hampden Park
Ground opened - 1903

John; Queen's Park, 'The Spiders'. I don't know the history behind the nickname, but I'll check it up on their website, or I probably won't. All of you will know that there is a huge amount of history behind the club, and the ground for that matter. When I was young, my dad took me to the Real Madrid versus Eintracht European Cup Final, played in front of a huge amount of people. I was also there when Joe Jordan scored that famous goal to get us into the World Cup. Great days.

43

My best memory of Hampden however was one sunny day at the Junior Cup Final, and for Craig's information, Auchinleck weren't playing, I think. Anyway, my memory is of me and my mate, John Berry, lying on the huge terracing facing the main stand getting stuck into a few cans of lager, the only way to watch a match. However, back to today's visit.

We had planned on going to Somerset Park to check out the Ayr United facilities. Craig knew somebody who had got us invited into the hospitality for a meal before the game. Everything was set, no pieces or anything to eat needed. Craig was a bit embarrassed as he is always slagging off people who go to hospitality. Just shows you how deep his feelings are. Bet he wasn't on the picket lines during the miners strike.

Anyway, the day was cold and sunny, too cold apparently. The park was frozen and the game was called off. So off to Hampden we went; flexibility is everything. Not easy at our age I hear you say.

The old 66 bus did the business no bother. We got off at the bottom of Holmlea Road and wandered round to gaze on our national stadium which looked pretty impressive in brilliant sunshine. Today was the first sunny day we had had in months. Pity about the cold.

There is a huge amount of building work being done in Lesser Hampden.We found out later that they are building a new supporter's club facility as well as facilities for the athletes at next year's Commonwealth games. Lesser Hampden will be used for a warm-up facility, and if it's as cold as today was, they will need them. So some lasting good is to come from all the money that is going to be thrown down the drain.

Craig; I was really looking forward to our trip to Somerset Park down in Ayr. Much effort had been expended in planning this trip, mainly by me. I had spent hours checking possible pubs to visit while we were there. To make that a little bit easier I had contacted a friend of mine who is one of the high heid yins on the committee of Ayr United FC.

He had made arrangements for us to have a tour of the stadium and even view the trophy room. Apparently this wouldn't take very long at all and we could then have lunch and a few beers in the club.

The one thing we didn't include in our plan was the weather. On that particular Saturday the weather had turned decidedly chilly, so chilly in fact that there had been a pitch inspection that morning. Apparently they had discovered permafrost or something like that.

Douglas McKenzie, my inside man down at Somerset Park, phoned to tell me the bad news and to suggest a few alternatives.

That was how it came about that John and I caught the number 66 First Bus and headed for the Battlefield area on the South side of Glasgow.

It is only a short walk from there up to Hampden Park, home of Queen's Park and occasionally a national football squad and sometimes known as our field of broken dreams.

John; I had checked one of Queen's Park's web sites and had found out that there was a supporters club bar, which was situated in an office block adjacent to Lesser Hampden. It was no nearer to being an office block than I am an author. It was just like a temporary hut builders use, only bigger. There were no signs to say where the place was and we were in and out of about three doors before a couple of workmen showed us the way and we found the bar. I'm glad we persevered. The place was just like a big box with a wee bar at one end. It was magic.

Marie and Jackie, the girls behind the bar were very friendly and great company. I was a bit embarrassed because I had no idea who The Spiders were playing. They had no idea either. A guy at the bar overheard us and told us today's game was against Annan. That was a bit of a conversation stopper. Craig told me Annan was down in the south somewhere. One of the girls even bought one of the two books I had brought. A great start to the day.

The girls introduced us to John Richmond, a lifelong Queens supporter, who spends all of his spare time helping to raise funds for the Youth Teams. He has taken them to competitions all over Europe. One of many famous clubs the Queen's youth teams have beaten is Valencia. There are many others, but my memory the next day had a few gaps in it.

John then introduced us to another great legendary supporter called Stuart (The Vicar) Hendry. The Vicar has hardly missed a game since he was 10 years old. I asked John why Stuart was called The Vicar, he said Christ knows! John and Stuart are at the heart of the supporters

45

who are keeping the team alive in these hard times. Before we left we were given complimentary tickets for a game in the near future. I hope Craig has the details. All too soon we had to leave this great bar as the job we have given ourselves is to check out at least 2 or 3 bars in the area. I would have been happier just to stay in the bar we were in, but Craig reminded me we were at work. Funnily enough, when I had a real job, getting pissed was a fairly regular event, so I have a great CV for this job.

Craig; We were not very sure if there even was a supporters club at the park or if we would be allowed into it.

As we strolled up to Hampden we had plenty of time to reminisce about favourite games we had seen played there. I don't actually remember what John's greatest memory was as I wasn't listening to him.

My favourite memory is of course the 1986 Junior Cup final. The soon to be legendary Auchinleck Talbot lifted the cup that day and set in motion a four day celebration which is still talked about in the village to this day.

After a bit of a false start we managed to find the Queen's Park social club. That was no mean feat as it didn't really look as if it was connected to the football club at all. In fact the building looked as if someone had been stacking porta-kabins together.

Just to avoid embarrassment I let John lead the way. We really didn't expect very much from the place but I'm happy to say we were greatly surprised. The club was great. It was certainly much bigger than we expected. Shades of the Tardis in fact!

The room was quite long and had a fairly low ceiling. It was very brightly painted and had a traditional bar at the far end.

When we arrived the bar wasn't very busy. That's another way of saying that yet again we were near the front of the queue at opening time.

We were served straight away by a couple of very cheery barmaids which immediately put us in a good mood. I was just a wee bit put out though by the fact that there was no Tennent's

Lager to be had in the club. The brewery is only a mile or so away from where we were standing after all.

Maybe I should have asked why this was the case as that would have saved me a good ten minutes of brooding. I can only assume there is some sort of sponsorship thing in place. Who knows?

Marie and Jackie

Anyway, I bravely put up with this serious lack of my favourite tipple and got wired into the Carling. After a couple of pints I couldn't have cared less who brewed it.

We got talking to Marie and Jackie, the barmaids, and learned quite a bit about Queen's Park supporters club.

It was around that time that I began to feel a wee bit guilty about some of the things I'd said to John concerning the look of the club. Earlier on I had suggested that the building the club was in looked like a stack of oversized Lego bricks. I may also have said that the place seemed to be furnished with old tables and chairs salvaged from a 1980s hotel function suite. The girls behind the bar told us that the supporter's club would be moving to brand new premises very soon so I don't think they'll hold it against me, for too long at any rate!

Of course it's not the fixtures and fittings which make a good pub or club, it's the people who run it and of course the people who use it.

Using the equation above I can honestly say that Queen's Park Supporters Club is a great club and I would highly recommend a visit to it. In fact if it was just a wee bit more accessible to passing trade it would make a great local for somebody.

It would certainly make a better pub than the next two places we were about to visit: more of that later.

John had somehow managed to flog the girls a copy of our latest book, which he just happened to be carting around with him. While at the bar we got talking to a chap called John Richmond, who apparently spends most of his free time raising funds for the youth programme up at Queen's Park.

It struck me that at every club we have visited so far there are small groups of dedicated supporters working away trying to bring on new footballing talent for the benefit of their chosen teams. Let's hope all this effort pays off eventually.

Before we left the club to find other supporters drinking dens Marie and Jackie told us that we were to get complimentary tickets to a future match.

It really is amazing how kind people can be. My only concern about this gift is that it would perhaps be a good idea for us to use the tickets before anyone at Queen's Park gets a chance to read what we've written about them in the next book.

John; The next bar we found was 'The Florida Park'; I wish we hadn't. It was packed with supporters watching their team get humped live on about six huge TVs. You could have cut the atmosphere with a knife, but Craig told me it wasn't the atmosphere he was worried about. We finished our pints and left as quietly as possible. You know what it's like with fanatics; I was worried one of them would ask us why we were leaving, but we escaped via the smoking garden.

'The Clockwork Brewery', where we landed next, was the complete opposite. It was very smart and filled with young upwardly mobile couples with prams and things. Real Ale was to the fore. This is the sort of place we usually hate, but it is a nice bar and we felt safer after the last place we had been in. The only bad thing was that rugby was on the tellies and England were humping Scotland, but quietly. I doubt if the owners would encourage a crowd of football supporters into it. It is a nice pub and worth a visit, but best to go after the weans are in bed.

Our final pub of the day was 'The Langside'. Craig used to visit it when he lived in this area. I don't think there are many areas where Craig has not lived, usually for a short time! He said it used to be called 'The Mission'.

Rachael & Laura

This was a great bar and the girls behind the bar, Laura and Rachael were good company. The guy I was talking to at the bar told me he worked for the Co-op Funeral Services. This was a coincidence as we met two guys when we visited Dunfermline who do the same job there. I suppose it is natural for Funeral people to be interested in Scottish Football, after all. It's dead on its feet!! 'The Langside' sponsors Queen's Park supporter's club, so it is doing a great service helping the club stay on its feet, away from the Funeral people.

Craig; Back down on Battlefield Road we decided to visit The Florida Park Bar. Many years ago I had wandered into this bar more or less by accident. It was the only one I could find which was still open on that particular Saturday night. I didn't stay long. In fact I was only there long enough to finish my pint, and back then I could really shift the beer.

The atmosphere in the place was what I would call malevolent. Knowing that John will ask I have decided to include

49

the dictionary definition of that word. Malevolent: adjective, 'having or showing a wish to do evil to others.'

That summed up the Florida Park back then and I think it sums it up now. Talk about walking into a bear pit!

To get a feel of what it was like walking into the bar that day try to imagine the atmosphere of a very crowded room full of half cut Rangers supporters whose team has just gone down two goals against Dundee United and then had a second player sent off. They were not chuffed, in the most extreme sense of the word. In fact they looked like they might be prepared to indulge in a little bit of human sacrifice. Not wishing to get involved in any of these quaint football rituals I suggested that we choke back our beers and leave the building at a rate of knots.

John was also eager to leave before anything other than the next game kicked off. Maybe it had something to do with being in an area called Battlefield.

I have no idea what the service in the pub was like. In fact I don't even remember tasting my beer. If it wasn't for the fact that we were writing a book about our experiences I would be trying very hard to forget being in that bar.

Our next choice was much more sedate. The Clockwork Beer Company is not the kind of place you would expect to find hordes of football supporters. It's the real ale capital of Glasgow's south side where you are far more likely to find an appreciation of the oval ball.

It was impossible to gauge the level of service in the place as the bar staff were far too busy to talk to customers. In this place even mentioning lager would ruffle an awful lot of feathers among the real ale nutters, so I'm afraid rating the beer would be pointless.

Actually I used to drink in this place back when I lived just up the road. I'm fairly sure we called it the Clockwork Brewery at that time. Even back then I felt guilty about ordering an ordinary pint of lager.

The bar staff were constantly on at us to try some of the horrible concoctions they brewed on the premises. In my opinion it's bad enough that they make soft drinks from dandelions and such like, but when they start making beer out of the scabby little weeds that's where I draw the line.

One pint of perfectly acceptable 'normal' lager was enough for me before we decided to go out and find ourselves a real pub.

We found a good one. The Langside, or the Mission as I used to know it, was a great choice. It's maybe a wee bit modern for my liking but the staff more than make up for this minor shortcoming.

Laura and Rachael put up with our daft patter without complaint. I think it was Laura who told us that the Langside sponsored Queen's Park. That was really good news as the last two pubs we had been in didn't seem to be the type of places which would part with any cash for their local football team.

John; We must have had a good bucket by the time we left, because the chips we bought next door tasted great, and they weren't, Craig threw half of his away. The man has no taste, or maybe it's me.

I devoured my chips while we waited for the 66 bus which left just on the other side of the road. This was good planning. We had planned to meet up with someone in a pub in East Kilbride, so there was a great excuse for another couple of pints before going home. As it happened, Craig got a text on the bus telling him that the bloke couldn't manage, so we had no excuse to go for more drink, so we went for more drink. Who said we ever needed an excuse.

Kate told me the next day I was in some state when I got home. I told here it was work and that she wouldn't be complaining when the money started rolling in. She said she doubted if that would ever happen, but if it did, it would be a change from me rolling in. What a cheek! I told her I had half a mind to stop this book lark altogether. She agreed with the half a mind bit.

Again I've got to admit that a lot of drink was consumed. I spend about £30, but we got about £6 from our book sale, and that disappeared somewhere 'Down your thrapple', Kate told me. She likes to talk old Scots sometimes. I am going to try to cut back, really I am.

Craig; When we had started out that morning the plan had been to have a bar lunch at Somerset Park. With our sudden change of venue we had not really thought through the food side of things. No pieces had been made, no small chunks of cold chicken had been packed and John was getting a bit cranky.

We needed food and fast. Instead, we settled for a large bag of chips each.

It was the largest bag of chips I have ever seen. Unfortunately the quantity was not matched by any degree of quality. They were manky. I probably saved myself a painful bout of indigestion and avoided losing a couple of weeks off my allotted life span by heaving them into the nearest litter bin.

After a wee snooze on the bus home it was unanimously decided that what we really needed was another couple of pints.

That's how we found ourselves propping up the bar in Shenanigan's in East Kilbride town centre. This bar seems to have taken over as our local recently.

Perhaps that's because of its central location or its friendly staff. Then again it might be because we rather like the fact that it is only £2.00 a pint. Whatever the reason this is where we will be planning our future journeys, but only if John can remember what we talked about.

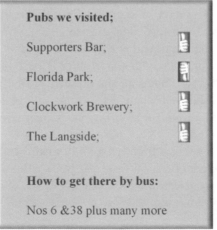

Pubs we visited;

Supporters Bar;

Florida Park;

Clockwork Brewery;

The Langside;

How to get there by bus:

Nos 6 & 38 plus many more

Raith Rovers

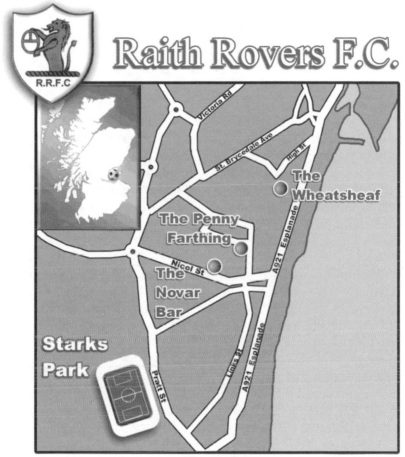

Starks Park
Ground opened - 1891

John; Raith Rovers, the web site I checked said 'Rovers' was the club nickname. Is there nobody in Kirkcaldy who could come up with a more imaginative nickname than 'Rovers'. Even 'Raith' would at least be unique. Is everybody in the town as dull and unimaginative as Gordon Brown, who gave himself the nickname 'Brown'. How about

'The Kirkcaldy Kings', or more apt, as I found out later could be 'The Starks' Stinkers', or The Raith Reekers'. Anyway, back to today's story.

A few weeks back we had visited Dunfermline and met up with some great supporters. Two of the guys worked for the Co-op Funeral Service and offered to pick us up in a Funeral Limo in Dunfermline and chauffeur us to some future game. The idea was to get a bit of publicity in the local paper both for the club and ourselves. We thought it was a great idea. We said we would take them up on their great offer the first time we visited Kirkcaldy as Starks Park is the nearest ground to East End Park and we didn't want to have the limo go too far. At least I didn't. Craig was all for taking them up on their offer next time we visited Ross County!

So today was the Limo day. I wanted to wear my long black coat and a top hat, but Craig said it was a stupid idea and we would just draw attention to ourselves. I thought that was the idea. As Craig says, you can't embarrass me. Anyway, I gave up on the black coat idea. I won't tell you his answer to my idea to walk in front of the limo like they do in real funerals.

With pieces in my pocket and a wave to Kate, I carried out the usual start to most trips, pick up Craig, the Old 18 into Glasgow Buchanan Street Station and then the bus to Dunfermline. We went into the wee shop in the station to get a paper and a can of juice only to discover that my regular paper, the slightly right wing 'Mail' had not been delivered. I had to make the decision on what alternative paper to buy. For no reason I can think of. I bought 'The Scotsman'. The only reason I've mentioned this is that as I went through the paper, I found a page I couldn't read, it seemed the letters were all mixed up. I showed this to Craig who told me it was Gaelic. Amazing! I hope Scotland's two Gaelic readers are aware of this. I wondered if this was a translation of the news in the English part of the paper, or is it news stories from the teuchter part of Scotland.

Craig; We had been making plans for a good week before this latest trip. Raith Rovers were playing Partick Thistle and I was more than a wee bit worried about it.

Not about the score or anything like that, but something with the potential to be really annoying. In fact there were two potential headaches connected with our wee jaunt to the East coast.

The greater nuisance of the two was the fact that John has a bit of history with one of the clubs involved in this particular football match.

There can be few people in the central region of Scotland, if not farther afield, who do not know that John, many, many years ago, was a ball boy at Fihill, Partick Thistle's home ground. He tends to bring it up in conversation several times a day, whether football is being discussed or not. I suppose we should all be grateful that he never reached the giddy heights of actually playing for them. There would have been no shutting him up if that had been the case. Fortunately an almost total lack of footballing talent ensured that he never got beyond ball fetching.

My great fear was that he would dredge up his greatest sporting achievement in front of some drink raddled Raith Rovers supporter, possibly one with an irrational hatred of Glasgow accents. That happens more often than you would think.

My other problem with today's journey centred on our transport arrangements.

A few weeks before this trip we had visited Dunfermline and had enjoyed a great day with a group of supporters at their club, 'Legends'. One of the guys, Kenny, contacted us a week or so later and made us an extraordinary offer. He arranged for a limo to pick us up in Dunfermline and take us to Kirkcaldy so that we could check out Raith Rovers and the pubs near to their stadium.

It was all meant to be a bit of a laugh but, unlike John, I can be embarrassed rather easily. Being huckled about in a big fancy chauffeur driven limousine is well outside my comfort zone. I was not looking forward to this part of the journey.

Our day started out like so many others. That is to say a long boring journey down to Glasgow on the number 18. Even after all this time I still cannot get my head round the fact that it can take an hour and sometimes much more to travel a distance of ten miles.

The journey itself was uneventful and we arrived in plenty of time to catch our bus to Dunfermline. John was a little bit put out when he found that the newsagents at the bus station didn't have a single copy of his beloved Daily Mail. I tried to console him by suggesting that maybe the Mail had at last fallen foul of the Trades Description Act by insisting on describing what they print as being a newspaper. It was after all just a matter of time!

John; It was a very dull and misty day, but by the time we arrived at Dunfermline the weather had cleared and we found our rendezvous point, 'The Commercial Bar'. It was a nice wee bar which sold lots of real ales. Craig, as you may know, hates any beer that's not Tennent's Lager.

Bob, our driver, phoned to let us know he would be with us in five minutes, so we downed our pints and went outside to await the arrival of our limo, and what a beauty it was. Three rows of seats and everything. Bob insisted on opening the doors for us every time we went in and out of it. The only downside was Craig would not let me wave to people as we went along the road.

Bob was from Kirkcaldy so he drove us around all the pubs that supporters frequent before he got us to the ground, Starks Park. I had told Bob that I had brought dark glasses and Blues Brothers hats to make any photos more authentic. He thought this was a great idea and told us that we would be passing a pub with statues of the Brothers outside, so we stopped at it and I got my photo taken with the gear on standing between them. Craig thought it was childish and refused to join in.

Back at the park it was very quiet, but as it was only about one o'clock, we assumed it was too early for the bar, if there was one, to be open. So after getting our photos taken, Bob dropped us off at 'The Nova Bar'. The idea was to have a pint or two there and try the ground later.

Craig; *When we arrived in Dunfermline we headed straight to 'The Commercial'. This pub is just along the road from the station and it was where we were told to wait for the limo driver to contact us. It was quite a nice place, despite all the real ale fonts nailed to the bar. We were served quickly and cheerfully by a very nice young girl. The pub was fairly busy with a mixed crowd of young and old customers. Meals were being served but thankfully the place was not too noisy.*

Actually up to this point I was still a wee bit sceptical about the whole limo thing. Somewhere in the back of my mind I had the notion that the whole thing was a bit of a set-up. I could just imagine all the Dunfermline guys we had talked to that last day waiting outside to have a good laugh at us. Thankfully I was wrong!

Our limo was waiting for us outside. I was really glad that there was no one around who knew me. John, on the other hand, was nodding and waving to passers by as if it was their fault that they didn't recognise him.

The drive to Kirkcaldy was very smooth and our driver, Bob, was a great source of information. We had actually come up with the idea of dressing up for our drive in the limo, but at the last minute I was overcome by a severe bout of common sense.

I was pretty sure that there was no danger of that happening to John and true to form, and for reasons I never really understood, he turned up dressed as the wee fat one of the Blues Brothers. At least I think that's what he was supposed to be.

If he was thinking about making a big entrance at East End Park he must have been very disappointed; it was shut. At first we thought the lack of noise was maybe down to the fact that Raith Rovers supporters are just unnaturally well behaved. But after a quick inspection of the stadium we realised that the place was totally empty.

Luckily for us our driver, Bob, knew exactly what to do. He drove us down to 'The Novar' on Nicol Street. He explained that this was where the Rovers fans tended to gather before the game.

John; The bar was very busy and I spied a group of young guys who seemed to be talking about 'The Rovers'. I went over and asked them who we were playing today. I wanted to sound like a Rovers supporter. They told me it was Partick Thistle, but that the game had been cancelled because of the state of the ground. I would be lying if I said I was disappointed as it made little difference to our day out.

The four guys were all fanatical Rovers supporters and members of 'The Jim McMillan' supporters club. This is a small club with its own bar in the ground. The members are dedicated to raising money for the youth team development. The four guys themselves have raised £62,000 in the last six years. Their only gripe was that in that time, only one half decent player has come through the ranks.

Michael, Craig, Denis and Andy asked us to join their company and we had a great time listening to stories of their adventures following The Rovers all over Scotland, and Scotland all over Europe. They reckoned one team is as bad as the other. The reason they follow Scotland is that it is the only way they will get to see their team in Europe.

When we asked them why the game was off, they said that it was because the week before they were at home to Celtic in the Scottish Cup, so the ground staff made the surface as rough as possible to try and stop Celtic playing. This backfired as they got humped anyway and the ground was still unplayable a week later. I didn't question the ground staff, so can't say if the story is true. I've got to say that in case the ground staff is a big bloke and takes offence at my comments. 'The Nova' is a great bar filled with crazy Rovers supporters. Well worth a visit.

Craig; *The building doesn't look much like a traditional pub. In fact it looks a wee bit like one of those old prefab buildings which were popular back in the 50s. That being said it is quite smartly painted. Inside it is a lot more traditional.*

We had only been in the place a few minutes before we got talking to a group of Rovers supporters. They turned out to be a great bunch of lads, well worth talking to.

They told us that the game had been cancelled because the pitch had been flooded. Apparently there had been an inspection earlier on and the game had been put off.

I'm quite glad that we hadn't got that information as we would probably have cancelled our trip. That would have meant missing a great day in a good pub with excellent company.

The boys, certainly had plenty of stories to tell. And some of them were printable. One of them told us that their team is the most important thing in their lives. To make his point he told us a story about his father. Apparently back in the 60s he cancelled his wedding when Raith got to the final of the Scottish Cup. Since his team went on to win it was seen as a smart move. I asked him if his mother thought that as well but apparently her comments were never recorded.

Michael, Craig, Denis and Andy

The Novar seems to be a favourite place for the lads to spend an evening. In fact they told us that a popular game they often play is to start at one end of the bar and have a pint from every font on the bar. It's a very big bar and there are a lot of different beers to be sampled. So far there have been many valiant efforts but the challenge goes on.

While we were enjoying ourselves In 'The Novar' I totally forgot to check out the bar and the service. The beer just seemed to arrive at my table. John must have been working overtime keeping the flow going so I really have to leave any assessment of the pub to him. All I know is the beer tasted great and the patter was well up to standard.

Our new pals may well have been great story tellers but they left a lot to be desired in their ability to gauge distances.

John; Time was getting on and it was with great sorrow that we said our farewells to the four guys and everybody else in the bar and headed down the road, round the corner and into 'The Penny Farthing'.

This was another good bar with great staff. Laura and Bill made us very welcome and we enjoyed a couple of excellent pints. I mentioned to Laura about the reason for the game being off. She said the story I had been told was not true. The real reason the game was off, she said, was because the park was too smelly for the players to play on. I was sure she was just taking the piss, but she insisted that was the case. She says the park is honking all the time, but that if it is cut up badly, it's unbearable.

I preferred her story, and when I told Craig, he said he remembered Billy Connolly, The Big Yin, telling the tale of getting off the supporters bus in Kirkcaldy and nearly being knocked down by the smell. It must have been bad when you notice it after being on a supporter's bus for a couple of hours.

The reason for the smell in the old days was because Kirkcaldy was the home of Linoleum making, which was a very smelly process. I can only think that Starks Park is built on the site of an old Linoleum dump and the smell seeps through to the surface. The factories must all be shut now because I stuck my head out of the door and all I could smell was the smoke from the smokers out for a fag.

I was all for heading for the bus when we left, but Craig was adamant that, for the sake of our art, we should visit another pub. It's all work, work, work with him. We walked along the High Street and went into the Waterstones to see if our books were on the shelf. They were, so we left and found a bar called 'The Wheatsheaf'. At least I think that was its name. Later we had an hour to kill in Dunfermline and went into a pub there, but by that time I had no idea what pub was what. What a state to get into! Anyway the bar we went into was not as good as the other two and the barman was a bit weird, but I didn't tell him that. We had a drink there and then headed to the bus station.

Craig; *We had decided it was time to move on and find another pub. Between them they agreed that our best bet would be 'The Penny Farthing' which, according to the boys, was down to the end of the road and then only twenty yards round the corner.*

To quote John, "Twenty yards, my arse!"

By the time we finally arrived at the Penny Farthing I really needed a pint. I was exhausted!

This pub was a bit more upmarket and I can't really see too many football fans choosing it as a pre-match drinking den.

It's a very good pub though and well worth a visit. We were served straight away by a very nice young lady called Laura. She was up for a laugh and managed to put up with our silly patter like a true professional.

However she wasn't too keen on me taking her picture and ran away every time I tried to get a shot. John claims it is my own fault. He says it takes me so long to line things up that people just get bored and move away.

I managed to solve my little photographic problem by roping in the barman, Bill. Once he agreed to have his picture taken Laura was more than willing to get in on the act. Although we were only in the pub for a short time we had really enjoyed our session in The Penny Farthing.

Laura and Bill

The beer was excellent and the service was top notch but time was moving on and John looked as if he could do with some fresh air.

We wandered round to Waterstones book shop on High Street just to check if our books were actually out on display. We hadn't had a re-order for a couple of weeks.

I realise that I really should have stopped John from re-organising the shelf displays but I have to admit I found it very amusing. We left before the staff noticed what was going on.

With half an hour to kill we decided that what we really needed was another pint and so a few minutes later we found ourselves sipping a brew in 'The Wheatsheaf'. As it turned out it was rather an expensive sip. We didn't get a chance to talk to anyone in the pub and the barman was also too busy to chat.

Perhaps at a different time of day The Wheatsheaf is a really good pub but we didn't really rate the place very highly. Obviously by the time we got into this pub any would-be Raith Rovers fans had long gone.

John; There was no direct bus to Glasgow, so we got one to Dunfermline, had a couple of pints in some pub or other there, and got our bus to Glasgow. As usual, I slept the whole way back and in no time we were back in Glasgow.

We headed straight back to the Central Station, but as we had about 20 minutes to kill till our train to EK, we went into the station bar and had a quick one. Why, had we no had enough? Irene picked us up at EK station and took us home, and so ended a great day out in Kirkcaldy, a run in a Limo, great company and no smell, or game for that matter.

I was well on when I got home. As usual, I hear you say! I think I spent over £40. The excuse I'm making today is that the drink in Kirkcaldy is pretty expensive. Two pints were well over £6. I think the Scottish Government is taking us all to the cleaners with their taxing policy on drink. There should be no tax on drink for pensioners.

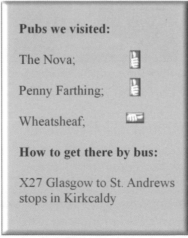

Pubs we visited:

The Nova;

Penny Farthing;

Wheatsheaf;

How to get there by bus:

X27 Glasgow to St. Andrews stops in Kirkcaldy

Kilmarnock

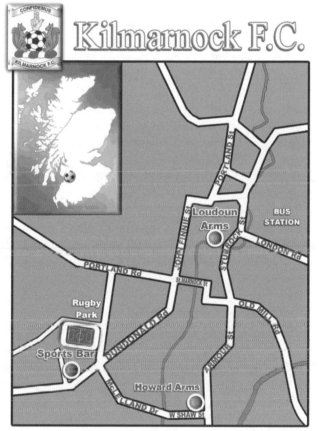

Rugby Park
Ground opened - 1899

John; Kilmarnock, nickname, 'Killie'. I think 'The Nockers' would have been a better nickname, but it might be taken the wrong way, never mind. I think Killie are one of the oldest clubs in the league. At the time of our visit on the 6th April 2013, it was our first trip to a Premier League Club.

Our previous trips to clubs in the lower leagues had all been great and we had made many friends and met great guys who are doing sterling work raising money to keep their clubs afloat.

Maybe it was because this was a Premier league club we decided to e-mail them the day before to ask if it was all right for us to visit the bar inside the ground, if there was one!

I checked Kilmarnock's web page and found that the secretary was a lady called Kirsten Callaghan. I received an almost instant reply to my mail with all the information I had asked for. One up to Kilmarnock.

Kilmarnock must be one of the easiest grounds for us to travel to. The old X16 takes us from the bus station in EK right to Kilmarnock, just one bus, magic. I had no idea where the ground was in Kilmarnock, but this is one of the hundreds of towns Craig has stayed in, and suddenly left, so I was leaving it to him to try and remember which pubs he was not barred from!

The bus was packed and I was sitting next to a lovely old lady who talked to me all the way to Kilmarnock. She was an amazing old lady who had lost her husband and son all too soon. I asked her what had taken her son so early in life and she told me all about him. He was one of the best Jewellers in Glasgow and one of the highlights of his working life was when he was asked to make a sword for David Murray on his retirement from Rangers. Retirement was not how I remembered it, but never mind. She told me he enjoyed a wee refreshment every day, and had his own stool in a pub in St. Enoch's square, where he worked. This is never a good thing, but I kept my thoughts to myself. Hope she doesn't read this book. She was keeping herself going though and was on her way to a hospital in Prestwick to visit a friend. When I told her what Craig and I were wasting our time doing she even promised to buy a book. What a great old lady.

Craig had said it was a 20 minute walk to the ground, but the walk passed in no time at all due to the fact that it was a glorious day and we were passing through a lovely area which did not look as if it would have a football ground at the end of it, but it did.

Craig; I was back on familiar ground for today's trip. Kilmarnock holds many memories for me. They say that your school days are the happiest days of your life. I am very happy to say that this is complete nonsense. Back in the late 60s I attended

James Hamilton High School on London Road in Kilmarnock. My school days at the 'Jimmy' were far from happy. Fortunately back then Kilmarnock had two picture houses and I spent many an afternoon watching badly dubbed German westerns instead of trying to make sense of Algebra.

While waiting for the picture house to open I spent a lot of time wandering around the town. This stood me in good stead for my later career as a beer drinker. I knew where all the pubs were. After leaving school I got a job with Western SMT and put my pub finding skills to good use.

Despite a lot of redevelopment over the years I was still confident of finding a few good pubs for us to check out on today's little adventure. It is just as well one of us knew something about Kilmarnock as John has a bit of a blank spot when it comes to this particular town. The last time we visited the place he enjoyed himself so much that he couldn't remember ever being there.

I have noticed that his memory does start playing tricks on him soon after his 6th pint. Frankly I'm surprised he ever finds his way home at night.

I was a wee bit worried that we might not get on the bus to Kilmarnock. There were an awful lot of small white haired women waiting at our stance when we got to the bus station. We managed to push into the queue behind the old yins and got the last two seats on the bus. I had to pretend to be studying my phone to avoid eye contact with the people left behind as the bus pulled away from the stop.

Maybe it was because the sun was shining or because we were both in a good mood, but Kilmarnock Bus station seemed almost reasonable looking when we got off the bus. Most of the time it looks really grim. It would be easy to believe that it had been transported to Kilmarnock from Eastern Europe in the 1950s.

I don't know why, but John didn't seem to believe that I knew the way to the football park. He doesn't have a lot of faith in me. He was very surprised when I took him straight there.

65

John; Opposite the ground is a very modern and unusual looking hotel called 'The Park'. It was one of the places the secretary had suggested we visited, but after a talk with some of the worthies in the 'Sports Bar', which was the bar in the ground, we gave it a miss. The 'Sports Bar' itself is a very modern and American looking bar, but the people inside were very traditional Scottish football supporters, unbelievably optimistic with a big touch of reality thrown in. Today they were playing for a place in the top six, if they won. The game was against Dundee, the bottom club, who were already relegated, so with traditional Scottish realism, no one I spoke to was confident of winning, and their depression was justified, they were humped 2-1 by the bottom of the league. It says a huge amount for the Scottish supporters that they follow their team every week. I am in awe of them.

We met some great supporters including three girls, a mother, her daughter and a friend who go to almost all of Kilmarnock's games. Most wives I know who have daughters go shopping every Saturday. I couldn't be bothered taking a note of everybody's name as I was not feeling great. I have had a touch of something recently. Craig was writing away furiously so I'm sure all names will be recorded.

Craig; The Sports Bar was very modern with lots of flat screen televisions all around the walls. I don't usually like very bright, modern, noisy drinking places, but this place was different.

Everyone we spoke to was very friendly and helpful. Even the two very large gentlemen standing guard at the door were up for a laugh. Take notice Dumbarton!

We got talking to a couple of Killie supporters almost straight away. They turned out to be brothers, Kevin and Stephen Paterson. We had a good laugh with the lads. They had high hopes of their team getting into the top six in the premier league by beating Dundee today. It would seem that once again we had put the kiss of death on the chances of one of our home teams. Dunfermline Athletic are paying a high price for making us welcome in their supporters club. I blame John.

We asked Kevin if he could recommend another pub where we might find more supporters to talk to. I thought he might suggest the Park Hotel, just across from the football ground. He didn't. I got the impression that perhaps we wouldn't fit in as the 'Park' looked a bit too fancy for the likes of us. To be honest I could see how that might be the case.

Stephen & Kevin settle their pre-match nerves

John; We said our goodbyes to a great bunch of supporters and wandered down some road or other and into a pub called 'The Howard Arms'. This is a great pub. We got into conversation with three supporters at the bar, one of them was the owner Billy Millar. Billy and his pals Sandy and Tivvy were great company and regaled us with some wonderful stories of Kilmarnock in the past. Again I will rely on Craig to give you some meat on my version of today's events, (remember, I'm no well).

Craig really enjoyed himself as the owner Billy was an Auchinleck man. I don't remember if he had lived there or if it was one of his relatives. Anyway, he knew everybody in Auchinleck. I asked him what the supporters were like and his answer was a shocker. To quote him, 'I'd rather have a crowd of Celtic and Rangers supporters in the pub at once than a crowd of Auchinleck fans'. Anyone who has been in a bar on match day with both halves of the 'Old Firm' in attendance will know just how bad Auchinleck fans must be. Craig was really happy with Billy's opinion of his beloved Auchinleck Talbot fans. It's a West of Scotland thing. If you don't know what I'm talking about, you shouldn't be reading this book. 'The Howard Arms' is a great and well run pub and well worth a visit if you're in the area.

67

I was all for heading back to EK when we left the pub, but I didn't want to seem like a wimp (although Craig knows I am) so I agreed to visit another pub on the way to the bus station. We found one round the corner from the bus station. From the outside, this looked like a pub we would like, a dump called 'The Loudoun Arms', but looks can be deceiving, though not in this case. Inside it was pretty old and run down looking; we loved it. It is great wee pub and a handy place to rest if the wife is shopping or keeping your place in the bus queue! We watched the Grand National and I don't think any horses were killed, although sometimes they try and hide this sort of incident.

Craig; Kevin suggested the 'Howard Arms' as a good place to meet more Killie fans. He told me that The 'Howard' was a favourite place for them to drink but suggested that perhaps if more of the fans would spend more time in the Sports Bar than the pub Kilmarnock FC might be a lot better off financially. While I was doing all this fact finding John had wandered over to chat up a group of female fans. The spirit is willing but everything else is weak. Old age is a terrible thing; it's a shame really.

The girls were very nice and chatted away to us for ages. Apparently they are season ticket holders. I was amazed. Any woman I have ever known would be more likely to be spending their three hundred quid on a week's self-catering in Tenerife than a seat at a football match. To be honest, so would I! I decided to take a picture and as I lined up my shot the doormen shouted over to a group of 'suits', who were sitting next to the girls, that I was from the taxman and they had better hide their faces.

As soon as we moved outside John once again cast doubt on my direction-finding abilities. He tried to wander off in the opposite direction from our next pub. Since he wasn't feeling too well I refrained from slapping him on the back of the head.

Instead I told him that if I was wrong about where the pub was I would pay for all the booze for the rest of the day. This always works.

For all the years I have been visiting Kilmarnock I have never been inside the' Howard Arms'. I wish I had, it's a great pub.

68

As soon as we stepped in the door we knew we had made the right choice. It's a very traditional bar. In fact it is more like a lounge bar with a small games room attached. I only got a quick look into the games room and it appeared to be more like a trophy room. The walls were covered with framed photos and football tops, all of them 'Killie' related of course.

My only criticism of the pub, and the Sports Bar for that matter, was the lack of draught Tennent's Lager. It's a very small criticism as the pints of Fosters in both places were excellent.

Billy, Sandy & Tivvy

The bar wasn't too busy as many of the supporters had begun to make their way out to the match. John, even in his weakened condition decided to strike up a conversation with three likely looking older guys.

Billy, Sandy and Tivvy turned out to be a right trio of characters. Billy Millar is the owner of the pub and has a few tales to tell about his favourite team. Being the nearest pub to the ground he has seen it all as you can imagine. Billy and his mates are very proud of the fact that one of Kilmarnock's legendary players was associated with their pub

Andy King who played for the club in the early 1960s, had his own stool at the bar. I really hope this was after the end of his glorious career and not part of his training regime.

Tivvy then told me about another Kilmarnock hero: Jackie Brown. Jackie was the team goalkeeper back in the old black and white days. It seems he was a bit of a character. He certainly liked to annoy some of the teams he played against, along with more than a few of their supporters. Apparently every time he played against Celtic he would wear an orange top and, just to balance things up, when the opponents were Rangers he would wear a green top. It's hard to say if all of this was meant to have a psychological effect on these teams or if Jackie was just arsing around.

The girls behind the bar in The Howard

By this time John was claiming that his poor state of health meant we really needed to head for home. I would have called him a hypochondriac but I knew this would just confuse him so I suggested that he was just being a wimp.

We compromised by heading up the town to the Loudoun Arms. What a place. It is on a rather dingy back street and it looks a bit manky on the outside. And it looks both dingy and manky on the inside. In other words it was perfect.

I like to think that the good folk of the Loudoun have only a vague notion of what wood laminate or brushed aluminium are used for. Being in this pub was like taking a step back in time. As I said to John, "You just don't get nostalgia like this anymore!" The only thing missing was a carpet that your shoes stuck to as you walked up to the bar.

John was feeling too ill to be amused by this remark so I did the laughing for both of us. One drink was enough for us due to John's failing health and we made our way round to the bus station.

I was feeling a bit peckish and decided to get something to eat out of Gregg's in the shopping centre while John kept my place in the queue for the X16.

John; I eventually got Craig out of the pub and we waited in the queue for the old X16. The bus down to Kilmarnock had been packed with the white haired on their way to Ayr for a day shopping or walking on the prom, so we were worried about getting a seat on the way back. Fortunately it was a double decker and we got a seat upstairs on the way back to EK. We got off the stop before the bus station and it was just a few yards from 'The Lum', our local and home to Russell, the world's greatest barman, who happened to be behind the bar. So after waiting about 20 minutes for a drink (only kidding Russell) we had a couple and then wandered up the hill to our homes. It was still only the back of six when I got in and Kate was surprised to see me so early and reasonably sober, well not completely pissed.

We had had a great day out in Kilmarnock, a place well worth a visit on a Saturday afternoon. I would give the football a miss though if today's result is anything to go by.

Today was one of the cheapest day's out we have had in a while. This is caused by drinking less. I think I spent about £25. I know some smart arsed woman will say that at about £3 a pint, it is still about eight pints and that is a lot. My answer is, stop going on and get a life.

Craig; *The woman who served me must have been desperate to get rid of her remaining stock. When I asked her if I could have a cold sausage roll she put it in a a bag before telling me that she*

71

didn't actually have any cold ones left but this one really wisnae that warm at all.

I was too stunned, not to mention too hungry, to argue. It was quite tasty but I couldn't help but worry that I might get some kind of food poisoning from eating a luke-warm lump of meat. I thought that I had better play it safe and have a couple of pints of lager as soon as we arrived back in East Kilbride. You can't be too careful you know.

We had enjoyed our day down in Kilmarnock. The service we received was first rate in all three of the places we visited and the beer was also very good.

The only worry I have about going round all these football grounds is that we seem to be jinxing the home team's chances of winning. If that gets out before we finish this project I think we might not be so well received when we stagger up to bar of the supporters clubs.

Pubs we visited:

The Sports Bar;

The Howard Park;

The Lowden Arms;

How to get there by bus:

X76 Glasgow to Kilmarnock

Partick Thistle

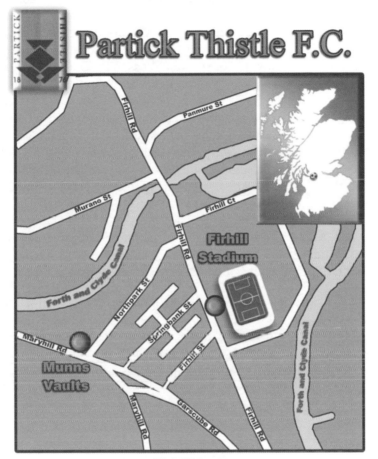

Firhill Stadium
Ground opened - 1909

John; Partick Thistle, The Jags, The Harry Wraggs, The Maryhill Magyars. Thistle are without doubt one of the best loved clubs in the country, with great nicknames, everybody has a soft spot for them.

They are also my favourite club. When I was young my dad worked beside Jackie Husband, a Thistle legend. Although Jackie was one of the best players in Scotland at the time, he still worked full time

73

in the Engine Drawing Office in Alexander Stephen's Shipyard in Linthouse. There was little money in football in those days, and remember, Thistle were playing in front of big crowds each week. Wonder where the gate money went. An uncle of my dad, Willie Ross, was the physiotherapist at Firhill for many years and treated me when my knee was damaged. I also did a couple of seasons as a ball boy. I used to get the underground from Govan Cross to St. George's Cross and get a tram, or just walk up Maryhill Road to the ground. Great days!

Mentioning the trams reminds me of a story an old workmate of mine, Hughie Flynn, told me. When he was young, which would have been very long ago, Hughie and his pals would catch hold of a cat, wait till an open top tram would come along and throw the cat by its tail into the tram. He said the screaming noise from the cat and the passengers was fantastic. This is probably not a very politically correct story, but is true, Hughie told me.

Up until tonight, all our trips had been on a Saturday, but my son Gregor had phoned me to see if I was interested in going to the Wednesday night game against Morton. If Thistle won it would almost certainly mean promotion to the Premier League. I said yes immediately, and invited Craig, so we could make it an official visit as well as watching the game, which would be a first, but it was Thistle after all. So I contacted Gregor and arranged to meet him before the game in the bar in the stand. It was a fairly fluid arrangement as Gregor works long hours and he can never be sure when he will get away.

Craig and I worked out the schedule for visiting pubs to collect stories for the book. The kick off was 7.45pm so we reckoned if we got a train at 4 o'clock it would give us plenty of time for research (bevy). Craig wisely pointed out that the cheap train ticket stops at 4 o'clock so we should go for the 3.30pm train. This would save us in the region of £3 each; the fact that we would drink more than that in the half hour was never discussed.

I collected Craig at 3 o'clock and we got the 201 along to Hairmyres and the 3.30pm train into Glasgow Central. I never tire of getting off the train in Glasgow. The buzz you get in the big smoke is magic, especially if your first port of call is 'The Horseshoe Bar'. We frequent this bar mostly on our way home from trips, but today was different. As Firhill is close to the centre of Glasgow (about 10 minutes on the bus) we reckoned there would be plenty of supporters in it, even at this early time, as it was the most important match of the season for the Jags.

Craig; I still don't know how he managed to talk me into it but once again John had managed to convince me that it would be a good idea to visit the home of his favourite team: Partick Thistle. I have heard all of his ancient tales of him being a ball boy at Firhill and how his family were involved with the team so often that sometimes I feel as if I had been there with them all. And I was absolutely certain that some poor bugger was going to have to live through the self-same stories again tonight.

Not only would we be visiting the pubs in the area, which we usually do, but I was forced against my will to actually watch the football.

It is not just the cost of getting into a match which annoys me but rather the quality of what you get for your money. That's not just the football you understand but the facilities. Usually Scottish football doesn't do much in the way of facilities.

Tonight's game was against Greenock Morton and apparently it was very important to both teams to get maximum points.

The one thing I do know about Firhill is that it is not surrounded by a vast number of really great pubs. Actually I only know of one pub in the area. Because of this we decided to start our investigation of the fans favourite pubs several miles from the stadium. I think it was me who suggested trying the 'Horseshoe' in the city centre. To be honest I just fancied a couple of pints in there and didn't really expect to meet any Thistle fans in the bar.

John; The pub was jumping with supporters of Thistle and Morton, a lot of people were making a day of it. We spoke to a crowd of Morton supporters who never miss a game. They were good company and told us some great stories. One was about an old owner of the club who took the roof off one of the stands so he could reduce his rates. They have a great song which Craig will, I'm sure, regale you with as he was taking notes. My mate Allan, his wife Elspeth and daughter Nicola turned up after enjoying a fairly liquid lunch. They were in great form (that means pissed).

Although 'The Horseshoe' is the home pub for Old Firm supporters, mainly Rangers, today it was a Thistle pub that also welcomed away supporters. The atmosphere was magic and we were sorry when the time came to move on closer to Firhill.

We cut through the wee lane from Renfield Street to Hope Street and stopped the first bus that arrived. Amazingly, the bus driver was very helpful, and although we were on the wrong bus, he told us which one to get. I thought I should mention this as we are always slagging off bus drivers, usually with good cause. The bus the driver told us to get, the number 40, turned up in about five minutes, and in no time we were getting off in Maryhill Road just along from the ground.

Morton fans gather in The Horse Shoe

Craig; Imagine my surprise when we found a lot of Morton fans enjoying a drink there. We eventually got talking to a group of them. They had been singing a very strange song and were keen to tell us what it was about.

Apparently, according to these fans anyway, the owner of Morton, Hugh Scott, likes to hang onto as much of this money as he possibly can.

The lads told us that one of his money saving schemes involved taking the roof off the enclosure. Apparently that meant that he would not have to pay tax on it. Unsurprisingly the fans were less than chuffed by this piece of financial wizardry, hence the following song!

"We don't carry razors
We don't carry chains
We just carry brollies
In case it f***in' rains.

So if you pass the cow shed
You will hear the cry
Put a bloody roof on
And keep us f***in' dry?

This led to a general discussion on how penny pinching the owner was. At this point I would like to stress that the song and all references to meanness and penny pinching by management do not convey the views of the writers of this book.

Anyway one of the guys, Matt Stewart, told us that he had once been invited in to hospitality. Apparently the single slice of pork he was allowed on his plate was so thin he could have read a newspaper through it.

John; Gregor had suggested that I nick up to the ground and get the tickets early as he had been told that it could be a sell-out, so while Craig walked up to our next pub, 'Munn's Vaults', I walked up to the ground to get the tickets. The lady at the desk told me the tickets had not arrived yet and they would be another half an hour. This was about 6.15pm and I thought they were cutting it a bit fine. I wasn't bothered; the worst that could happen would be that we would miss the match.

I went back to 'Munn's Vaults' and found Craig in amongst a crowd of supporters belting out of their anthems. It was a riot of noise and I had no idea what was happening. It was like being in a pub before an old firm match, without the violence and hatred.

Two Thistle supporters we met had driven up from Newcastle and were going straight home after the game. Now that's what you call dedicated supporters, or slightly mad, as most Thistle supporters are. We had a great time and spoke to lots of crazy guys who struggled to make themselves heard over the noise. To finish off a perfect visit, the landlady came round with free pies, which were great. Needless to say Craig did not have one, he reckoned someone must have touched them to get them onto the baker's board. What a fusspot he is.

Craig; The journey up to Firhill only took about ten minutes or so and as planned John headed up to the park to get our match tickets while I got on with the important task of getting the beers up in our next pub, Munn's Vaults.

There are probably some very good and interesting reasons for naming this pub Munn's Vaults but I couldn't be bothered finding out what they were. All I will say is that it is not very catchy or even friendly sounding. I'm happy to say that this did not seem to be putting the drinkers off: the place was mobbed. The Thistle supporters were in good voice, singing some songs with totally unprintable lyrics. I really thought that we would be going without our beers as the crowd was four deep at the bar. Luckily I was completely wrong and got served in just a couple of minutes. The bar staff were on top form.

Just as I found a space to set down the beer glasses John walked into the pub. He said the ticket office was shut and we would just have to get them when we went up to the park. Personally I think it was a ruse on his part. His real ploy was to hang around outside the pub and wait until I had done all the donkey work up at the bar.

I am constantly amazed at the dedication of football fans. Let's face it it's only a football game! Anyway, the first person I talked to had travelled all the way from Newcastle for this game. God knows how much it was costing him and his pal to travel up here and stay overnight. I think I would have settled for reading about it in the paper the next day.

We moved up to the top end of the bar where we got talking to another dedicated Partick supporter called Phil Steven. Phil told us that he had been following his team for years but the scariest moment he had ever had was during a game against Rangers in 1989.

Apparently Phil and a pal had only just managed to get into the game. They eventually found themselves sitting in the highest tier in the Rangers stand. Against all expectations Partick scored the first goal. The image of two very lonely Jags supporters surrounded by several thousand bears is indeed a frightening one. As you can imagine the lads kept their celebrations to a minimum.

We didn't stay too long in the 'Vaults' since we needed to buy our tickets for the game, the cost of which never ceases to amaze me. For this kind of money there should be a helluva lot more than 90 minutes of football on offer.

Phil Steven chances his luck with a pie

John; We left the pub about 6.45pm and headed up to the ground, and what a sight met us. There were thousands of supporters queuing up to get in. The streets round Firhill were mobbed. It was a fantastic sight, and one that has not been seen there for many years. I felt the clock going back to when I was a ball boy in the days of 30,000 plus gates. I was filling up with nostalgia. Craig wanted to fill up with lager, so we went into the bar in the main stand. I got the tickets; two adults (Gregor and his pal) and two concessions for Craig and me cost £58. I was shocked, but shouldn't have been. People with very little disposable income are paying much more that that every Saturday at most grounds. When I was young football used to be for the poor working classes, now it's the playground for the people on social security. Only kidding!!

The place was jumping and I had to join a long queue for a pint. As we were expecting Gregor and his pal any moment, I bought four pints. As usual Gregor was late and Craig and I had to try and down the other two pints. At least Craig was happy.

We were thrown out of the bar as it was closing because of Scotland's crazy drinking laws and met Gregor and his pal across from the stand just minutes before kick off. There were still thousands of fans trying to get into the ground so it was obvious that the kick off would be delayed, and it was. It was eight o'clock before the game started. It took us ages to get a seat and we were separated from Gregor and his pal John. The three stands were packed and the atmosphere was electric. I bought a Pie before the kick-off. Craig didn't as he reckoned the baker must have touched it!

Craig; The supporters club at the park is really very large. It looks like the function suite of a slightly run down hotel. Since I had braved the crowds round at 'Munn's Vaults' John felt obliged to do the honours here. There must have been fifty people in the queue.

Although the room was huge there wasn't a table to be had. In fact there was barely enough room to squeeze past the drinkers who had been smart enough to get in there early. I managed to find a small space over at the back wall and waited there for a good, fifteen minutes. Eventually I get bored and squeezed my way back over to the bar just in time to see John get served. Almost immediately he found an empty table. I hate it when he does that.

Although the beer was quite good and we did eventually get a table I really don't think I would advise a visit to the Thistle supporters club. It is too big and to be honest not very comfortable. I do realise that the bar staff are doing their best to serve the punters quickly and efficiently but the place was just too crowded.

By the time we actually got into the ground that had become far too crowded as well. We couldn't get a seat. Eventually a less than helpful steward pointed us in the direction of what were quite possibly the last two empty seats in the stadium. And I think I know why they were empty.

Nobody in their right mind would ever describe either John or me as tall. If you will pardon the pun, we would be 'stretching' a point to suggest that we were anything more than of average height. So just exactly who these seats were meant to fit is a mystery to me. Even that 'very well-known budget airline' gives you more legroom!

John; Now as you all know, this book is not about the matches themselves, so all I will bore you with was that the place erupted about 10 minutes before halftime when the Jags scored a sensational goal. It turned out to be the only goal of the match. This was just as well as we decided to leave just after halftime. Craig was in a lot of pain, caused by lack of drink.

We said our goodbyes to Gregor and his pal and got a bus back into Glasgow and somehow ended up back in the 'Horseshoe'. While we were in they were showing a Champions' League match between Paris Saint Germain and Barcelona. Nothing in the match from the park itself to the players and the style of play, bore any resemblance to what we had been watching at Firhill.

It just goes to show you, you can't beat Firhill for thrills, no football, but plenty of thrills.

Craig was so hungry by now that he suggested we get chips from 'The Blue Lagoon'. The chips taste great when you're drunk and Craig reckons the burning fat (or creash if you're from Ayrshire) will destroy anything that will damage your insides.

Irene met us at EK station and ran us home. I had an empty, as Kate was down in Kilwinning looking after her sister Margaret who had just had an operation which men don't talk about. You all know the areas I'm talking about.

So ended our visits to the bars around the Firhill area, and great they all are, and so are the Thistle.

If you are interested I spent in the region of £40 today, or maybe a wee bit more. Mind you, £12 of that was for a discount ticket for the match, and a Pie before the match, which was great. So all in all, I came home with a wee glow in me.

Craig; I was ever so glad when John asked me if I would rather call it a day and head for home, via the pub obviously.

I don't know what the link is between alcohol and deep fried food but it is certainly a strong one. As soon as we left the Horse Shoe the aroma of rancid chip fat started working its magic on us.

You would think that by now I would realise that most of the chips I was about to purchase were going to end up in the bucket. John, on the other hand, always manages to scoff the lot. Either he has the constitution of a horse or he long ago lost all sense of taste. Since he also drinks Belhaven Best I must assume it is the second of these two possibilities.

A combination of the Best and the hot chips meant that I didn't hear much from John on the journey home on the train.

Pubs we visited:

The Horse Shoe;

Munn's Vaults;

Firhill Bar;

How to get there by bus:

No 17 from (and many others) from Hope Street

Rangers

Ibrox Park
Ground opened - 1899

John: Rangers, The Gers, The Teddy Bears and many other nicknames, some which are politically incorrect, are spoken in association with Rangers. Love or hate them, and there is no middle ground for most people in the West of Scotland, and other places, they, like Celtic, are a hell of a size of a club.

But as you all know in our book, size does not matter. In fact a small one can often be what we want. Of course it's pubs I'm talking about.

Today is all about finding out what the pubs round about the ground are like, and if we are well received in them. Ibrox is a fairly easy ground to get to from East Kilbride, compared to Aberdeen anyway. The train into the Central Station and a bus along Paisley Road will do the trick. That was the plan.

We got the wee orange M1 bus, which was the 'right' colour for todays visit, from the bottom of the road along to Hairmyres to catch the 12 noon train. As usual on a Saturday, it was a big four coach train and the conductor was nowhere to be seen, so this meant getting our tickets on the platform at the Central Station, which always annoys Craig. But this did not matter. We're not in a hurry as there are plenty of buses that take you along Paisley Road to the Cessnock area where there are a bunch of traditional Rangers pubs.

Craig; This was the big one, the one we have been waiting for: Rangers. To be honest it was only one of the trips we have been waiting for. Not being a football supporter I feel that I am in a perfect position to tell the unvarnished truth about anything we find out about the bars in and around our football grounds.

Although I'm from the West of Scotland I never got caught up in the whole Rangers / Celtic thing. I have no idea why not. Having talked to a fair few sports fans from the East coast I get the idea that most people there think we are all nuts in the west.

They might be quite close to the truth actually. I know a Rangers fan who refuses to drink out of a green cup. Just for a bit of balance, I also know a Celtic man who refuses point blank to eat Blue Riband chocolate biscuits. Now you really do need to be a die-hard fan to pass up the chance of a nice cup of tea and a choccy biscuit for something as daft as deeply held religious beliefs.

Anyway, today's journey into the land of the ' Blue Noses' started with a bit of an omen. We were waiting at the bus stop for our first bus of the day when we saw this wee orange bus coming along towards us. You just don't get more apt than that!

There was something very wrong with my seat on this bus. For some reason it could swivel round by 45 degrees. I assume that this is to help disabled passengers. My seat seemed to be loose and kept swinging around every time the bus went over a bump.

Given the state of our roads you can imagine I was getting a bit dizzy by the time we got off at the train station.

Actually I thought I was seeing things when we were walking through the car park. A car had rolled backwards down the slope and bumped into another parked car, At least two people were in for a bit of a surprise when they got back from Glasgow.

Once again the conductor didn't bother his bum selling us any tickets; this of course meant another queue when we got to Glasgow.

John; The first one we tried was 'The District'. It was a nice and friendly pub. All the walls are covered in tasteful Rangers memorabilia, tasteful that is if you're a Rangers fan. We spoke to a very nice crowd of supporters. I'm not saying I was surprised how nice they were, but I was. Just goes to show you can't believe all you read in the papers about football hooligans. All the supporters in this pub were great guys. Craig took a couple of photos to remember them by and we said our goodbyes, and after a couple of 10 minute handshakes we were on our way to our next port of call.

Little did I know that by the time we had walked the 200 yards to our next pub we would have witnessed something we had never seen before. Two mounted Police officers (a man and a woman) turned right off Paisley Road into Harvie Street. Just then a car turned in from the other direction and raced past them. Help ma boab, did the two mounted screws not take off after them in the style of The Lone Ranger, as you would do near Ibrox. After racing across a small junction, they caught up with the Starsky and Hutch impersonators and stopped them, it was amazing. There were wee Jakie boys filming it on their expensive cameras. They told us it would be on Facebook in a few minutes. I would have loved to have seen the film, but I have no idea how it all works. Maybe Craig will find it.

With shouts of 'Hi Ho Silver Away', which I admit was a bit childish, Craig and I went into 'The Louden'. Now this is where you start to get into world of 'Old Firm' fanatical pubs. The entire pub, outside and in was Red White and Blue, nothing wrong with these colours I hear you say, or the bluenoses amongst you, and there isn't. There wasn't an inch of wall that wasn't covered with photos of Rangers legends, past and present, but mainly past. The big tellies were showing videos of Rangers matches. All the time we were in the pub, Celtic never scored, but they picked it out of the net a good few times. The locals were in heaven, blue heaven.

Now I've got to make something very clear, the pub was packed, but everyone was in good form. I never heard bad language, although some of it might have been religiously leaning towards the proddy side of the great divide. The service was quick and friendly. I'm not suggesting you go in dressed in green hoops, but that apart, it was a great pub and we enjoyed ourselves.

Craig; Out on Paisley Road West we found our first refreshment stop of the day. 'The District' is a fairly tradition looking Scottish pub, except of course for its decoration. At the time I remember thinking that I had never seen so much blue used in a pub's colour scheme. I was in for a bit of an education later on that day.

We got talking to a group of fans who were down to see the match all the way from Montrose. This was them here for a home game! The lads, Greg, Craig, wee Dite and Brian, apparently manage to get to most home games.

I'm not sure if they were kidding us on or not but they claimed that Craig had a very famous cousin and of course I was supposed to guess who that was. Little did they know that if they were expecting a knowledgeable sports fan to rattle off a smart answer they were barking up the wrong tree. They eventually gave up and told me that his cousin was in fact Sandy Lyle.

I toyed with idea of asking," Sandy who?" But I thought better of it. We enjoyed our short stay in the District and would recommend it. The service was great and so was the beer. I'm not sure of the prices as John is in charge of the kitty nowadays.

The Montrose boys told us where we could find another good pub, and it was only just down the road. Outside I took a picture of two police officers who were passing by an horseback.

Just after I took the photo they galloped off down the road. I thought it was a strange reaction to a camera but it turned out they were chasing someone.

Greg, Craig, Wee Dite and Brian

We spent the next five minutes laughing at the poor soul who had just been caught after a high speed police chase. That's probably what he will tell his mates anyway. The shame of being caught by a couple of polis horses would be too much to bear. The Louden Tavern, the first one not the second one, was a relevation. It certainly wasn't what we expected.

It was much better. We must have looked really out of place, with me wandering round taking pictures. An old boy at the bar came over to tell me that the place wasn't as good as it used to be. Apparently the owners had taken down his favourite picture of Jim Baxter. I couldn't see where there would the room for another picture. It would take hours to check every photo on the walls,

Once again the beer was really good and the service was very efficient. One of the customers told us where the other Louden Tavern was but said it would be very busy by this time, We decided that busy or not we had to visit it.

John; We had been told by one of the guys in 'The District', that the pub opposite Ibrox underground station was the one to visit for characters, so leaving 'The Louden', we headed along towards Ibrox underground. By the way, when I was young, this station was called Copland Road, I wondered why they changed it, it's still on Copland

Road. This means Francie and Josie and Johnny Beattie will have to change the words of that great classic, 'The Glasgow Underground'. Mind you, now I think about it, some of the other stations have also changed, and I think at least Francie is dead. Getting old is hellish.

John, looking the picture of health

The pub was called 'The Louden Vaults' I think. It was just a much bigger and louder version of 'The Louden'. The pub was absolutely packed, we could hardly get in the door, but we had come this far and we decided to give it a go. I managed to get to the bar, everyone in my way moving aside and when I got to the bar, the service was instant and friendly. Rangers may be struggling a bit recently, but their supporters know how to run bars.

This bar was just a bigger and louder version of the last one. I must say that if anyone has never visited this bar, or one like it, if there is one, it is worth a trip, probably not on the day of an 'Old Firm' match. I wonder if Celtic have a similar version of such pubs. We will find out soon as a visit to Parkhead is coming up.

We enjoyed the banter of the people next to us. We couldn't hear for the noise, but we just kept nodding our heads and saying things like 'you're right there big man'. The pub was starting to empty as the crowd was heading out to the game, so we followed them, but headed to the underground station to get a train the one stop to Govan Cross. The crowds we have seen today are incredible. There seemed like millions of them. I hope they won, I have no idea, but the support deserves it.

Craig; Had I known just how far away it was I might just have stayed where I was. Round at the other Tavern we could see it was busy long before we got to the door. I didn't fancy our chances of getting a pint to be honest.

This was probably the busiest pub I have ever been in. The strange thing was that as we edged our way in the crowd parted to let us through. Even at the bar itself people stood back to let us in.

We were served in a few minutes. Eventually we even found a wee place to sit our beers down and take in the flavour of the place, In all the time we were in there we never heard a single cross word spoken. Everybody was laughing, joking and generally having a good time. So were we.

The troops assemble at their HQ

After the Tavern we made our way to the underground station at Ibrox. We were the only people travelling in that direction. In fact we almost had the whole carriage to ourselves.

John; Leaving Ibrox behind, but not too far, we got off the train in Govan, my old stamping ground. God knows what they have done to Govan Cross, but it looks a mess.

I gave Craig a running (or slow walking) commentary on our way along Govan Road and into 'Brechin's Bar', one of the oldest, and unchanged, bars in the world, or anywhere else for that matter. I always hope to see someone I know in this bar, but Craig, very unkindly, told me that there was nobody in the bar as old as me. I looked around and I am sure there was an old guy at the end of the bar about my age, but the depressing thing is that he looked really old. So I just shut up and drank my pint.

We had really enjoyed our day so far, and the great thing was that it was only about half three. Now my better half Kate was down in Kilwinning looking after her sister who is recovering from a wee operation, so I could go home without Kate knowing what state I was in. Who am I kidding, she knew I'd be pissed. All she ever asks me is to try and remember to eat something, anything. Craig, on the other hand is his own man, so he kids himself on, and says he can go home whenever he wants, so the day was our oyster.

The problem is that at our age, the way we drink, we can only enjoy ourselves for about five or six hours maximum before we fall down, or I do anyway, Craig claims he can carry on all night, and he may be right.

Craig; At Brechin's we sampled a few more beers and failed to speak to another soul. The service and the beer were once again really good but after the last three pubs this one was far too quiet for me.

John loved the place, which in my opinion tells you all you need to know about John. What I'm hinting at is that Brechin's, like my old friend, has seen better days. We had a couple of pints to give John time to get all nostalgic and check out the customers for a familiar face. I tried to tell him that after 40 years it is unlikely he will find any old friends in Govan, Those who haven't already passed on are unlikely to still be visiting pubs on a Saturday afternoon. Maybe he should be looking in local care homes.

John; Our plan was to get a bus into Glasgow, the train to EK, and have a couple in 'The Monty' before heading home, but because of the train times, we had time for a pint before the train. We could have sat for ten minutes and waited for the train, but that would be sensible, and that's not us.

Craig was starving, so on the way to the Monty, we got a couple of bags of chips and ate them outside the pub before heading for our last drink of the day.

We had a nice time in the 'Monty'. I met my son Alasdair's wife Mary's father, Jackie, in the bar and we had a chat about Mary and Ally's new addition to the family, which was due the next day. We are both delighted about the extra babysitting we will be involved in. Grandparents just love their grandchildren, for an hour at a time I hear you say. I think Jackie had had as good a day as me, he certainly seemed to be in the same state as me, happy! We were sensible and got a taxi home after only a couple, or so.

So ended a great day of sampling the bars in the Ibrox area. The problem is that there are so many of them and the area is so large that we are thinking we may need a couple of visits to Rangers and Celtic to take in the vast amount of pleasure palaces in their vicinities.

I think I blew in the region of £40 today, that did include a bag of chips and half a taxi and a wee bit for the underground as it's not free, which is ridiculous, so all in all, not to bad, or is it?

Craig; *Round at the bus station we asked a bus driver which bus we should catch to get back into the city centre, He tried to put us off by telling us to take the underground instead. What he failed to tell us was that we could catch a McGill's bus just a few yards away which would do the trick. Maybe it was just a bit of rival company loyalty, but we were not amused.*

Back in Glasgow we decided not to stop for our usual couple of beers. Actually it was a ploy of mine to avoid a visit to John's favourite chip shop. I was trying to avoid another cholesterol bomb going off in my arteries.

Up in East Kilbride we stopped off at the chip shop in the village. I would have splashed out and had a full fish supper but John was in a hurry to get his feet back on the sawdust. The girl in the shop insisted on wrapping my fried-to-perfection chips in newspaper. That was a very traditional touch which at the time I really appreciated.

For once I was really enjoying my chips Unfortunately weather conditions were optimal for a personal disaster to occur.

There was a perfect ratio of chips to wind speed. A gust of wind caught my chip paper and the whole lot went flying. It's just not fair.

The only good thing was John had gone ahead to get the beers up. He could have done himself a real mischief laughing if he had only waited a few minutes.

After a couple of pints we called it a day and got a taxi home. I was surprised that John wanted a taxi rather than get me to phone Irene to come and get us. It was only much later that I realised he didn't want Irene telling Kate what kind of a state he had got himself into.

Pubs we visited:

The District;

The Louden;

The Louden Tavern;

The Brechin Bar:

How to get there by bus:

Nos. 9A/10/38 etc

Dundee

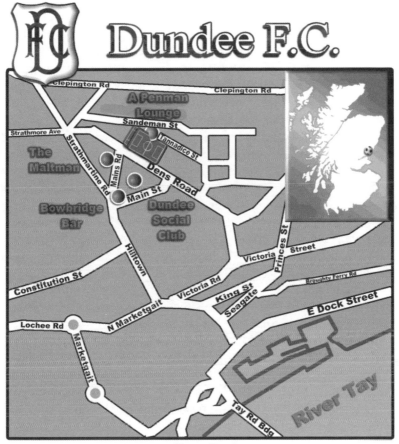

Dens Park
Ground opened - 1899

John; Their nicknames are The Dark Blues, or The Dees. Although I'd never heard of the Dees until I checked the web page before our visit, it's a good nickname, so 'The Dees' it is. Don't know why I've given you all this information as it has nothing to do with what we are about in this masterpiece.

It was a last minute decision to go on the trip as my son Alasdair's wife Mary was due any day and I may have been called away to do something, probably drive somebody somewhere or look after the other two kids. Fortunately, the happy event, a healthy girl, did not interfere with the important things in life - bevy!

The night before the trip I booked us seats on the bus, so technically we had to pay 50p each, so the bus was not completely free. The reason I booked was that Craig and Irene had a bad experience coming back from Dundee after delivering our books once and have worried ever since about being stranded in Dundee. I can assure you that there are much worse things that can happen than a night out in Dundee, especially if you know the legendary 'Bush Bar'.

Craig said that he had nothing to put on pieces so we decided to rely on fish suppers. It's very, very unusual for Craig's Irene not to have a bevy of options for Craig's delight on the days of our trips, I wonder if she is getting as fed up as my Kate is at organizing stuff for pieces every week or so. I will check with Craig after he's had a few.

The morning dawned bright and sunny and I had a spring in my step as I went down the hill to pick up Craig. An uneventful journey on the old 18 took us into Buchanan Street Bus Station to pick up some soft drinks and crisps to have on the bus.

The Dundee bus turned out to be one of these fairly new giant double deckers. The design of the bus means that there are very few seats downstairs, and by the time we got on we had to go upstairs. There is dam little leg room on these buses and although I am no Jack Reacher, the real one, not the midget who plays him in the movie, I found the leg room pretty tight. At least it gave Craig something to moan about at the start of the day.

It was a lovely journey up to Dundee; the only thing worth mentioning was that there were two young couples in front of us who shouted at each other in a semi-jakie type talk. At one stage one of the boys mentioned, in a loud voice, that his pal, who had recently lost about £40,000 on some house deal had just spent £285 on a Bagetti Kettle. I think that is the company who make the so called super cars. Youngsters sure know how to spend other people's money today.

Craig had checked up on the locality of the pubs round about Dens Park, but we felt we needed some local input, and a pint, so after getting off the bus we headed straight to 'The Bush Bar', one of our favourite bars in the country, to ask Harry the owner to fill us in on the bars in the area. Sod's law was at work and Harry had just left the bar and wouldn't be back that day. He was off with the wife shopping. Didn't sound like Harry, must be getting old and henpecked. This turned out not to be a problem as his brother-in-law Jeb, who we had met before filled us in with bar details and how to get a bus to the ground, so we had all the information we needed as we left 'The Bush'.

I had already told Craig that the bus we needed left from Albert Square, I had checked on the web-but Craig reckoned I had been watching Eastenders and was mixed up. Following Jeb's instructions (I wondered what Jeb was short for, I just assumed his mother liked 'The Dukes of Hazzard') we walked round the corner and found the bus stop, well two bus stops. There was no sign of Dens Park on any of the stops. Luckily there were two guys in bus driver's uniforms, so I asked them and was told to go round the corner into Albert Square and get a 1A, a 1B or a 1C. I knew it was Albert Square, Craig was crushed.

After having to put on a bit of a spurt, or our impression of someone putting on a bit of a spurt, to get the bus, we were whisked up to the Dens Park area. The people in front of us must have been listening to our conversation, things must be quiet in Dundee, and they told us which bus stop to get off at. We still had a wee walk up a hill to the ground. We wanted to have a look and see if there was a bar inside the ground, and there was. The bar was called 'The Andy Penmann' lounge after one of Scotland's greatest inside forwards. Come to think on it, Dundee have produced some of the greatest players in Scotland, but all a long time ago.

Craig; *With remarkably few hitches we found ourselves sitting on the Megabus M 90 skelping along the road and the miles to bonny Dundee.*

We were on our way to check out the facilities in and around Dundee football club. This would be the first time we had moved away from the city centre area of Dundee so there had been a great deal of planning. Despite all of that we decided that we had better call in at our favourite pub,' the Bush Bar' for a bit of advice.

The pub wasn't very busy for once, and we had plenty of time to talk to the barman. Our old pal, Harry the owner of the Bush was away on domestic duties, but his stand in, Jeb, was very helpful. He even told us which bus would take us up to Dens Park

95

Given that we didn't know how long it would take to find a good drinking establishment we limited ourselves to a single pint each. John insisted that the bus we needed to get left from an area called 'Albert Square. I thought he was talking nonsense. This led to a good ten minutes of 'Eastenders' jokes.

In my best cockney accent, which is far from convincing, I suggested that maybe he was still a bit badger and skunk from a night out on the old hit and miss. Actually I have no idea if that makes any sense whatsoever. But it sounded right at the time.

I had checked out our route on Google street view the night before and it actually felt as if I'd been along this road before. To misquote somebody whose name escapes me, 'It was Deja vu all over again.' I have a feeling that I've probably said that before, perhaps more than once.

John; A donation of a pound each got us into the great wee bar filled with the real supporters who follow their club through thick and thin. Like most clubs recently it has been a bit thin. We spoke to a few supporters, and a great bunch of guys they were. A father and son, both Bob Walkers, had driven down from Aberdeen to see the game. The young Bob having just arrived back from Dallas, Texas the day before and this was the first thing he wanted to do. I said they were great guys, I never said they had any imagination. I've said it before, but I'll say it again, these guys are the backbone of Scottish Football, or what's left of it.

There was a big table filled with sandwiches, cakes and pies which were all free, and after being told how great the pies were and to help ourselves, we both had a pie, or as they say in Dundee, pehs, so Pies are Pehs in Dundee! How's that for a bit of local knowledge. No need for you to make a fool of yourself if you're ever in a bakers in Dundee.

Craig; *Our idea was to stay on the bus until we caught sight of the floodlights at Dens Park. It seemed like a perfectly good plan but it could have ended badly.*

The passenger in front of us had overheard our master plan and had some surprising news for us. Although the driver told us the bus went past the park he didn't mention that it would be in a different street and completely obscured from view.

We managed to get off within walking distance, if not within sight of the stadium. Everyone we had talked to had told us that Dundee didn't have a supporters club at their ground. But John was determined to go up and have a look. Just to humour him I agreed to have a look. I really hate it when he is right, but since that doesn't happen very often I can't really complain too much.

Of course he did try to go into the wrong club but a friendly bouncer soon put him right. That's not a description you can usually attach to the large gentlemen who block our doorways. I think it must be an east coast thing. As I've said before, people on the east coast are much less grumpy and threatening than the west. Anyway they pointed us in the right direction and even took one of our leaflets.

The Twa Boabs

In the Andy Penmann lounge we got another friendly reception. The lounge is well set out and was not too busy when we arrived. Up at the bar John asked the young barman if he and the rest of the bar staff were all Dundee supporters. The young guy looked a wee bit nervous when he replied that only half of the staff were. Since there was only one other person behind the bar I said "I take it you're the one who isn't' ? He nodded and I got the distinct impression that his loyalties were with a team several hundred yards down the road.

We decided to leave the nervous young man to his glass polishing and moved on to find some actual supporters to talk to.

The lounge had a family friendly atmosphere but I decided not to hold that against it. It was worth putting up with a few noisy weans scuttling around the room, after all the beer was good and reasonably priced. We found a couple of seats and immediately got into conversation with a couple of Dundee stalwarts.

Actually they were Aberdonians, but that doesn't matter. The younger of the two gentlemen introduced himself as Bob Walker, then added, nodding at the other chap, "So is he". I got the impression that he has done this before as he had a good laugh at our expressions. It turned out that they were father and son.

Travelling a couple of hundred miles to see a home game certainly defines dedication. While we were chatting I decided to ask a question which has been bothering me for a while. I asked the two Boabs what was the difference between Dundee and Dundee United. After a good ten minutes of in depth discussion I was not one bit better informed.

I did get some really vital information 'frae auld Boab' though. Apparently the bucket 'Oor Wullie' sits on every week in the Sunday Post is called a luggie. As far as I'm concerned that made the whole trip worthwhile.

Usually I don't touch food at buffets: too much chance of catching something nasty. But on this occasion I decided to risk it. Dundee might never win any prizes for their pies but being free and freshly out of the oven I thought they were pretty good. I resisted the urge to get my money's worth by filling my pockets with unclaimed pies and settled for another pint of lager.

The two Boabs were really good company but eventually we needed to be on our way to pastures new. 'The Maltman' had been recommended to us by Jeb down at the Bush Bar.

John: The guys also filled us in on the best pubs in the area, or at least the ones where Dundee supporters would be found, so it was with fond farewells and cries of awa the Dark Blues that we left Dens Park and headed up a wee hill to our next Pub, 'The Maltman'. The bar was packed, which was great to see, and after getting a couple of pints we had a chat with Jamie and Tam, a couple of young lads who follow the team each week. When I asked them why they do this, they both said it was just the way they were brought up. I think that following your local team each week is a great thing to do and it gets you meeting other people instead of sitting in front of a computer all day. Good luck to them all, and Dundee. The pub had a great atmosphere and spontaneous singing was breaking out in all corners. Craig and I just mimed.

Tina was 'Simply the best'.

'The Bowbridge Bar' was our next port of call. As it was about three o'clock, the bar was quieter and we had no trouble getting to the bar and ordering a pint. The owner and the lady behind the bar seemed quiet and reserved, but we got them talking eventually and they were very nice. The lady was called Tina and we had a good time chatting away to her. This is another nice bar with a good atmosphere.

We had forgotten the way to the next bar we were trying to find and we ended up asking directions from a guy outside the 'Dundee Social Club'. He suggested we come in for a pint and we both spontaneously agreed. Inside it was nice and fairly busy, mainly with people of our age group, old! The guy sat with us and we had a great time. By the way, his name was Bobbie McGhee, honest. Today we met Jeb, Tina and Bobby McGhee. I think the people of Dundee used to like old American TV programmes and Country and Western music. No offence meant to any of them, they're great names, and great people. Like all social clubs, the atmosphere is great and the prices are very reasonable, and this was the case here, another great place to visit.

Craig; To be honest I didn't like the look of it from the outside. That might have something to do with it being painted pink, or maybe it is peach. But I'm glad we did go in. The lounge

99

was very crowded and we didn't fancy our chances of getting served quickly so we came back out and walked round to the bar. It was just as crowded but we were in great need of refreshment so we waited our turn at the bar. Actually it was John who waited as I really needed to get rid of some excess liquid before I took on any fresh supplies. It turns out that the bar and the lounge are joined together meaning we could have just walked through rather than going out and round. Anyway, by the time I got back john had got the round in.

And a very decent brew it was. There was a good range of ages in the bar and the supporters were in good voice, belting out their team songs. As far as I know there were no Hearts fans in the pub. We had seen a few making their way up to the Park but either they don't drink or they were in the pubs up on the street.

By the time we got our second pint most of the Dundee boys were leaving for the game. Only a few hardened drinkers, and us of course, were left in the bar. John asked one guy, who looked as if he was well on the way to an alcohol induced blackout, if he was a Dundee supporter. He said, actually slurred would be a more accurate term, that he used to be, but the drink had taken over. Besides he could buy a fair bit of booze with the money he saved by not going to the matches. It's good to meet people who are dedicated to their art.

We decided it was time to move on so we said farewell to our new pal who by this time was alternating between staring into space and staring into his pint.

Up over the hill we found 'The Bowbridge Bar'. It's a really traditional pub both outside and in. There were very few supporters left in the place by this time but we were told that the Bowbridge is a favourite with the fans. Up at the bar John discovered that that they sold both 70/- and 80/- on draught. He was really excited about this which I found a wee bit strange since he was now on the vodka.

The barmaid told us that her name was Tina and I am fairly sure she regretted telling us that almost immediately. I lost count of how many times John asked her how Ike was doing these days. It's a pity we couldn't have seen this pub earlier, or on a day when the team were playing an important game. Apparently this place is a favourite with the fans, usually.

We had heard of another place where we might be able to meet some supporters. It was called the Taxi Club, or something like that. Somebody gave us some very sketchy directions on how to get there but I didn't hold out too much hope of ever finding it.

As we were walking back along Main Road I noticed a sign on a building down a side street. It turned out to be the Dundee club. The group of people standing outside having a smoke were a bit of a giveaway I have to admit. John asked them if they could tell us how to get to the aforementioned Taxi Club and to be honest the blank expressions on their faces told us we were backing a loser.

So, to cut our losses, we decided to have a beer in their club. It didn't look like much from the outside but it turned out to be a very large and comfortable place on the inside. I was reminded of the working men's clubs you used to find in every town back in the 1970s BT (that would be Before Thatcher of course)

We sat down with a chap we had talked to at the front door. Bobby McGee was a good man to talk to as he was a Dundee supporter himself. We had a couple of drinks with Bobby and reminisced about the good old days.

That seemed to be apt as the club was in a bit of a time warp itself. Having said that, there was a good mixture of ages among the customers, everything from 18 to 80 in fact. On match days they always get a good crowd in. And so they should as the prices are reasonable, the beer is good and the service was great.

John; After a few 'y'all have a great day', we left and headed back to 'The Bush' for a quick one before getting the bus back to Glasgow. I don't remember anything about the journey back except it passed in about two minutes. I think we had chips from the 'Blue Lagoon' before getting the EK train. That's all I remember of the journey home, it was a hell of a day.

101

The only down-side of the day, apart for the vast amount of money I spent, was that I managed to lose the leaflets we had taken with us to distribute in the pubs we visited. We had 5000 printed recently. This is one of Craig's ideas to increase sales of the books through the publicity we will get from leaflet distribution, if I don't lose the damn things first.

So ended our trip to the Pubs in the area of Dens Park, and great places they are.

Craig; Somewhere between the Dundee club and the Bush Bar, where we headed for a last wee refreshment before catching the bus back home, John misplaced the leaflets he had been carrying around all day.

Of course I wasn't too bothered about this even though I had spent weeks designing them. But John felt bad about losing them, so I let him.

After a drink, possibly two, in the Bush we set out for the bus station and home. Back in Glasgow we visited a certain chip shop where yet again 1 bought a small bag of creash with some chips in it. Usually I make a heroic effort to eat the chips but this time I decided to cut out the middle man and threw the lot in the bin. I knew I would reap the benefits of this action the next morning.

Pubs we visited:

The Andy Penmann
Lounge;

The Maltman;

The Bowbridge Bar;

Dundee Social Club;

The Bush Bar;

How to get there by bus:

M9 Buchanan St to Dundee
1A/B or C from Albert Square
Dundee to ground

Hamilton

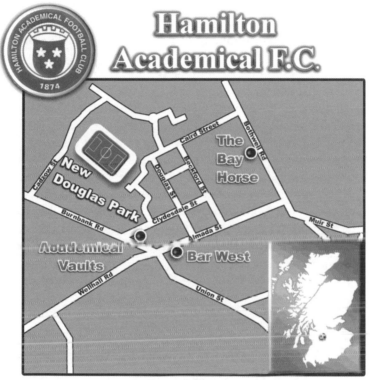

New Douglas Park
Ground opened - 2001

John: Today we were visiting Hamilton Accics. The new John is not going to be politically incorrect, or racist and tell you all what Hamilton Accies used to be slang for in Glasgow, anyway you all know-don't you? 'The Accies' is a not bad, but not great nickname. It is certainly better than calling the new ground 'New Douglas Park'.

But back to today's politically correct and depressing world, the New Douglas Park was built, courtesy of Sainsburys, who bought their old ground, Douglas Park, and have built a supermarket on the site. I know you may say that you cannot hold back progress, but the new ground, although there is nothing wrong with it, has the atmosphere of a morgue, and is just as clean and tidy. The only difference is that in today's world, there are probably more people in the morgue. Never mind.

Hamilton is the nearest ground to East Kilbride, so getting there was a dawdle, 25 minutes on the old 201 would do the trick. This meant we would be leaving at about 12 o'clock, so a long lie was in order, or that's what I thought until Kate told me on Friday that we were meeting Irene and Craig down in the old Crooked Lum for Breakfast. The bar would not even be open! I think the girls are determined that we will eat something before the hard work of bevying starts.

We met Craig and Irene at 10.30am in the Lum and had a great breakfast. This meant we would not have to spend any of our drink money on food. Craig and I managed to get away from the girls at about 12 o'clock and headed down to the bus station for a 201 to start the day's work. We still tell the girls that we are working on a Saturday. Kate tells me it is just like when I had a real job, the coming home drunk bit.

Craig; *Today's trip didn't have a lot going for it right from the start. When we were sitting around planning our next journey I voted for Hamilton, not because I particularly like Hamilton Accies but rather because they play their home games less than ten miles along the road from us. It suited me to be back at a reasonable time of day as I was going out on Sunday afternoon. At least that's what I thought was supposed to be happening. John agreed that we needed an easy day as he wasn't feeling too great.*

As it turned out I had got my dates wrong and John also managed an all-day session despite any lingering illness.

After the biggest breakfast I've had in more years than I can remember we were ready to set off to check out the pubs around Hamilton's stadium.

We had been tricked into going to the Crooked Lum for breakfast. I believe the thinking behind this was to make sure we actually had something in our stomachs other than the produce of a brewery. And since it was an all you can eat deal we ate our way

104

to a standstill. It only took us ten minutes to waddle down to the bus station to catch the 201 to Hamilton.

John insisted that we had to check out the stadium for signs of a social club despite the fact that everyone we talked to said there was no longer a club there. I toyed with the idea of waiting in the pub while John carried on with his wild goose chase but I felt too guilty. Besides I really needed to walk off that mammoth breakfast.

As predicted it was a complete waste of time, there was no sign of a club down there. Our first, and long overdue, beer of the day was served to us by a very nice girl in the Academical Vaults on Clydesdale Street. It is a really sturdy looking pub from the outside and a fine traditional one from the inside. The Vaults is the nearest pub to the stadium and is a favourite with the home support.

John; The bus dropped us at Hamilton West train station and we wandered down a wee lane to the park. The idea, as usual, was to see if there was a bar in the ground where supporters meet before the game for a wee refreshment. My mate Allan, who along with his son Fraser is a season ticket holder at Hamilton, had told me that he thought the bar was shut. It was. But just as we got to the ground Allan, Fraser, and Allan's son-in-law Ross were just about to go in for a meal in the hospitality lounge before the game. We had a chat with them before wandering back up the lane to find our first place of business, 'The Academical'. This was the pub we were told where the home supporters meet before the match. It was a nice pub with great atmosphere, the type of bar we like. No food or kids, and any women in the bar were 'Accies' supporters, so that is all right.

The first laugh we had was when the bar manager, a lovely girl called Irene, attempted to put skooshy soda water into Tam's white wine with ice. Now Tam was a big hard looking guy who had just introduced himself to us, so I didn't like to comment on him having a white wine spritzer with ice in case he banjoed me. Anyway, back to the story. The top of the skooshy thing was loose and the soda water went everywhere. Everybody within a ten yard radius was soaked. What a laugh!

105

You'll be served smartly by Irene in the Academical

The bar was quiet, but it was only one o'clock and it soon filled up with a fairly subdued lot of Accies fans. One fan I spoke to was a girl called Sandy who has been a season ticket holder for 40 years. She looked about 30, so standing in the freezing cold to watch the Accies must be good for keeping age at bay. She told us her father would give her a lift over the turnstiles to get in when she was a wee girl. She never told me how she got out. Craig was keen to take a photo of her, but she said she always looked Glaikit in photos. That's a great Glasgow word.

We had a smashing time in the bar, but felt we should check out the other bars on our list, so we said goodbye to the girls behind the pub, and Spritzer drinker Tam, and headed along the road and into our next bar, 'Bar West',

Craig; The Vaults is a fine traditional pub which has my most favourite of all pub fixtures, apart from beer fonts obviously. You just cannot beat a comfy bar stool. While I was sitting at the bar I got into conversation with a fellow stool-user. His name was Tam and he was a retired cooncil worker. He told me that the Academical was his favourite pub. So much so that when he retired he decided to take up sitting in it as his new and possibly only hobby.

106

Tam also told me that this was possibly the busiest pub in Hamilton and it got especially busy on match days. Depending on who the Accies were playing, it could also get a bit rough.

This inspired me to ask if there were any really rowdy pubs in the vicinity. We like to view the broad spectrum of a town's drinking establishments. Let's be honest there is so much more to write about when you visit a right manky bar.

Apparently we had missed our chance to view one such bar, by more than a couple of years. 'The Clansman' had to be seen to be believed according to Tam. Every town has a place like this. Actually quite a few towns have more than one. It's the one where all the knuckle-draggers eventually end up drinking, a case of downward mobility perhaps.

Anyway, according to Tam he was going to an interview or something and told his wife that he would be going for a beer in the Clansman afterwards. His wife was shocked and told him he couldn't go in there wearing a suit and tie as the clientele would quite likely crucify him. They would not take kindly to an authority figure, someone looking like a probation officer, social worker or worst of all, a bloke from the jobcentre wandering into their pub. I was sorry to have missed it but I do know what she meant.

I have been in some pubs where you have to watch what you are doing in case the locals get upset. For example in certain rural pubs it is advisable to read your Daily Record from the back pages to the front in case the bar-flys think you are a passing intellectual stopping by to mock them.

We got talking to the barmaids who were very interested in our day trips. John saw his chance and handed them some of our very colourful, well designed and informative leaflets which they read before putting them behind the bar. The idea was to hand them to punters, once they had had a drink, or preferably two, and in no time at all we would be worth a fortune.

Unfortunately someone, and we are not allocating blame here Irene, knocked them onto the floor, where they stayed, soaking up all the spilt beer and puddles of soda water.

John; Now, the name 'Bar West' should have given us a clue; who calls a bar, 'Bar West'? It was very modern, slate tiled floors, big windows, kids in with their well-to-do parents and food served in huge bowls full of salad and other modern things. Mind you, the bar manageress Yvonne was nice and made us very welcome. She told us away supporters frequent the bar. As the bar was nearly empty, Cowdenbeath, who the Accies were playing today, cannot carry a big away support. Craig was disappointed with the place, but I had promised him that the next bar we were heading for was really great. I had been in it a few times before and I staked my reputation on Craig loving it.

Yvonne at the bar in Bar West

Craig; We got directions to our next pub and made our way out onto the street. After I had stopped John from taking off in the entirely wrong direction we walked round to Bar West. To be honest we both felt the name of this place was telling us all we needed to know about the calibre of its customers. When they take a bog standard pub in the south side of Glasgow and slap a name like this on it, they call it gentrification. We tend to call it a waste.

Our first impression of Bar West seemed to confirm our worst thoughts. It was quite busy with ladies lunching and kids being annoying. There was a definite lack of old geezers knocking back pints and speculating about the chances of the Accies actually winning something.

108

The barmaid and the manager were very nice so we changed or minds about the place. Apparently Bar West is popular with away supporters.

The beer was quite good and the facilities were very clean so I was more than happy. John knew of another pub we could visit but was less than convincing about knowing how to get there. You could have knocked me down with a feather when he led us straight there.

John: When we went into the bar, 'The Bay Horse', I nearly died of shock, as there was what I assumed was a children's party in full flow at the far end of the bar. Craig gave me a look that would have turned lesser men to stone. Craig went to the toilet right away, I think he wanted to throw up-and I ordered the pints. When Craig returned I bent over to let him kick my arse, which he did. This is no mean feets for Craig with his arthritis, so he was definitely not happy.

We got talking to the two girls behind the bar, who were both great company. They were called Mhairi and Denise. They told us it was not a children's party but a First Communion. She said it was the start of the season for them, so there you go.

Denise's dad, Gerry McCabe, who was a great player in his day, had just been paid off by Dunfermline. He was the assistant manager there. Dunfermline are in a hell of a state at the moment. Hope things improve by the time you are reading this book.

Another great thing about this bar is that there is a fantastic Indian Restaurant right across the road and the same guy owns both places, so if you've had a few and can't be bothered leaving for a curry, the curry comes over the road to you. How good is that?

We had a great time in 'The Horse', and by the time we left, Craig admitted it was one of the best bars he had been in and that if he lived in Hamilton, this would be his local. He even tried to un-kick my arse.

Craig; *As you can imagine John was insufferably smug by the time he opened the pub door. His smugness was very short lived though. The sound hit us straight away and I thought we had landed in a nursery by mistake. There were weans everywhere. And they were running wild. I can just about put up with weans* being in the pub, just about. But there were balloons and streamers everywhere.

Talking about balloons, John was looking embarrassed and more than a little nervous. This was supposed to be a really special pub after all.

By the time I got back from the toilet John had found the only relatively quiet area of the bar. My first words to him were, "Assume the position". He had no argument to make and bent over. Luckily for him my best arse kicking days are long past and I only caught him a glancing blow. A pint of very acceptable lager later and I was feeling a bit better.

We didn't get a chance to talk to any of the customers about pub facilities, the friendly service or even the quality of the beer. That wasn't because they were in any way unfriendly or too far gone with the booze. No, the problem was that the majority of the customers stoating around the bar were under nine years of age. Luckily the barmaid, Denise, made up for the lack of amusing patter from her customers.

Mhairi & Denise provide the entertainment in The Bay Horse

Denise told us that the Bay Horse can get quite busy on match days and even more so when the racing is on at the Hamilton course.

I made the mistake of talking football to her before it became abundantly clear that she knew an awful lot more about it than I did. She was kind enough not to rub it in too much.

With quite a bit of imagination I could see that The Bay Horse would be a great wee pub once any person under the age of 25 had been shown the door.

I would certainly recommend a visit to this pub. The only downside I would point out is its location. For someone, like myself, who is unlikely to stray far from the main bus route for fear of never finding the way home, the Bay Horse seems a little bit off the beaten track. But to be honest, if I was a local, I would be quite glad about that as you can't beat a bit of elbow room up at the bar.

One of the things which really impressed John about this pub was that there was a very good curry house straight across the road from it. This might sound like a great idea but speaking from experience I think a night on the lager with easy access to hot spicy food could be a recipe for disaster. Not just for the consumer but quite likely for anyone unlucky enough to find themselves in an enclosed space with him. Back in East Kilbride we decided to stop off at 'The Lum' to gather our thoughts on our highly successful trip to Hamilton.

John; Two or three pints later, we said our goodbyes and walked up the road and got a 201 right away. It had been one of our most sober trips, so to celebrate we visited 'The Lum' on our way home and had a couple there. Even after all this work I was still home before six.

I think The Accies got humped 3-1, I think we are becoming a jinx to the clubs we visit. It was a very enjoyable day and the pubs in the Accies area are all worth a visit.

You are going to find this hard to believe, but I think my spend for the day was only just over £20. Some of you will say that as we spent nothing on food or travel, it is still in the region of seven pints which is a lot of drink. To you I say, get a life.

111

Pubs visited by us:

The Academical Vaults;

Bar West;

The Bay Horse;

How to get there by bus;

X1 First Glasgow
Glasgow to Hamilton

Inverness

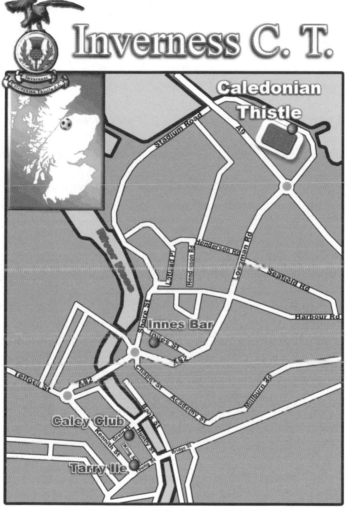

Inverness Caledonian Thistle
Ground opened - 1996

John: 'The Caley'. Not to bad a nickname, not great either, but I don't have time to think of a better one, need to concentrate on today's story.

It's a hell of a long way to Inverness, but I've never said our job was easy. That being said, the legendary Gold Bus makes the journey so much better. But more of that later in today's adventure to the teuchter land.

We've been to Inverness before in previous outings, but today's trip is for a very specific reason - and you all know what it is - to get pissed!

I went on the web and booked us return tickets on the Gold Bus. They're not really tickets, just a booking slip, but it gives us the security of knowing we should get on the bus, with the free coffee, scones, tiny sandwiches, tablet, lavvies and everything. There is talk now and then of the Scottish Government stopping the bus pass. If they suggest it again, Craig and I are marching on the Parliament Building, wherever it is.

The Gold Bus was leaving Buchanan Street at 8.30am, so after checking the web, I reckoned I had to get Craig at 7.15am. The things we do for our book! Craig said he was going to go back to the old tradition of bringing pieces to save a bit of money, so that was something else I had to remember before going to bed on Friday night. The other thing I did was to phone my brother Robert, who runs a bed and breakfast with his partner Ruth near the town centre in Inverness. He told me things were going well and I was to give him a phone on Saturday so we could meet up for a couple of pints after Craig and I had visited the ground and probably another pub. It was going to be a busy day, for our livers anyway.

The Gold Bus was full and we were one of the last on, so when we got on there were only single isle seats left. Craig sat on one side and I sat opposite him beside a crazy looking lady who kept standing up and peering out of the front of the bus. Just before the bus left, she got up and raced up to the driver. This was the second time this happened. This time she got off the bus, I think she must have been expecting someone. Anyway, this meant Craig and I got to sit together. This was great for me as Craig's Irene, as normal, had lots of extra things in with his pieces. She had even put in a packet of chocolate raisins for me. What a woman. Hope my Kate is reading this.

The bus was about a quarter of an hour late leaving because of all the faffing about with the full bus and everything, and the weather was very dull and wet. I was just mentioning the dullness of the day to Craig when he reminded me that the Gold Bus has darkened windows, so it was not as dull as it looked. It's just something else for me to remember.

I had a read of my right-wing 'Mail' to find out what was happening in the real 'get to work or die you lazy bastards' world and Craig his left wing rag, 'The Daily Record'. I usually buy the Record as well when I'm not with Craig, but I don't tell him that.

By the time we had put the world to rights (or right in my case), the scones and coffee were being served. I've said it before, but this Gold Bus service is great, the seats are really comfortable and the food is brilliant and free. If they could just put wings on the thing it would make the flight to Tenerife ten times better than Ryanair. The only down side is that you cannot get a wee bevy on the bus. Not that I'd want one at nine in the morning!!

It is one of the nicest runs in Scotland up the A9 to Inverness and the three and a half hour's run fairly flashed past. The weather had brightened up and was dry when we got off the bus in our Highland Capital. My brother says the weather in Inverness is much better than Glasgow. It could hardly be worse.

Craig; *This latest journey was one we had been looking forward to. Not because we are great Inverness Caley Thistle supporters but because to get there we would be using the fabulous Gold Bus. This just has to be our favourite way to travel I love the comfort and service while John enjoys watching me make a mess of trying to butter scones and or pancakes.*

John; As a wee aside from our trip, at the time of writing this, 'Father's Day' was just a few weeks away and we had decided to do a promotional drive to see if we could sell any extra books, so Craig had designed and produced posters, leaflets and end of shelf publicity to send to each Waterstones Store. To save the postage we decided to pop into the Inverness store as we would be passing it, hand them in and try to talk to the manager about taking more books.

When we went into the store, I asked the first employee we bumped into if we could talk to the manager. It turned out that she was in charge. She was the assistant manager, a lovely girl called Sharon, who was really great and on the ball. When we told her our plans and showed

115

her the publicity material, she said it was a great idea. She said they had plenty of books at the moment, but if we had a few minutes to spare could we sign them all, so we did. She has put up the shelf end material and the books are well positioned, so we hope all dads in Inverness will get a book for 'Fathers Day'. But back to the real reason for today's visit to Inverness.

Craig; We were aware that the Thistle could qualify for European football if they were to win today and to be honest that worried me more than a little. My reasoning was that almost every game we have covered so far, where the home team needed a win, they ended up on a loser. One of these days some large and easily annoyed fan was going to twig that we are complete Jonas as far as football is concerned. Teams which at any other time would have sailed through the qualifying stages of the cup or gained promotion to a higher division are failing miserably and it is entirely our fault.

It's getting to the stage that I'm too embarrassed to wish the fans good luck before we leave their club. Anyway back to today's match, Inverness versus Dundee. I don't think we actually saw a Dundee supporter all day, That's a bit of a pity I have to say as we had made some good friends among the Dundee fans just a couple of weeks earlier, Then again maybe they would have remembered we had wished them good luck as well, just before they got humped when we were up at Dens Park. Life can get dangerous out there for a couple of old, well meaning, bus pass travellers.

The trouble was, as far as I could see it, Inverness Caledonian Thistle stadium was a fair distance away from anything interesting. Of course I was under the impression that there was no social club at the ground. It was only when John phoned the stadium that we found out that there was indeed a good chance we could get a drink out there.
John was all set for making straight for the ground but, after an hour on the bus into Glasgow and then three and a half hours on the Gold bus, I was ready for a pint, Fortunately John saw the errors of his ways and agreed to stop off for a quick brew.

John; While we were in the store I phoned the ground to ask if there was a bar in the ground. There was, so off we went in the direction of the ground. One of the bars Craig had found on the web was called 'The Innes Bar', on Innes Street. It seemed to be roughly on the way to the stadium so that was our first port of call. It turned out to be a really nice, and atmospheric bar, even though there were couples with children in view. I suppose in today's economic downturn you cannot turn anyone away! The owner Craig, and his assistant Colette were great and we had a good time. It was still early, about one o'clock and they said most of the supporters would be arriving soon. This is a lovely wee pub and well worth a visit if you are up north anytime.

Colette and Craig at The Innes Bar

Craig gave us directions to the ground. He said 'turn right at the end of the road and that is the road the ground is on'. What he failed to mention was that it was a hell of a walk, Highlanders are a tough lot, distances mean nothing to them! To be fair, it was a lovely walk along the river past a lot of skips and industrial estates, but by the time we got to the ground Craig was knackered and had decided we would get a taxi back.

Craig; *Once again I had researched our targeted town on my computer, and found a likely looking pub in Innes street. Cleverly they had decided to call it the Innes Bar. I liked that but would have been more impressed if they had named it The Innes Inn. One way or another it would be hard to forget its name. Finding this pub was a great feat of*

117

navigation, I thought, but John didn't believe I knew where I was taking him. The Innes Inn was a great wee pub. Actually it is quite a big pub and not too busy when we arrived.

We were served straightaway and it was a really good pint. The barmaid was very nice and chatted away to us. Without too much persuasion the gaffer, Craig, agreed to have a wee picture taken.

There was a fairly good mix of ages in the bar and things were very civilised. A bit strange for a pub near a football park, but there you go. We didn't want to stay too long, not because we didn't like the place, we did, but because we had no idea how long it would take us to walk to the stadium.

As it turned out that wasn't a daft idea. On the map the idea of how long it would take us to get to the stadium. ground doesn't seem to be too far away from the centre of the town. I think that the map might have been drawn by someone who had never visited Inverness, It was miles away. In the pub the owner told us that it was only about a 20 minute walk to the park. He obviously hadn't seen us walk into his pub.

The stroll from Innes Street to the stadium could quite easily become an Olympic event, either that or a good training regime for special forces soldiers. I nearly didn't make it. John, once again, didn't trust my navigational skills and had to ask a passer-by if we were on the right road. To be totally honest I was beginning to think that maybe we had taken the wrong road. The scenery left a bit to be desired it has to be said. There seemed to be an awful lot of refuse trucks and container lorries roaring up and down the road. It might have been better if there had been a bus or two, but we struggled on.

Manfully I managed to keep my whining to a minimum but I was beginning to think that I might never see the dammed stadium.

John, to his credit, refused to leave me behind. Right enough I hadn't given him my share of the kitty money, but I prefer to think it had something to do with loyalty; who knows?

John; There were lots of fans and a pipe band milling around in the sunshine when we approached the security man at the door of the 'Sports Bar'. He said we had to pay the entrance fee to get into the bar. We had the same problem at Dumbarton and it took us ages to talk our way in there. This was different. The man on the door was a guy called Mackay, and when I told him my name and why we were here we were ushered in right away. There are a lot of Mackays in this area and further north. The Mackay Clan come from the Sutherland area, all great men. I remember being in Dornoch with Kate and our pals Dave and Helena, and we were looking at a war memorial. Almost ever name on the memorial was Mackay, Dave's comment was that the place was full of deid Mackays.

Where was I, yes, we got into the 'Sports Bar' in the ground. It was more like a 'Spartan' than 'Sports' Bar. The floor was wall-to-wall concrete and the walls were not much better. But none of that is important. It was a great bar with great supporters. The girls behind the bar, Donna and Dunell (I think) made us very welcome. We spoke to a few of the supporters and we, but mainly Craig, had a long conversation with a supporter of my age (an old bloke) called Dougie McKendrick who told him all about the birth of this club from two, or maybe three highland clubs. I was surprised by the hatred some of these supporters have for each other's clubs. There arc seemingly some guys who will go up to Dingwall rather than watch the Caley. I thought it was only in the West of Scotland that real hatred abounded.

We had a great time in the bar. Today was a very important day for the club. If they won today against Dundee United and Celtic beat St. Johnstone, which they did in an earlier kick-off game, then the Calcy would be in Europe next season for the first time ever. What a day; they got humped! Hope it's not us that arc a jinx. This is the third time in a few weeks something like this has happened. Kilmarnock and Dundee have suffered at our hands.

Craig; *When we eventually got to the stadium we found the supporter club defended by two large men. Apparently the club is for home supporters only, but they had reckoned without John and his famous brass neck. A couple of minutes after telling us that we could not get in, the bigger of the two guys was ushering us through the door.*

John said that the only reason we were allowed into the club was because the big man was a Mackay, and therefore belonged to

119

the same clan as himself. I said that I had my own idea of what Klan he belonged to, but the ex-grand wizard and Daily Mail reading Tory pretended not to know what I was talking about.

The decor of the supporters club came as a bit of a surprise. It didn't have any! I thought we were standing in the hallway to be honest. The stadium is relatively new and I suppose we should have expected a really modern design but bare concrete is a bit hard to take.

Functionality must have been what the designer was looking for when he dreamt this place up. Either that or the club was too skint to lavish even a few quid on anything other than a large bucket of white paint. However the starkness of the place didn't seem to bother any of the fans who were enjoying a drink and a laugh before the game.

We chatted to the barmaid and told her what we were up to in her bar. Donna and her friend were up for a laugh and posed for a picture even though they were very busy.

There are very few things which can put me off my beer but those thin, flexible plastic beer glasses come very close to doing just that. I hate the way the beer splashes over the top when you lift them off the bar. But since the floor of the place is just bare concrete I don't suppose it matters much.

The girls serve up a few laughs at The Sports Bar.

The next problem we encountered was the lack of seating. There were only a few stools scattered around and even fewer tables. I was exhausted and really needed to sit down. Eventually we found a couple of stools over in the corner. We were joined by another older gentleman by the name of Dougie McKendrick.

He looked as knackered as I felt so we found him a stool. He reminded us that Inverness Caley Thistle had been created from two teams. Unfortunately the fans of each team didn't appreciate the amalgamation and now boycott the team. The result is that Inverness now has a team in the Scottish Premier League and only manages to get an average attendance of around four thousand fans.

How they manage to keep going is a mystery. Although it does kind of explain why the supporters club looks like the inside of a bomb shelter.

We had a couple of pints with our newest pal before it was time to leave. I told John that we really needed to get a taxi back into town as my feet were in revolt and refused to take another step. To be honest I think he was quite pleased because, let's face it, he's not getting any younger.

John; We said our goodbyes in a highland accent and wandered out into the sunshine. We only waited for a few minutes before a taxi dropped supporters off and picked us up. When we told our driver, a Romanian Caley supporter why we were up in Inverness, he told us we would get a special rate. We found out in the pub later that the fiver he charged us was a pound more than the usual. I suppose he did tell us it was a special rate, special for him!

'The Caley Club' was where we found ourselves. This is an old club and inside was just like any working man's or woman's social club. They were all built about the same time and have that old depressing look about them, but Craig and I love them. The drink is reasonably cheap and the people and staff who frequent them are always friendly and great company, and that was the case here. We had a great time. This is another place that is a must if you are in Inverness and much more fun than prancing about looking for a monster. Mind you, there were a few monsters in the bar, if you know what I mean.

Just as were getting settled in, my brother Robert and his better half Ruth arrived and we enjoyed another pint with them, while still chewing the fat with the crazy locals. When we finished our second pints we said our fond farewells and wandered up the riverside, which is really nice, and into a pleasant wee pub called 'Tarry Ile'. What the hell that means I have no idea. I made a mental note to find out, but we had had about half a dozen pints by then and I forgot altogether. It was great catching up with Robert and Ruth. If you're ever up in Inverness you must stay with them at The Rossmount in Argyle Street. You'll have a great time and be made most welcome.

Craig; *Our Romanian taxi driver spoke remarkably good English, far better than most Glaswegian ones, or John for that matter. He dropped us off at the Caley Club and I think John was a wee bit disappointed. Maybe he thought we were going for a wee dance.*

The Club was a lot bigger on the inside than we had imagined. Given the attendances at games these days I would think that the whole lot of them could manage a pint in this place before kick-off.

The club itself was a fairly standard layout for a working man's club, maybe a bit more comfortable than most but nothing unusual.

I had to use the facilities almost as soon as we got to the bar. Usually this would be seen as a rouse to avoid getting my round in but, since John was in charge of the kitty, I could not be accused of any wrong doing. It's not often I'm lost for words but the toilets in this club fair took my breath away, in a good way. They were immaculate. If there is ever a competition to find Scotland's best bogs I'll be voting for Inverness Caley Supporters Club.

There were automatic towel dispensers as well as air dryers. Best of all the doors opened outwards. This meant that I didn't have to touch any door handles on the way out, magic! Unfortunately many men do not bother to wash their manky hands after using the toilet. Personally I think they should be fined or at the very least smacked about the head for this kind of behaviour. Pardon the rant but it is one of my pet hates.

Back at the bar a pint of very acceptable lager was waiting for me. We chatted to a couple of locals as we waited for John's brother to appear,

Although it was nice and comfortable in the lounge and the beer was reasonably priced and good, we decided to move on. We had asked John's bother, Robert, to show us a pub in the city centre where he thought football supporters might gather before a game.

We have found that there are always some stragglers left behind when kick-off time approaches. Actually it usually ends up that some of the less fanatical supporters, who might have left the house with every intention of going to the match, get a little too comfortable in the pub and give the game a miss entirely. Well-oiled and opinionated football fans can be a great source of information to the writer. They can also be a huge pain in the arse, but that is the kind of risk we are prepared to take to produce a quality book.

Unfortunately we were out of luck in the 'Tarry Ile'. There were no fans in, straggling or otherwise. The pub was fine. It was clean and tidy and the beer tasted exactly as I expected it to. I would say that it was a pub worth visiting if you are in the area. It just wasn't what we were looking for.

John: By the time we left the 'Tarry Ile', which is another great wee pub, it was time to wander back to the bus station to catch the 5.30pm Gold Bus home. This time the bus was fairly empty and we had our choice of seats. Why we chose to sit next to some young bloke who never stopped asking us questions I'll never know. Just bad luck. We were going to move, but you know what it's like, you don't want to be seen to be insulting some poor bloke, even if he is a bit of a bore.

Between sleeping and eating our free pieces, we were soon back in Glasgow and heading down to 'The Horseshoe' for a nightcap or two before getting the train back to EK. We had a great time on the train talking to our fellow passengers and trying to sell them books, although we didn't have any with us. I had booked a taxi to get us up the road as

123

we were incapable of walking any distance by this time and our two better halves had been out on the piss as well during the day.

Taking pieces meant that I saved a bit on food, but meeting the brother meant that more rounds were bought than usual. We also got a couple of taxis. You'd think we were making money out of this! I think the total for the day was about £40. I know some people will say I am an alky, but I don't smoke or gamble, so there!

Craig; We were both looking forward to a good sleep on the bus home but I'm afraid that didn't happen. We attracted the attention of a nutter who wanted to talk. And talk he did, all the way down from Inverness to Glasgow In fact he talked us sober so we had to drop into the Horse Shoe to top up again.

Pubs we visited:

The Innes Bar;

The Sports Bar;

The Caley Club;

The Torry Ile;

How to get there by bus:

M10 Gold Bus from Buchanan St
Stagecoach 27 from Inverness
(a couple of stops) or a 20 min walk

Hibernian

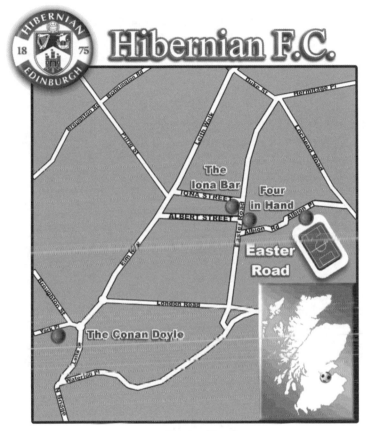

Easter Road
Ground opened - 1893

John; Hibs, *The Hibees*, good nickname, today's trip was to Edinburgh, Scotland's capital city. Like most people from Glasgow, I don't particularly like Edinburgh, but I think it is just a traditional thing, and not to be taken too seriously. On the other hand, one of the real things I hate about the place is trying to get into it. The traffic is a nightmare. The only way to get in quickly is to go by train, and it costs a fortune. The Bus Pass should be changed to the 'Truss Pass', so we pensioners could get on the bus and train for nothing. With the money this government is throwing away what difference would it make to let us on the trains for nothing.

Today was the last day of the season and I don't think any of today's team had much at stake, except pride. Hibs still had the Scottish Cup Final to take part in, so I suppose they would be holding something back in reserve, but to be honest, I have no idea.

There is a bus to Edinburgh every quarter of an hour from Buchanan Street, so there is no need to book or worry about times, you just turn up and get on the first bus that is leaving.

To change the subject slightly, at the time of the visit it was coming up to 'Father's Day', and Craig and I agreed, for the first time, that this would be a great opportunity to sell some of our books, so we (or Craig) had produced posters, fliers and shelf ends to give to all the stores to increase sales. Pretty impressive I hear you saying. We posted the material to most of the stores, but as we were going to be in Edinburgh, I suggested we visit the stores in Princes Street and George Street, so we could be ignored in person by the stuck-up Edinburgh managers who believe two old drunks bevying around Scotland is not a topic for Edinburgh snobs. Maybe I am being a bit hard on them, but we would soon find out!

But to get back to today's adventure. With our promotional material in hand, we left EK on the old 18 and headed to Buchanan Street. It was a dark and wet day, miserable, and this was near the end of May. To make things worse, Craig and I had had a heavy day yesterday and we were both feeling a bit worse for wear. Serves us right I hear you say! By the time we got into Buchanan Street it was lashing down.

I got a couple cans of Diet Coke while Craig went to the toilet. Craig spending 30p to pee meant something was not right with his innards, though he said he felt fine; the old Auchinleck spirit. The Edinburgh bus, the 900, was only about half full and left right away. The weather got worse as we headed East. By the time we were in Edinburgh the rain was the heaviest I can remember. Thankfully, we both had our umbies.

Because of all the diversions caused by Edinburgh Council's determination never to finish the tram lines, we ended up getting dropped off on George Street, right outside one of the two Waterstones we planned to visit. So we dived straight in. I had very little hope of anyone even talking to us, let alone getting an order, but, lo and behold, (that's the Edinburgh version of bugger me) the manager originated from Ayrshire, and even though it wasn't Auchinleck, (so Craig hated him), he was very nice and agreed that the books should sell well for 'Fathers Day' and promised to get back to us with an order. At the time of writing this there is still no order, but you never know, though I've got a dam good idea - nothing!

With fond Ayrshire farewells, we went back out into the rain and walked down onto Princes Street, with the Castle on the hill and everything, and went into the Waterstones Store. This was more like the Edinburgh thing, the staff were ok, but only just, and we left not really knowing what had been said. That usually happens to me later in the day.

We just missed the number one bus, which was the one we wanted, but after wandering about in the rain checking to see if there was another bus that would take us to Easter Road, we went back to the stop and waited 15 minutes for the next one, a number one. Talking about a number one, that summed up the journey to Easter Road, it was shit. It must have taken about an hour to do a journey advertised as taking 10 minutes. We could have walked it in about 20 minutes if we had known where we were going. By the time we got off the bus it was nearly 2.30pm. The only interesting thing about the journey was that the bus was one of these that ran on lecky some of the time and then the engine would suddenly come on. This may be energy efficient, but to me it just sounds like two things that can break down.

Craig; For today's little adventure we had decided to head for the east side of Edinburgh. Easter Road stadium, home of Hibernian was next on our list of places to visit. We had a couple of good reasons for wanting to visit Edinburgh and at least one good one for not going anywhere near the place.

Firstly we had a couple of book shops to supply with advertising materials before going on to the most important business of the day: beer.

On the down-side we were going to have to suffer the traffic chaos of the city. Getting to Edinburgh is very easy- unfortunately getting through it is a very different story.

We have been to Edinburgh quite often and I have to say that as far as I can remember, we have never travelled the same route twice. Even the bus drivers don't seem to know what is going on. Our driver actually stopped the bus to shout over to another bus asking which road was the best one to take to get us to the bus station. That doesn't tend to fill the traveller with a lot of confidence.

By the time we got off in George Street the rain was bucketing down. I got soaked in the time it took to get my umbrella up. After delivering the stuff to Waterstones shops John decided to give us both a bit of exercise by marching us up and down Princes Street searching for the correct bus stop, before settling for the first one we had come to.

We were very glad to see our bus eventually coming along the road. Little did we know that it would have been far quicker for us to walk to Easter Road than take this bus. It was standing room only, which did nothing to cheer me up. I'm pretty sure that at no time did the bus get above five miles per hour, most of the time it just sat motionless. The one consolation of that was the bus was one of those hybrid thingys. This meant that it wasn't belching out exhaust fumes for the entire hour it took us to travel the mile and a half journey out to the Hibs ground.

On board the bus the passengers were all a bit less than chuffed. Between the lack of speed and the steam rising off 50-plus very damp people there certainly wasn't much to laugh about.

To lighten the mood I suggested to a group of fellow travellers that what they really needed here were some trams. I have always said that Edinburgh folk have no sense of humour and once again I was proved right: nobody laughed.

Almost everyone on the bus was going to the game so we were fairly sure that we would be able to get off at the right bus stop, for a change. Because it had taken so long to get to the stadium we had very little time to find the supporters club and choke down a drink. But we managed.

John; We followed the crowd up the hill to the ground and after going to the wrong place, we found ourselves at the entrance to the season ticket holder's lounge. The couple at the door explained to us why we couldn't get in, but in a very nice and helpful way. The girl called Linda was very pleasant, as was the bloke, and after I had told them the reason for the visit, they agreed to let us in. I could get a piece at any door. Craig was amazed.

The set up was great. The downstairs bar allowed kids in, but the upstairs one didn't, so upstairs we went. It was a very large, but nice bar and the staff were very friendly. All in all a very nice place for a pint before the game. We didn't have a lot of time as it was near kick-off when we arrived, but we still had a nice time. I was starting to worry about Craig as he ordered a coke instead of a pint. This is never a good sign. He assured me that death was not round the corner and he would have a pint at the next port of call.

Craig; After a lot of pleading with the wee lassie at the door John succeeded and we were allowed into the club. It was up two flights of stairs and by the time we got to the top I wasn't really in the mood for a pint. A small cylinder of oxygen and a large armchair would have suited me better.

The club itself was huge, as you would expect, and it was very busy. We were served straight away by a friendly barman who's name was Derek. John explained to him what we were up to and he seemed genuinely interested. But as soon as John had finished his spiel Derek started his own pitch. Apparently he is an insurance salesman through the week and only works as a barman for Hibs home games. I explained to him that we were well past it as far as building of a pension plan was concerned.

John; The next port of call was a pub called 'The Four in Hand'. The place was nearly empty as all the supporters had left to go to the match, but it was a reasonable sort of bar and the two girls behind the bar were friendly. Craig found out what the name of the place meant, but kept it a secret. Meanwhile, I was trying to keep out of the eye line of the barman. We had been in this bar a year or so before and had slagged off the lazy bastard in our last book for ignoring us. Mind you the chances of him reading the book, or even being able to read were slim, but I didn't

129

want to take a chance of telling him who we were. Craig told me I was a big fearty.

Craig; *The crowds were still making their way to the stadium as we walked back to the main road in search of our first pub of the day. That pub turned out to be 'The Four in Hand'.*

Actually we had been in this pub a year or so back, and we had not been impressed. There were no football fans in the bar but we did manage a wee chat with the bar maids. They were very nice and I would have taken their picture if it hadn't been for the barman coming over. We had been less than complimentary about him in one of our earlier books and I thought it was better if we didn't draw attention to ourselves, hence the lack of pictures.

The girls did let us into a little secret. We had been wondering what the name of the pub, The Four in Hand, was all about. I had imagined that it had something to do with a legendary achievement by Hibernian Football Club. It seemed fairly logical to me. I was wrong, as usual.

Apparently the place used to be a coaching inn and the name came from the number of horses it took to pull the coach. The driver would have the reins of the four horses in his hand.

The beer was quite good and I think it was reasonably priced, for Edinburgh that is. I had checked out Easter Road on Google Earth and had found a few more pubs.

John; One pint later we wandered out and down the road. We passed a pub called 'Iona', but from the outside it looked a bit fancy, so we carried on down the road and were approaching a dump of a place called 'Tamsons' when a youth appeared round the corner, only to be set upon by one, and then a group of hooligans who started battering this boy, who only managed to escape by getting into the pub. Craig told me most of this as I found it hard to see while running away!

After getting our breath back we decided to give the 'Iona' a chance, so in we went. It is a great wee bar with a great atmosphere. The staff were brilliant, and Tracy one of the three or four girls who were serving, was great fun. We had a great time and all too soon we had to leave. The girls told us the best way to get back into the city, and off we went.

130

Craig; *A few hundred yards down the road from 'the Four' is the Iona Bar but when we arrived outside it we decided that it looked a bit upmarket for our purposes and we moved on.*

A little further down the road I spied 'Tamson's. It looked suitably grotty and more likely to be a supporters pub. We were chatting away as we approached the pub when I noticed a young chap walking towards it. Suddenly another guy jumped on his back. To be honest I thought they were just a couple of young guys mucking about. Then another bloke joined in and I realised that it was more serious.

It wasn't exactly a display of martial arts, more a big Jessie slapping match, but it was not nice to see. I turned to say to John that we should maybe give Tamson's a miss only to discover that I was talking to the back of his head, a head which was getting further away by the second. Suddenly the Iona Bar looked a good prospect.

It was much better than we thought it would be. Inside it was very nice and cosy. The girls behind the bar were friendly and chatty. In fact they were quite shocked to hear about the fight just down the road. Tracy told us that it was very unusual to have any trouble in this area. Once again the beer was good. So good in fact that we stayed on for another pint.

One of the girls showed us a good shortcut which meant we could miss out all the congestion we had experienced before

John; I knew the area we were in now and we got off the bus and went into a bar called 'The Conan Doyle'. Although the bar was not the type that we liked as it was very up-market, it is the company that makes the bar, and we met a great couple called Scott and Sandra who were visiting the city to see Ghost, which was on in the Playhouse. They were great fun and insisted on buying us a drink. We had a grand time and all too soon they had to leave to see the show and we wandered round to the bus station to get the 900 back to Glasgow.

We got on the bus and the next thing I knew was we were coming into Glasgow. I wish I could sleep that well in my bed. Craig was fully recovered and feeling like a new pint, so we walked down to 'The Horse Shoe' and did what we do best, had a couple of pints.

After that it was the train back to EK and as both our better halves were out partying, we got a taxi home. The day had started a bit slowly, but by the end we had had a great day at Easter Road, home of the 'Hibees'.

The day started very cheaply for me as I only had a fiver on me and had to tap Craig before I remembered a hole in the wall. Even though we got a round bought for us, I still managed to blow in the region of £30, I've no idea how!

Craig; We caught a bus within a couple of minutes of us arriving on Leith Walk. After another couple of minutes travel on the bus John decided that he knew exactly where we were, a phenomenon which doesn't happen too often, and demanded we get off to visit a pub he knew. I'm glad he did as that pub was the Conan Doyle.

Sandra and Scott get in the spirit

This was a very nice wee pub, very traditionally furnished and spotlessly clean, I was a wee bit wary as it was just a bit too much like a restaurant but it turned out fine. That is to say, the beer was good and there was a space at the bar to lean on, all the requirements of a decent boozer in fact!

While we were evaluating our day so far and knocking back our pints we got into conversation with a very nice couple from Aberdeen. They told us that they had come down to Edinburgh to see the play 'Ghost' at the theatre.

That was a bit of a mistake as it inspired John to tell us about every play, musical and concert he has ever seen.

Andrew had a familiar look about him but I couldn't put my finger on who he reminded me of. Eventually he told us that he had once been mistaken for the former president of America, Bill Clinton. He must travel in very exalted company when he's not having a lager in Edinburgh.

We had a few laughs with the two of them before it was time to head back to the bus station. John decided that he needed something to eat on the bus so he bought a large packet of Malteasers. It occurred to me that he would never be able to finish them all himself so I didn't bother buying anything. As it turned out we had both made a big mistake.

We hadn't even made it out of the bus station before he opened the packet. Actually the packet didn't so much open as explode. Malteasers flew everywhere. They bounced off the seats, the floor and a couple of innocent by-standers.

All of the passengers around us had a good laugh and even the driver got in on the act. As the bouncing sweets found their way to the front of the bus he opened the door and let them out. Very amusing! The rest of the journey passed without incident or anything to eat.

Pubs we visited:

Hibs Social Club;

The Four in Hand;

The Iona Bar;

The Conan Doyle;

How to get there by bus:
M90 every 15 minutes
from Buchanan St to Edinburgh
walk from bus station

Celtic

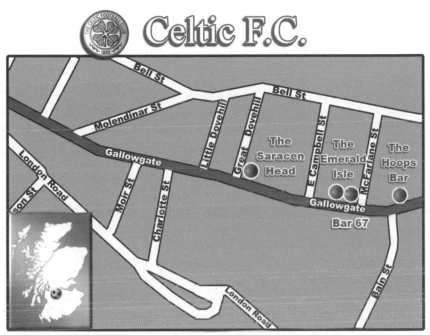

Celtic Park
Ground opened - 1892

John; Celtic, 'The Bhoys', one half of the 'Old Firm', a club known all over the world and the East End of Glasgow. You cannot visit the world using the Bus Pass, so it was off to Glasgow's East End on a sunny, but cold Saturday in May.

Being born and brought up in Govan, and going to Govan High School, like Alex Fergusson and other famous people too many to name, or remember, I was a Rangers man, whether I liked it or not. It wasn't that I didn't want to support Rangers, it was just that everybody in the school did, it went without saying.

I had a very unbigoted upbringing, and although religious bigotry was the norm, my parents would have none of it. The reality is that for most normal people at that time, you left school, got a job and met people who were from the 'other side'. If you were lucky enough to be normal, you soon realized that we are all 'Jock Tamsons Bairns'. I have no idea if I have used that in the correct context, or what it means exactly, but I think you know what I mean.

Unfortunately, by the time a lot of boys and girls leave their segregated schools in the West of Scotland, the hatred is too deeply rooted, and we are left in the situation we are in. Bigotry is still rife in certain sections of the community.

Enough of this brilliant, but serious, historical rhetoric. We were looking forward to visiting the bars around the Parkhead area. The problem is, like around Ibrox, that because the clubs are so huge, there are hundreds of pubs to visit. Am I mad, did I just say it was a problem! As far as Craig and I are concerned, the more the merrier.

We sat downstairs near the front of the bus into Glasgow and Craig was convinced there was a psychopath sitting at the back. Almost everyone who came on, women with toddlers, a one legged man with two sticks, and a blind man all fought their way upstairs. How the blind man knew there was a psychopath up the back is anyone's guess. I even asked Craig if they were all going upstairs for a smoke. He assured me they weren't. We looked around when we got off and there was nobody there!

Anyway, back to reality. The plan was simple. The number 18 to the Barras, some of Danny's delicious donuts, a wander round the Barras and out onto London Road where there are loads of pubs, all of the Celtic persuasion. By the way, Danny's Donuts are magic. I'm sure they're just solid grease made into a circle. I bought five, I thought Craig might have one. He had two and a half the swine.

It was a beautiful day, the sun was blazing down, so you all know what day it was, and we spotted about five pubs from where we were standing.

Craig; *It was time to pay a visit to the other half of Scottish football's' 'Old Firm'. Celtic has a huge following and we were on a mission to check out some of the pubs the Bhoys use for a light refreshment before taking in a game at Parkhead.*

136

John claims to know all of the pubs used by Celtic fans so I let him plan this latest trip. I really should think things through before assuming he knows what he is talking about.

Warning bells were definitely ringing when he tried to lead the way into a shop. Granted the place was painted green and white and had very loud music playing but the window display should have been a bit of an indicator.

Since we didn't have far to travel we didn't have to start out until ten o'clock. All of the pubs we would be visiting were in the area around the 'Barras'. I'm still not sure if this whole trip was a legitimate attempt to check the standards of pubs serving the Celtic faithful or a cunning plan to get John within striking distance of 'Donny's Doughnuts'. He really loves those doughnuts!

As soon as we got off the bus he made a beeline for the kiosk. To humour him I agreed to try one or two of his favourite hot snacks.

While I am no food nutritionist I am fairly certain these things are deadly. They must be at least 90% creash. They're also delicious!

As everyone in the west of Scotland knows the Barras is a place where you can buy just about anything you can think of, and a sack load of things you never dreamt of.

One of the shops I saw in there a few years ago had an advertising slogan above its door which sums up the ethos of the Barras. In large gold lettering it said, 'We buy rubbish: We sell antiques'. It's the kind of place where you are well advised to keep your hand on your money at all times.

We managed to navigate our way through the stalls and the highly suspect tobacco dealers without parting with any more of our money.

John; There was no doubt about which one was first, the legendary 'Saracens Head', or the Sarry Heid as it is sometimes called. In we went and were immediately made to feel welcome by a great barman - Shug, and he looked like a Shug, if you know what I mean. Over a couple of pints he told us all about the bar and the films that have used the bar as a background. The only sad thing is that the bar is only open on Saturday and Sunday unless it is being used for a function. There had been a funeral in it last Monday. Craig told Shug he wanted to use the bar for his. Shug told him he could arrange it for next Wednesday! Some man.

Shug keeps the beer flowing

There was a sign warning people not to dance on the bar, I asked him why such a measure had to be taken. He said his niece had fallen off the bar once. When I enquired if the wee girl had been hurt, he said no, and she was 39. He showed us the dent in the floor.

We knew nothing could match 'The Sarry Heid', but it is our job to check all facilities, so we said goodbye to Shug and the locals and wandered out into the sunshine. It's funny how everywhere looks nicer when the sun shines, even the Barras, and that's saying something.

Craig; On the far side, across the road from the famous Barrowland Ballroom we found our first pub of the day, and what a pub it was. The Saracen's Head is probably the most atmospheric pub I have ever been in. It would be quite easy to spend an hour or two just looking around the bar at all the memorabilia which has been collected over the years.

It is all authentic unlike so many 'theme' pubs'. Our barman, Shug, was a fund of information. Apparently the pub has been used in quite a few films, The Angel's Share and Sunshine on Leith to name two.

The Famous Sarry Heid

The patter of some of the old boys at the end of the bar was well worth listening to. I doubt if any of the four of them was under 70 but they were behaving like a bunch of 17 year olds. They were taking it in turn to threaten each other with random combinations of, 'a square go, a doin and a right good slap'. Needless to say none of the above ever took place.

We were enjoying our visit so much we decided to have a second pint. Shug told us that on match days the place would be jumping. When he is in charge of the door no more than 130 people are allowed into the pub.

It is changed times though as the pub is only open a couple of days a week which is a shame. 'The Sarry Heid', as it is known locally, should be on a heritage trail with busloads of thirsty historians visiting a real gem of a Glasgow pub. However it might be an idea to give it a miss on match days.

It can be unfortunate when a nice place gets a bit of a reputation. The Saracen's Head suffers a wee bit from that with people, who have probably never laid eyes on the place, telling tales of hard drinking punters ready to fight at the drop of a jacket.

The artist Peter Howson once had an exhibition of some of his paintings and sketches at the Gallery of Modern Art. He had sketched nine or ten victims of the war in Kosovo and, unfortunately, followed that up with a series of drawings of the 'Sarry Heid' punters.

The pictures were hung back to back in the gallery. I will not name the gallery guide, you know who you are Sheila, but somehow both sets of drawings managed to get mixed up. The thing is, nobody noticed.

John; We had a look inside 'The Emerald Isle', but it looked out of place for this area and there was nobody in it. It looked as if it should have been in a housing estate and serving food for kids. Just my opinion, mind you. Almost next door was 'Bar 67', named in memory of the Lisbon Lions, a team of players who all came from within a few miles of the bar we were in. How times have changed. It was very busy and noisy and the walls and ceiling were covered in Celtic memorabilia. It was hard to get a word with the barmaid who was rushed off her feet, but she was very nice and the bar was really great. It took about 10 minutes to pour my pint of Best, so we only had the one. The bar is certainly worth a visit.

The next bar we visited was 'The Hoops'. The front door of the bar was closed and it took us a minute or two to discover that there was a side door. We found it and in we went. It was a strange place, all very modern, but it looked as if the owners had run out of money about a month before opening. There were one or two unfinished things. We had a great time though. The barman Neil was a great bloke and told us all about the financial troubles pubs in the area are having with there being no Rangers in the league. This was another pub that was struggling financially. We had a great chat with Neil and this is another bar well worth a visit. It goes without saying that they are all great pubs to visit if you're not a Rangers fanatic.

Craig; *We didn't have far to walk to our next pub. The Emerald Isle was a bit of a culture shock as it didn't have any. If you want cheap beer this is the place for you, if you like good beer, keep walking.*

To be honest it is laid out more like a café than a bar. And when I say café I'm talking about the greasy spoon variety.

I can, however, see the attraction this place has for its customers. We bought two pints and got a fair amount of change

140

from a fiver. The fact that it was far busier than the 'Sarry' tells its own story. They do say you get what you pay for and although it might seem a little out of character for me, in this instance I would be prepared to pay more for a better pint, quite a bit more.

In my humble opinion this pub falls into the category of 'no very good'.

Govan meets Galway

Bar 67 was our next pub and it was a much better prospect. It even looked like a pub. I can also report that the beer was of a much higher standard. The service was excellent but the girl was far too busy to stop for a chat.

Even though it wasn't a match day the punters were getting a bit frisky, singing a variety of songs and practising their chanting ahead of the cup final the next day. There were quite a few guys in the bar who had made the trip over from Ireland for the game and we managed to chat to a couple of them. They were certainly up for a laugh.

Not being much of a football fan I didn't really know what the significance was of the pub's name until much later. I'm really glad that I didn't embarrass myself by asking.

There was no doubt in my mind about the meaning behind the name of the next pub on our list. The Hoops Bar is located at the end of one of the newest buildings in the area and the bar itself is very modern.

At first we thought that it was shut but I noticed a bloke taking supplies in the side door. John made an executive decision and we slipped in the side door as well. Once John gets a taste of the beer there is just no stopping him.

There were only two other customers in the bar so we didn't really get much of an idea about the usual atmosphere in the pub. The barman, Neil, was very interested in what we were doing and even suggested a couple of things which could help us with advertising the next book.

The bar itself is bright and spacious. I think it would probably suit a younger clientele, especially on busy days. But the beer suited us just fine. In fact we enjoyed it so much that we had another one.

We felt it was only fair to help with the cash flow of Neil's bar after he told us how much the local pubs have lost since the regular Old Firm matches stopped.

It is to be hoped that these great wee pubs survive the wait until normal service is resumed.

John; We had had a great time in all the pubs we visited. Just as we were about to leave 'The Hoops', Craig got a text from his Irene to let him know she was in Glasgow with his sister having a wee cocktail in the Merchant City. As this is only a few minutes walk from where we were, and it was his sister after all, Craig felt we should wander along to meet them. The only saving grace was that we had been to our allotted pubs and were meeting them in a bar, if you can call the up-market 'Metropolitan' a bar. But they sold pints of Tennents Lager, so Craig was delighted until the waitress told him the price. I thought he was going to have a heart attack. I was on the point of phoning 'The Sarry Heid' to make the funeral arrangements, but he was ok, and even bought me another pint.

Craig and John 'Hooping' it up behind the bar

A great day ended with us walking down to the Central Station, without going into 'The Horse Shoe', and getting the train back to EK.

This was one of our more sober days. I think I only spent about £25, and that included £2 for five of Danny's finest. Craig probably spent £25 for the four pints in the 'Metropolitan'. What a day!

Craig; We rounded off our day out by strolling into the Merchant City to meet up with Irene and my sister Janice. They were having a sophisticated afternoon out on the town. We soon put a stop to that.

I really don't think that the Metropolitan gets much of the overspill from the Celtic bars on the Gallowgate but just in case the odd hoops fan wanders in I feel a warning is in order.

DO NOT DRINK IN THIS PLACE. If you do I'm fairly sure you'll end up watching the game on the telly because you'll be too skint to get into the park.

Pubs we visited:

The Saracen's Head;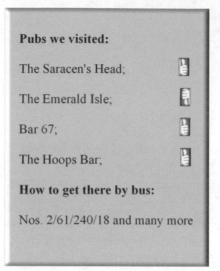

The Emerald Isle;

Bar 67;

The Hoops Bar;

How to get there by bus:

Nos. 2/61/240/18 and many more

Falkirk

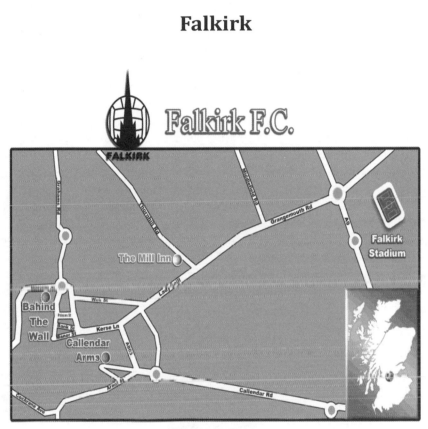

Falkirk Stadium
Ground opened - 2004

John; Falkirk, 'The Bairns', another very famous and historic club who have produced some of Scotland's greatest players. At the moment I can't remember any of their names, but it doesn't matter. They know who they are, if they are still alive that is.

Falkirk Stadium is a crap name for a football ground, it doesn't have the same ring as Brockville, but I suppose it is the way progress is going. At least it is called Falkirk Stadium, and not the name of the sponsor, in this instance Asda, who bought the ground in the centre of town to build a supermarket and paid for it by building a brand new purpose-built stadium on the outskirts of town. But we are not here today to bother about trivial things like football stadiums, or players for that matter, it is the pubs that are the stars in our eyes.

Craig had the possibly brilliant idea of visiting Falkirk and carrying on to visit Stenhousemuir which is just a few miles along the road. Stenhousemuir allow East Stirlingshire to share their ground, which has the great name of Ochilview Park, a premier league name if ever there was one. So if everything panned out as planned, we would have covered three teams, or three lots of pubs in the one day. Actually, it is only two lots of pubs as it turned out that there are only a couple of pubs in the Ochilview area, so the supporters share them too.

So back to the start of our day. The usual number 18 took us into the Buchanan Street Bus Station, only it didn't. The route has changed, so instead of going round George Square and up to the bus station, it carries along St. Vincent place, up Hope Street and onto Bath Street on its way somewhere west. I had asked the driver for tickets to the Bus Station, but in true West of Scotland fashion he just ignored it and went on his own way. I suppose his attitude is that since we are getting the trip for nothing, it doesn't really matter where we end up. But I got the last laugh, cause I don't care. We got off and walked to the Bus Station.

Craig and I had independently worked out completely different routes to visit the grounds, so we went with Craig's. It's easier, and he really suffered. The bus to Falkirk was a right wee bone shaker and took forever to get there, visiting every town on the way, and some that weren't.

I haven't mentioned it, but the reason we chose Falkirk today was that we had received an order for five Cheap Way Rounds from the Waterstones there, so we killed two birds with one stone, or bone shaking bus. So first things first, we delivered the books. The young guy in the shop was very helpful, and gave us directions to the first pub we planned to visit. It is called 'Behind The Wall', and is a bar supporters use and meet in for away games. We had found out that there are no pubs at the ground. Thanks Asda.

Craig; Visiting three clubs in one day seemed like a good idea to me. The fact that it was my idea has nothing to do with it.

146

What really amazed me was that everything turned out exactly as planned. Well almost everything.

To be honest things didn't start quite as well as they might have as we missed our first bus into Glasgow by two minutes. Had we managed to catch it we wouldn't have had to sprint along the road to the bus station. Obviously when I say sprint I am using quite a large slice of poetic licence.

I still don't understand why our driver decided to keep secret the fact that the bus no longer calls into Buchanan Street bus station. I suppose we should be grateful that he took us into Glasgow at all. He probably thinks he's doing well slowing down to let passengers off.

The journey up to Falkirk would have been fine if the bus we were on had been equipped with any kind of shock absorbers. As it was, my back was killing me by the time we got to the bus station. I needed a couple of pints to kill the pain.

John; 'Behind the Wall' is a great bar and the two guys serving, Craig and Graeme, were great company and filled us in on other pubs and how to get to the ground. This is a pub well worth a visit, although it is a bit hard to find. Craig told us that we had just missed meeting Alex Totten, a Falkirk legend, who had left just before we arrived.

My Craig was still keen to visit the ground, so we eventually found the bus stop and 10 minutes later we were at the ground. The stadium is brand new and very impressive in a no atmosphere sort of way. Zippo's Circus was setting up in the land beside the stadium and I'm sure I saw the fat lady. Craig said it was Falkirk's centre half, back for the first day of training..

We couldn't see any sign of a bar, or anywhere there might be one, so we walked about halfway back to the city centre before jumping a bus for the last bit. Seemingly the bus passed a bar that we could have gone into. Who cares.

Craig; *We had been told that a pub called. Behind the Wall was a favourite with Falkirk supporters, so that's where we headed The pub is on Melville Street and we would not have found it without very good directions.*

It would have been a pity to miss it as it turned out to be a great pub. From the outside it looked like many other small pubs, but it is huge inside. There is a long modern bar and lots of seating and through the back is a restaurant area. The barman told us that there was also a sports bar upstairs.

Craig and Graeme behind the bar
in Behind The Wall

At first I wasn't sure about the 'BTW', as it is called. It is just a wee bit on the modern side for my liking but I have to admit that they do serve a really good pint. Our barman, Craig (what a great name for a barman), was very friendly and told us all about the pub and the football team. Apparently the pub runs a supporters bus, charging fans a fiver to get to games. For that not only do you get a seat on the bus but you also get a pint. Sounds like a bargain to me.

Between them, the barmen, Craig and Graeme managed to work out a plan for us to get out to Falkirk's stadium. It sounded fool-proof to me but then again I was travelling with John.

After walking in circles for ten minutes we jumped aboard a bus and pleaded with the driver to take us to the park. Fortunately he was going that way anyway.

Falkirk's stadium looks huge and, if like me you know nothing about football, suggests that the team is very successful. I suppose you could say that they successfully got Asda to build it for them.

After five minutes staring at a building which was very obviously shut we headed back to the nearest pub. That is not entirely true unfortunately we managed to miss the Mill Inn on Thornhill Road which we had been told was a good supporter's pub.

Make a date to visit Laura, Allan and Abby at The Callendar Arms

John; We got off the bus at the bus station and went right into the nearest bar as we were both in need of the facilities. It was called 'The Callendar Arms', and as soon as we were inside and relieved, we thought it was not the sort of pub we liked, all up-market and serving food. How wrong we were. As we have always said, it is the people in the bar that are the most important thing, and the staff were great. The two girls behind the bar, Laura and Abby were brilliant, as was the manager, Allan. At least I think he was the manager. The owner, Val, came in later and she was good company as well. Not only that, but the locals were great fun and kept us in hysterics, especially me. I am easy to please after a few pints.

A wee guy with big shoulders came over to us and introduced himself. He said 'my name's Robert Sole, but you can call me R Sole' that's the sort of patter that went on all the time we were in. Another funny guy, Tam Cole, who owns one of the local bus companies, told us a true, but terrifying story of a family of 37 Pakistanis who were sleeping

149

in a single bed when it collapsed, killing several of them. The police are putting the blame on Al-Ikea. It was that sort of pub, the locals didn't seem the sort of people who would frequent such an up-markety sort of place. Allan even set us up a round. Famous authors like what we are meet a lot of really good guys.

It was with a heavy heart that we had to leave the pub, and Falkirk. The two pubs we had visited were brilliant and well worth a visit. Tam, the comedian and bus owner advised us on what bus to get to Stenhousemuir, the C-1, which, by coincidence was his bus.

Craig; Eventually we found our way to 'The Callendar Arms' on Callendar Road. This place had just been refurbished and I have to say that once again I didn't particularly like the place initially. As soon as we got talking to staff however I changed my mind. It was a great pub. At one point the customers were queuing up to tell us jokes and stories.

We also got some very precise instructions on how to get to our next destination. For once we were confident about which bus to get as the bloke giving us the instructions was also the owner of the bus.

Just to round off a perfect visit, the gaffer, Alan, bought us both a drink. It might not look like a typical football supporters pub but I would certainly recommend a visit.

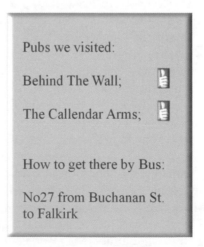

Pubs we visited:

Behind The Wall;

The Callendar Arms;

How to get there by Bus:

No27 from Buchanan St. to Falkirk

E.Stirlingshire, Stenhousemuir

Ochilview Park
Ground opened - 1890

John; Stenhousemuir and East Stirlingshire. We had a lovely run, in bright sunshine, from Falkirk to Stenhousemuir, and after getting off the bus, we wandered round to see the park. It is not a stadium like Falkirk's, but a great old-fashioned park. An interesting fact is that it has an artificial surface, which looked great. We were able to wander about the place which was very nice in a slightly run down sort of way. A bit like Craig.

Stenhousemuir, 'The Warriors', a great nickname, and East Stirlingshire', 'The Shire', a not so good one, share the ground. I'm not sure, but can only assume that this is because of financial reasons, and not out of choice. But there's nothing Craig and I can co about this. The sad thing for us is that it is fewer pubs to visit.

Craig; We caught the bus from Falkirk up to Stenhousemuir and the driver actually stopped the bus and showed us where the football park was. This guy wouldn't last ten minutes on the East Kilbride/Glasgow run.

We didn't see much sign of a social club at Ochilview Park, but apparently there is one and a small bar under the main stand. We didn't actually see them as the ground was shut when we visited, but it was quite nice to see an old fashioned stadium. I can only assume that Stenhousemuir can't be needing a new supermarket in the centre of town, not just yet anyway.

John; There were only two pubs in the main street, and one was in a hotel. So first of all we tried the pub, 'Gilmour's Bar'. From the outside it looked like a very tough sort of place, so I told Craig to put on his hard man walk into the bar. Inside it was the same. But it was a great bar, the type Craig and I love, nothing fancy (that is an understatement) but we had a great time in it and the barman, Douglas Hamilton was good company. Come to think on it, Douglas Hamilton is a fairly posh, up market name, just shows you; he was as tough as nails. The pub is worth a visit.

Craig; It didn't take us long to find a convenient boozer though. Gilmour's looked a little bit rough from the outside but once inside we realised that impression was wrong. It was a lot more than a wee bit rough.

To blend in I thought about asking for my pint in a dirty glass but I was afraid that the wee hard nut behind the bar might take it the wrong way. We didn't stay long.

Just before we left John asked the barman if there was another pub in town which Stenhousemuir / East Stirlingshire supporters frequented. I thought he was tempting fate using words like frequented in a rough place like Gilmour's but the wee man didn't take offence.

He told us that there was a hotel just up the road called 'The Plough', but he didn't think it was much of an attraction to the average supporter. To avoid any embarrassment and possibly physical assault we decided to tell the wee bloke that it didn't sound like the kind of place we would like either.

Needless to say we took the long way round to The Plough, constantly checking to see if the wee fellow was watching us. By the way, he was right about The Plough. I really can't imagine too many fans wandering into this wine bar and paying well over the odds for a very ordinary pint. It's the type of place where you feel compelled to wipe your feet before entering.

We tried talking to the young chap behind the bar about the town's football team but to be honest he looked surprised to hear that there was one.

Although we had finished our mission to visit the pubs around the two football stadiums there was one more place to visit. Having worked for a bus company I am rarely surprised by the strange routes thought up by people who obviously have never set foot on a bus. Travelling from Stenhousemuir to Glasgow by bus requires some serious thought. Unfortunately John was in charge of the thinking.

I have never heard of Carron Shore before. I doubt many people have. But that's where we landed up. As it turns out I'm quite glad we did. The Carronshore Bar was a great wee pub. I think we laughed from the minute we entered the place until the time we left, two pints later to be precise.

The barmaid, Melissa, was a good laugh and told a few stories about her customers and the four or five who were in the bar joined in.

We were shocked to discover Dick Van Dyke sitting at the end of the bar. The customer sitting on a stool just along from us was a dead ringer for the veteran American comedian. The resemblance was amazing.

His fellow drinkers were having a great time taking the mickey out of him and we felt that we should join in, just to be

153

sociable you understand. As you can imagine there were a great many references to his relationship with Mary Poppins, most of which were unprintable. The bloke took it all in good humour. I suspect he gets it a lot.

Dick Van Dyke Pops into The Carron Shore Bar

Unfortunately we had a bus to catch so we had to leave our new friends after a visit which was far too short. I can't really see how I will ever manage another visit to Carron Shore but if I do get the chance I will certainly take it.

John; Since there were only two watering holes, we had to visit the Hotel 'The Plough'. It was not easy to find the way in, but eventually we got there, and the surprise was that although the Hotel itself looked run down and unused, the bar was very modern and recently refurbished. Although very nice, it was not the sort of place that we like. Now earlier, I hear you say, we went into a pub in Falkirk a bit like this and it turned out to be great because of the people behind the bar. Well the man behind the bar was not unpleasant, but did not go out of his way to make us feel welcome.

We had been told in Falkirk by Tam, the bus owner, which bus to get to take us to Carron Shore, where we were to change buses to get one to take us to Kincardine. Now it will seem to some people that this is going away from Glasgow, but I knew that we could pick up the St. Andrew's to Glasgow coach, which is a very comfortable coach, unlike the bone shaker we got up to Falkirk, and takes half the time. After waiting about 20 minutes for the number six bus, it turned up and we were whisked to Carron Shore, only to discover we had almost an hour, or two pints, to wait for our next bus. Luckily for us, there was a bar round the corner called 'The Carron Shore Bar'. This was another wild looking place from outside and in, but again, it was a great bar with a great barmaid called Melissa and great locals who kept us amused with their stories. We enjoyed a couple of pints and the company before saying our goodbyes and promising to return.

An interesting thing about Carron Shore is that it is called a Shore, not because it's near the beach, but because there's a wee river running through the place. I said to the local who told me this that I thought rivers had banks, not shores. He said, 'what the hell do you know about anything'. My smart come-back brain was numb.

Craig; We needed to catch a bus to Kincardine from where we would be able to get a bus to Glasgow. However we were both suffering the two major side effects of a day on the sauce. We both needed a pee and something to eat There is only one food group which can cure the hunger which is brought on by alcohol use. We needed chips.

Once on the magic Citylink bus it took only minutes to get back to Glasgow, at least that's the way I recall it. As usual John insisted on a visit to the Horse Shoe before we caught our train home.

The only incident of note was a short exchange of pleasantries with the train guard. Apparently I wasn't walking fast enough for him. Strangely I managed to get on to the train, walk up to the next carriage and sit for a couple of minutes before the doors closed and the train moved out.

It must be a Glasgow thing where customer service is replaced with customer abuse. I just hope there is an intensive retraining of all bus drivers and rail workers before the Commonwealth Games hit town.

A bit of exposure to our service industries should do wonders for the tourist trade. Fortunately we didn't have to depend on

155

public transport for the last part of our journey. Irene was waiting for us at the station and drove us safely home.

John; Our next bus, the number 15, took us over the Forth on the famous Kincardine Bridge and into the town of Kincardine. If we had hurried, we might have got a coach right away, but we both needed the toilet and chips, so we had a bag of chips, found the local pub and had a couple before the next coach arrived. This can't be good for us.

We had a lovely journey back to Glasgow, but discovered that if we hurried down to Central Station, we would just miss the train, so that meant we had to visit 'The Horseshoe Bar', our favourite in Glasgow for a quick one before getting the next train, which we almost missed. Craig had a bit of a run-in with the conductor who was trying to get him to hurry on to the train, but the less said about it the better. Irene picked us up at EK Station and ran us home.

So ended a fantastic day visiting three clubs, but only two grounds. All the pubs were worth a visit, and most of them were fantastic. Falkirk, Stenhousemuir and East Stirling might not be doing as well as they would like, but they have great pubs around them, for what it's worth.

As usual I spent a lot of money, thank god the last pub we left was not next to the house or I would have been in an even worse state when I got home.

Pubs we visited:

Gilmour's Bar;

The Plough;

The Carron Shore Bar;

How to get there by bus:
X27 to Cumbernauld
H1 to Stenhousemuir

Forfar

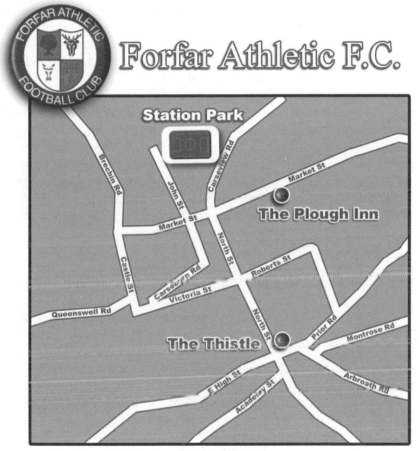

Station Park
Ground opened - 1888

John; Today's trip was planned for the 15th July. This is not during the Football season, but it doesn't matter. As you know, we are only interested in the pubs around the grounds, so it is not too important if there is a game on or not, especially for the wee teams where there may not be facilities inside the ground.

Other reasons for doing the trips off-season is that the weather is sometimes better, which makes a hell of a difference in Scotland. Also, we would never be able to make our publication date (that's a laugh) if we only visited grounds on match day.

This is the first time we have tried four clubs on one day, so I'm sure we'll end up pissed. Mind you, we end up pissed when we only do one club, so there you go, talking piss already and we've not started the trip yet.

As you can imagine, getting to our first port of call, Forfar, meant a hell of an early start. I was worried for Craig, but this 'four in a day' was his idea, so Hell mend him! I got up at 6.15am, that's early morning, and collected Craig at seven. Now Irene, his beloved partner (they live in sin), is away in her beloved Millport this week with her daughter and grandson, I think. Anyway, I just hoped Craig had got to his bed at a reasonable time. He's a nightmare when he's a free agent, bevy and late nights to the fore.

We had both been on the web checking bus times and I had booked us passage on the trips to and from Dundee, in case the buses were full. Craig had checked up on the pubs and their position near the grounds. You can only laugh!

The four clubs we were visiting today all have great nicknames, except one, or so I thought. Forfar are The Loons', Montrose 'The Gable Endies', Arbroath 'The Red Lichties'; I wish I had taken the time to find out how they all came into being. Brechin, on the other hand, have a crap nickname, 'The City'. Could they not think of a more original name, and Brechin is surely not a city. So how can they call themselves 'The City'?

I was wrong, now there's a surprise! I found out in one of the pubs we visited that Brechin has an official Cathedral, so it is a Cathedral City, so they are allowed to call themselves 'The City'. Fair enough I hear you say, but even so. It's still a bit unimaginative, they could have called themselves names like 'The Glebes', or even 'The Angustoorie Bitters'. Now there's a name.

I collected Craig at about quarter to seven and we got a really quick bus into George Square. I still can't understand why the bus company will not run a bus from EK right into the bus station in Glasgow. EK is a big place and deserves a bus into the bus station. I'm going to write to someone. The walk up the hill from George Square to the bus station is a nightmare early in the morning.

158

We sat in our seats at the front of the queue at about quarter to eight, 40 minutes early! The time fairly flew in watching bus after bus unloading kids returning after three nights without sleep from T in the Park. Talk about the walking dead. As each bus arrived it was about five minutes before anyone got off. The driver had to go round the bus trying to waken them all up. I'm sure the girls wore clothes when I was young.

Just about our departure time a wee bloke came up and told us our bus was delayed about two hours. No explanation or anything. He told us to go to another bus bay and they would get us on a bus about nine o'clock. To cut a long story short, I'm sure Craig will bore you with it anyway, our new bus left at nine, stopping at every place on the way to Dundee. The driver was a bit of a comic. A woman rushed up to him in Dunblane and told him he had passed her stop. His instant reply was 'it's up to you to tell me where you want off, it's no up to me to guess', magic patter.

We reckoned we would be about an hour behind schedule when we arrived at Dundee, and if our bus arrived when it was supposed to we would only have two minutes to catch our next bus if we didn't want to fall further behind. We were on the edge of our seats as our bus pulled into the bus station in Dundee and saw our next bus ready to go. I got up quickly and got off the bus first and fairly belted along to our next bus to ask the driver if he could wait half an hour for Craig, only kidding Craig.

We were keen that nothing else would go wrong as we had spent a lot of time planning this trip. We had maps of all the towns and everything. An hour behind schedule was not a major disaster as all it meant was that we would have an hour less drinking time at the end of the trip in our favourite watering hole in the East, 'The Bush'. That was probably a good thing.

Craig; As readers of our three other books will realise it takes a lot to annoy me. I'm usually quite laid back about all the little problems which can occur when you take to the open road in search of decent pub. But Buchannan Street Bus station is the one place we can be certain that if something is going to go wrong on our day out, that's where it will start. The latest piece of mismanagement really had me fizzing.

We were sitting, patiently waiting for our bus to Dundee when a flunky in a yellow waistcoat sauntered over to inform us

159

that our bus was running two hours late. Telling us this obviously exhausted the wee soul as he didn't have enough energy left to let us know why it was running so late.

Maybe that information was on a need to know basis and being on the bottom rung of the travel business we just didn't need to know. Eventually we did manage to get on another bus to Dundee, albeit a very slow one. Although the journey up to Dundee was very slow nothing else happened to annoy us.

We arrived in Dundee with exactly three minutes to spare before our next bus left so I would like to apologise to the half dozen or so passengers we knocked out of our way on our sprint through the bus station.

Alex Ploughs on with her work

John; Forfar was our first port of call. We had our map out and knew where we were getting off, and it worked. Off we got and walked up North Street, along Market Street, which is right beside the lovely wee park, and into 'The Plough'. This is a nice wee pub and the girl behind the bar, Alex, was brilliant and made us very welcome. For most of the time we were the only ones in the bar. Mind you, how many people want a pint early doors on a Monday morning? We do. Alex told us that the bar was packed on match days, which is more than the ground probably is. Anyway, we had a great time in a lovely wee bar, well worth a visit.

We walked back down North Street, passing 'The Caledonian' which, like many pubs nowadays, was shut, and went into the pub which we reckoned was next nearest to the ground, 'The Thistle'.

This was more like a traditional 'Spit and Sawdust' bar, and it was great. Karrie, who was not in the slightest fat, was great fun and full of enthusiasm for our books She even gave Craig her e-mail address so he can send a photo of us to make a Facebook page about our books. What a girl. I left Craig to the technical talking as I had no idea what they were on about. Certainly not pub talk. People like me think everything in the West is best, but there are some great pubs and people in the East.

Karrie says you won't get stung
in 'The Thistle'

Craig; On the trip up to Forfar, apart from the driver having a long running argument with a jakey-looking young man the journey passed quietly. The argument was a long running one because the bus could only travel a few hundred yards at a time due to traffic conditions. This gave the Jakey time to catch up with the bus and make a series of rude gestures in at the driver. The boy may well have been a complete moron but you would have to give him a ten out of ten for creative gesturing.

161

Once in Forfar we walked straight up North Street. We had been told we would find the nearest pub to the football park up there. The Plough looks like a traditional small Scottish hotel and that theme continued on the inside. I was so busy looking around the bar area that I failed to notice that there was a single step down at the bar.

Fortunately I did not fall flat on my face as the embarrassment factor would have been very high. But talk about whiplash. Manfully I kept my whimpering to an absolute minimum but I'm pretty sure that I managed to put a new kink in my spine.

Anyway the young barmaid was really nice and the beer was pretty good as well. The Plough gets a lot of business when there's a football match on up at the park, and although we didn't actually get as far as the ground we were told it was only a five minute walk from the pub.

With a lot of ground to cover today we couldn't stay too long. We had passed our next pub on the way up to the Plough so for once we actually knew where we were going.

There is great potential for confusion with the Thistle Bar. In the Plough we were told it was actually called Mr D's but our map said it was called the Thistle. Just to be sure I checked on Google Earth and in the picture of the place it was named Mr D's. We were just glad that there was a pub there and were not too fussy about what it was called.

Needless to say when we arrived at the pub the name above the door, and everywhere else, was The Thistle and that's where we had our next pint.

Being on the corner of North Street and High Street makes the Thistle a good navigation point should you ever find yourself in Forfar for the football (Try saying that after a couple of pints)

The pub is actually a bit more modern on the inside than I thought it was going to be. Once again we found this pub to be a really friendly place with everyone more than willing to chat to a couple of auld yins from the west coast.

We were served by Karrie, who is the daughter of the gaffer, and a very nice lassie. We chatted for ages and somehow managed to convince her that buying one of our books would be a good idea. Usually when young people agree with us I assume they are taking the pish, but Karrie actually sent me an email the next day to tell me that she had bought a book on Kindle. If we were still doing the old Russell Standard the Thistle would obviously qualify for the full five pint glasses

Pubs we visited:

The Plough;

The Thistle;

How to get there by bus:

M9 Glasgow/Dundee -No20 to Forfar

Brechin

Glebe Park
Ground opened - 1919

John; Leaving Forfar behind, things were picking up. Our next bus, the 21A, whisked us through lovely countryside to Brechin, where, because of our fantastic maps, we got off at the right place, next to the pub we had read about on the club's web page. 'The Stables', this is a fantastic bar with great staff and locals. The fact that they are all crazy just makes it better. The owner Allan and his daughter run the place and were magic company. They even bought us a drink, and they were not the only ones. Two locals, Jack Renils, who used to own the pub, and his pal Jordan were great fun. They also got us a drink. What a fine crowd they were. Jack regaled us with epic stories, all of them true. The only downside to our visit to Brechin was when Jack told us that the local Distillery had been broken into the night before we arrived. Seemingly two Chinese gentlemen broke a window to gain entry. One of them asked the other 'is this Whisky', the other replied, 'not as Whisky as breaking into a Bank'. Brechin is some place. By the time we had left, drunk, there was no time to go to any other pubs. They could not have stood up to 'The Stables'. We will return some day.

Jack and Jordan at The Stables

Craig; Finding the nearest pub to Brechin City's ground was easy and very lucky all at the same time: easy because we got off the bus just outside the place and lucky because it is a great wee pub.

The Stables is just about everything we both love about a public bar. From the moment we walked into the bar until we left an hour and a half later we were met by nothing but really friendly helpful and generous people. What a place!

The present gaffer, Alan, was hilarious and insisted on buying us a drink a move always calculated to get you on the best of terms with two auld yins travelling around the country in search of a good pub.

I was chatting to Alan and a couple of his customers when another drink arrived in front of me. John came in to explain that it had been bought by one of the guys sitting outside. He was the previous owner of the Stables and obviously still enjoyed the odd thirst-quencher in his former premises. We spent the rest of our stay outside in the beer garden having a laugh with him and his pal. The day just got better and better

Pubs we visited:

The Stables;

How to get there by bus:

M9 Glasgow - Aberdeen service
change at Dundee
X27 Dundee to Kirriemuir
change at Forfar
No.21A Forfar to Edzell
get off at Brechin

Montrose

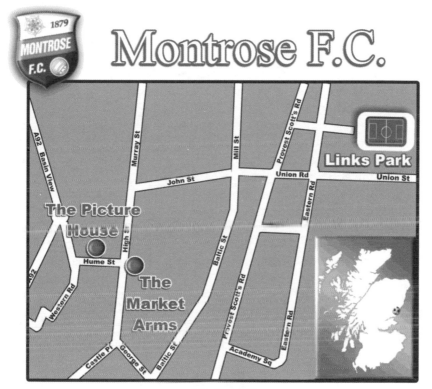

Links Park
Ground opened - 1887

John; God knows how we found our next bus, the MW Nicol number 30. Thought you'd like to know. The 30 minute journey from Brechin to Montrose sobered us up and we stepped off the bus feeling no pain. For some reason, nothing to do with the drink, my map reading skills had disappeared and I had no idea where we were, although we should have been next to the sea. Craig claimed it was all my fault that we were lost. Mind you, now I come to think on it, he didn't shout up about how to get anywhere. Also, it was a burning hot day. You don't often hear people complaining about that in Scotland. We had planned to visit 'The Golf Inn' and 'The Legion', if they would have let us in. Apologies to them, I'm sure they are great bars. Anyway, we just went into the pub we happened to be standing outside, 'The Market Bar'. We had actually been in this bar before on a previous visit, or so Craig told me, and very nice it was too. The barmaid was very nice and told us where all the pubs we were looking for were, why she bothered I'll never know. I could hardly walk. We had a nice time and left to go across the road for our next bus.

Many of you will find this hard to believe, but there was still about 30 minutes till our bus, and there was a 'Picture House' across the road which was a pub. Montrose is a great place. In we went for more drink and talked to a lovely lad called Jamie who was running the bar. He seemed very interested in what we were doing, god knows why, and took some of our leaflets to pass on to the locals. East of Scotland people are great, or great actors. Who cares, I like them. Jamie lives in Arbroath, our next port of call. Come to think of it, almost all the bar staff we met live in a different town to the one they work in. Isn't that amazing?

Craig; Actually that is not entirely true, Montrose was a bit of a let-down. We failed miserably to find the football ground. As it was an incredibly hot day I was a bit concerned that John, being so much older than me, might not be up to trekking around the town. So in all honesty we didn't try too hard to find it.

After 15 minutes searching we gave up and wandered into the Market Bar. It wasn't great but since the beer was cold and we were on the point of collapse through heat exhaustion, we put up with it. Actually we were the only customers so there was very little chance of any banter developing, friendly or otherwise

Once outside again we checked out where we had to catch our next bus from then realised it would be the bus stop straight across the road from a pub. It was almost as if we had planned it.

The Picture House is, as you might expect, a converted picture house. The old movie theme is featured in the decor of the place and I suppose some people might find that amusing and or trendy. But not me! However the young lad serving was a good laugh and joined in on our usual nonsense patter so this bar gets a better rating than it might have.

Pubs we visited:

The Market Bar;

The Picture House;

How to get there by bus:

M9 Glasgow to Dundee
X7 Dundee to Montrose

Arbroath

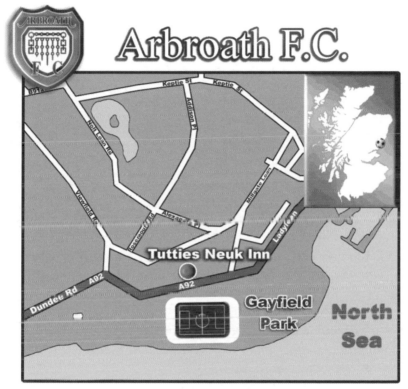

Gayfield Park
Ground opened - 1925

John; Our next bus, a Stagecoach Number 30, which was the same number as our last bus, although a different company, arrived and took us the scenic route along the coast from Montrose to Arbroath. We knew the bar we were looking for and after a 15 minute walk along the front, we found it opposite 'Gayfield Park'. The park is right on the edge of the sea, and although today was a scorcher, it must be a nightmare of a place on a miserable day. The pub 'The Tutties Neuk' is a very up market sort of place, but it is still a great bar. Carol, the barmaid was good fun and told us some great stories. Seemingly, there is intense rivalry and hatred between Arbroath and Montrose. The Arbroath supporters call the Montrose supporters 'Scumtrose'. Makes the Old Firm pretty tame! She told us how the pub got it's name. Hope Craig can tell you, cause I've forgotten. We had a great time in this smashing wee bar and all too soon had to leave and walk along the front in brilliant sunshine to catch our next bus, the old X7 Aberdeen to Dundee coastal rider. What a great name for a bus!.

Craig; Following on from our failure to find the football ground in Montrose John insisted that we had to at least clap eyes on Arbroath's ground. I agreed, not because I had a great desire to see the park but I had been told that straight across the road from it was a very good pub. It was a fair walk from the bus station but it is well worth the effort.

Tutties Neuk, given its position, gets a good turn from football fans on match days. The barmaid, Carol, could quite easily be described as a larger than life character; she could start a party in an empty hoose.

Like every other football team Arbroath have a great rivalry with their nearest neighbours, in their case Montrose. Carol told us they refer to them as Scumtrose. Not very catchy but it certainly gets the insult across quickly.

Apparently the good folk of Montrose are none too keen on their neighbours either and the police have to escort Arbroath fans to their derby games up in Montrose.

Carol told us that Tutties Neuk gets its name from the days when cattle were allowed to graze on the village green for a fee. Tutties were the drovers apparently and the Neuk was the toll where they paid their dues. So ends today's history lesson. How accurate that history is I do not know so please direct all questions and or corrections to Carol in Arbroath.

Our day was almost finished and we had managed to visit the pubs closest to four of Scotland's senior football teams and thoroughly enjoyed doing so.

Carol keeps the beer flowing in Tutties Neuk

John; Although Dundee was only a starting and finishing point, we had planned enough time to visit the legendary 'Bush' bar. A couple of pints later and we were on the bus home for about one and a half hours' sleep. It must have been about eleven before we got into Glasgow, so it was straight home, and no stopping for a nightcap on the way. Just shows how sensible we can be, or how drunk!

The four clubs we visited all have great pubs near them and all of them are worth a visit. I don't know if it had anything to do with the sunshine, but all of the towns looked really nice.

I don't know if I mentioned it earlier, but Kate was also away for an overnight somewhere, so she never saw the state I was in when I got home, no idea how much I spent, but it was a lot.

Craig; *However, bad news awaited us down in Dundee. With a lot of planning we had managed to arrange an hour long visit to a favourite bar before catching the bus back to Glasgow.*

Since we started our epic bus adventures the Bush Bar in Dundee has been a wee bit special to us. The owner, Harry has been a good friend to us old yins even though he's just a young guy himself.

175

It seems that the Harry is moving on and while we wish him well I really question his sanity. Surely owning your own pub is the pinnacle of all human achievement. Everything in life would be downhill after that.
After this devastating news we made our way home.

Pubs we visited:

Tutties Neuk Inn;

How to get there by bus:

M9 Glasgow to Dundee
X7 Dundee to Arbroath

Airdrie

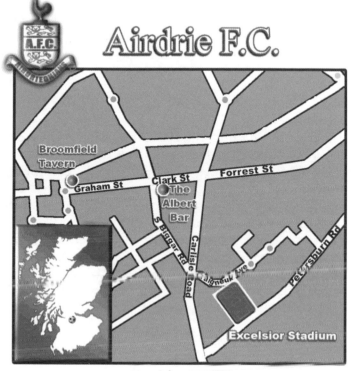

Excelsior Stadium
Ground opened - 1998

John; This was the second time we had done more than one club in a day, it was still summer and the country was in the middle of a heatwave. It was a magical time.

The three clubs we planned to visit are all fairly near EK so it would not be such an early start as previous multi-club visits.

The plan was to go to the furthest ground first and work backwards so that our last trip, when bladders would be under pressure, would be the shortest. That was the plan anyway.

Craig's Irene was having a week in Millport, and Irene always makes Craig's pieces, with wee extras and everything, so Craig had asked me the day before if I was taking pieces. I told him that I was making my own pieces as usual, so he decided to buy pieces at the local Sainsbury's in the morning.

Kate needed some shopping so she ran me down to meet Craig at 9.30am outside Sainsbury's. Pieces and papers bought, we said goodbye to Kate and jumped onto an old 201 which arrived right away. A good start to the day. It's a long and convoluted run to Airdrie on the 201. It would almost be easier to tell you the places it doesn't go through. Some of the places it does go through are right rough looking, Craig even thought he was back in Auchinleck at one point.

The plan, which I had arranged, I must admit, was to get off the 201 in the centre of Airdrie and get a local bus down to the new ground. To cut a long story short, if we had just stayed on the 201, it would have taken us right to the ground. Mind you, the wee local no. 26 did the business in a more, 'has this bus got a licence' sort of way. The Excelsior Stadium looked very nice in the bright sun-shine. Just like the day we went to Falkirk, there was a Circus setting up at the ground. It was called The Vegas Circus, the biggest in the country and it looked great. On the way to the ground, the wee rattly bus took us past the 'Albert Bar', which we had discovered on the web was the closest to the ground, so we got the same wee bus with the same driver back up the road and got off near the bar.

Craig; *This trip looked like being the easiest one we were ever likely to make. Visiting Airdrie Coatbridge and Motherwell all in one day meant that for the most part we would be using a single bus service*

The First Bus 201 would take us to all these towns and as luck would have it the bus passed by my front door. It was a perfect plan, or so it seemed.

Things started going wrong straight away. As I was alone that week, Irene being away on her annual summer visit to Millport, it was up to me to arrange my own food for the journey. I dare say I will surprise no one when I admit that I forgot to get any fresh bread in for my pieces. Actually I also forgot to get anything in to put on the bread I didn't get. So instead of getting

178

the bus from just outside my front door I had to trudge down to the town centre to buy some sandwiches.

On one of the hottest days of the year I was already feeling the strain. I had forgotten how uncomfortable the run to Airdrie was on the old 201. These buses are alright for short trips but on the long-haul to Airdrie they are quite literally a pain in the butt.

The bus shoogled and bumped through housing schemes, rumbled through large potholes and chugged along through heavy traffic until we got off the bus in a part of Airdrie we both recognised.

As it turned out that was a bit of a mistake. John had asked me to find a bus which would take us out to the park for a wee look around and that is exactly what I did. Therefore I take no blame for what happened next.

As we wandered around the outside of the stadium a number 201 came rumbling past. If we had just stayed on our old rattle trap for another couple of stops we could have been at the ground 20 minutes earlier.

John of course tried to blame me for this but I stood my ground and pretended I couldn't hear him. We noticed that a large circus had pitched their tents beside the park and wondered if it was just a coincidence that Falkirk FC, who we had recently visited, also had a circus set up next to their park.

Perhaps the football clubs see allowing them to set up on their land as a way of making a little extra cash during the close season.

My personal view is that these football clubs have so many clowns playing for them that they let them do a bit of moonlighting in the big top as a cheap form of training.

John; 'The Albert Bar', like most bars at this time of day, or morning, was very quiet, but it was a great looking bar inside, the type we love. We got talking to the barman, Gavin MacKenzie, who was the owner. He was a great guy and told us the background to the bar, and even showed us a lovely photo of his grandchildren, which his son had brought in. We felt like part of the family. He even bought us a round.

What a great guy. The pub won the SFL Supporters Pub of the Year a few years back. If you're ever in Airdrie, walk along a couple of hundred yards from the pedestrian bit; it is worth it to visit a brilliant bar.

Craig; I would like to take credit for finding the pub nearest to the football ground but to be honest we found it totally by accident. The Albert is a good old-fashioned man's pub. I would imagine that if a woman ever walked into the bar everyone would drop their dominos in shock.

Although that would not have been much of a problem on the day we were there as there was only one other customer in the place. I really thought we had made a mistake staying for a pint in such a quiet place but once again I was proved wrong.

The owner of the Albert started chatting away to us, telling us a little about his pub. He told us that the pub used to be a big favourite with fans going to the match. In fact the pub was named SPL pub of the year some time back. But these days the place is not so busy on match days. I think this has more to do with the fortunes of the football club than the popularity of the pub itself.

John; Sadly, we had to say our goodbyes, and we wandered along the street towards the busy bit. Just before we got to the pedestrian area, we saw a bar called 'Broomfield Bar'. I don't think I have ever seen a bar that looked so grotty from the outside, so needless to say, in we went. The other reason we had to go in was that Broomfield was the original ground in the days of Ian McMillan. What a player. Inside, the bar was a riot of noise, and it wasn't music, it was all coming from the two customers who were playing pool. One of the guys, Michael, must be a helicopter pilot, loud was not the word for it. But he was a great guy and very friendly.

The barman, Billy Tullard amazed us by recognizing us as soon as we walked in. He had read one of our books. Didn't want to ask him why he didn't read the other two, that would have been pushing our luck. It was definitely a Bluenose bar, which is not unheard of in Airdrie. Billy's arms, which were all we could see of his body, were covered in tattoos which you don't see so often nowadays. They were, how can I put it politically correctly, from the old days, or the bygone days of yore, in Billy's case.

180

When Michael, the Helicopter Pilot, heard we had written a book, he got us to sign one of the leaflets we bring with us to spread through bars to promote our books. Michael was going to keep it and sell it for a fortune in the future to put his first grandchild through University. I don't know which is the craziest, us ever being famous or his grandchild going to university. Only kidding Michael, We will be famous some day! Billy also gave us a free round. This is turning into a great day already.

Billy and the rest of the customers were a terrific crowd and we were saddened by the news that the bar was closing next week for ever. This type of bar is rapidly disappearing from our towns, to be replaced by Wotherspoon type places which are, in our opinion, crap.

Craig; After leaving the Albert we made our way along to a famous old pub. Talk about going from the sublime to ridiculous. I don't think I've ever been in a noisier pub. What makes that last statement a bit odd is the fact that at no time during our visit were there more than seven people in the pub, and four of them were keeping very quiet indeed.

The three younger men in the pub must have some sort of medical condition, one that has played havoc with their hearing. They apparently couldn't hear anything said to them at a level under 80 decibels.

Two of them had fallen out with each other and spent most of our stay screaming death threats at each other. I wasn't really worried which one would do in the other, it was what would happen to the witnesses that was worrying me.

The other chap was quite friendly actually but in a very loud sort of way. The barman turned out to be an old pal of ours from a previous visit to Airdrie. He told us that if we were still reviewing pubs we had better get a move on as this one was closing in a week's time.

We would have finished our beers and snuck out of the place but our pal, Billy Dollard, bought us another drink and I'm ashamed to say that our liking for the booze overcame our fear of an imminent doing and we stayed on.

Eventually we did manage to leave, uninjured. I did feel a wee bit guilty about leaving behind the other customer, a tall quiet man of about our age. He had that 'rabbit caught in the car headlights' look about him. I wonder if he ever made it out.

Pubs we visited:

The Albert Bar;

The Broomfield Bar;

How to get there by bus:

X11 Buchanan St. to Motherwell, then 201 to ground

Albion Rovers

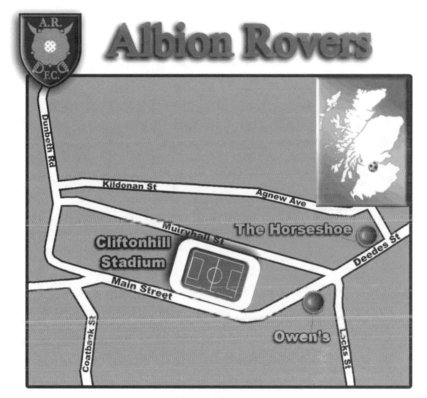

Cliftonhill Stadium
Ground opened - 1919

John; So it was with great sadness, and our ears ringing, that we left Airdrie and 'The Broomfield' to its sad end, and wandered through the modern pedestrian precinct to get our bus along the main road to Coatbridge, home of the once mighty Albion Rovers. The Wee Rovers, as their supporters call them. This is another of the many club nicknames that lack a bit of imagination, the 'Wee Albi' would have been a great

183

nickname. I think I'll put it on my 'Bucket List' to ensure all Scottish clubs have great nicknames. At least Airdrie have 'The Diamonds' as their nickname, after the shape of the red diamond on their shirts. Anyway, back to today's trip.

Craig; Our next pub was in Coatbridge the home town of Albion Rovers. 'Owens' is not too far from the stadium but to be honest it seems a wee bit upmarket for your average football fan. I think there might be a bit of a culture shock. Although very busy, the pub staff were nice to talk to and seemed interested in our adventures. Only time will tell if that translates into book sales.

Kelly gets hassled by an old guy at the bar

While we were sipping our beers we got talking to a very nice young girl called Kelly. She is a teacher and was waiting to meet some friends in the bar. Unfortunately she made the mistake of asking John what we were up to in Coatbridge. That was his cue to go into sales mode, as unsuccessfully as ever it has to be said.

The contrast between the customers in this pub and the last one we were in could not have been greater. I would certainly recommend a visit to Owen's and since the Broomfield is thankfully about to close forever I don't have to tell you what I would recommend for it.

184

John; We went into the bar nearest the ground, 'Owens', or 'Big Ownies' to it's regulars. This a lovely bar with a nice restaurant and beer garden and obviously makes most of its money from food. For the ordinary person there is nothing wrong with it, but to us it was too fancy. The couple running the bar were very busy all the time we were in, which is great for the bar, but the atmosphere was too fancy for us. Maybe on match days the place will have a better feel about it. Having said all that, normal people will find it a lovely place to visit.

The only regular who spoke to us was the lovely Kelly, a primary teacher on her summer holidays, in to meet a couple of pals, and if they are like the primary teachers I know, get wrecked!

Craig; *There was a fair old contrast between 'Owen's' and our next pub. 'The Horseshoe' is a bit more down to earth than its predecessor and therefore gets a decided thumbs-up from me. From the moment we go to the door we were treated like regulars, that is to say the barmaid took none of our nonsense and continued to run the bar like a well-oiled machine. Talking about getting well-oiled John had started knocking back the vodkas. I remained true to my beloved lager. Looking back on it I would have been much smarter settling for a couple of pints of cool tap water.*

The old boys at the bar were having a good laugh and not always at our expense. The barmaid Pauline, while joining in on the fun, kept all us older guys in line. This is another pub I would definitely recommend. It was handshakes all round as we left to catch our bus to Motherwell

John; Our next port of call was 'The Horseshoe', which was just a short walk along the road. Now this is what we would call a real man's bar. The barmaid Pauline and four locals were all great fun and kept us going all the time we were in. At one point I asked one of the locals if they came to the bar every day. Twice a day was his answer. We go home during the afternoon for a wee sleep before returning. Now they are real men, although their livers must be in a worst state than mine. This bar is certainly worth a visit if you are our on your own.

185

Pubs we visited:

Owen's;

The Horseshoe Bar;

How to get there by bus:

900 BuchananSt. to Garrowhill
then No.2 to ground

Motherwell

Fir Park
Ground opened - 1895

John; Like all our journeys today, I had planned the Coatbridge to Motherwell section. A change of bus was needed, which never works for us. It's really me it never works for. However, after much wandering around between stops and Craig complaining about the heat, (when do you hear that complaint in Scotland), we managed to get our second bus which took us to 'Fir Park', home of 'The Steelmen'. Now I know

Motherwell are sometimes called 'The Well', but that is another crap Nickname, so 'The Steelmen' it is.

Motherwell have a social club across the road from the park, so we thought we'd give it a try first. It looked closed at first, but there was a nice girl who asked if she could help us and signed us in. It was fairly quiet and lacked atmosphere, but again this was to do with the time of day and the fact that it was lovely outside which gave the impression of the place being dark. We had a word with the barman and two or three of the older locals. I worked for Thomson Litho for about 30 years or so and the owner, Matt Thomson was Motherwell's full back and captain for many years. He used to tell me stories of his playing days when we shared a few drinks together in the old days. Unfortunately Matt has passed away and the business has closed. The older guys remember him as a very hard player, a very very hard player. One of the best!

I'm sure the club is rocking during match days, it certainly is very handy for the ground. We said our goodbyes and following instructions given to us by the barmaid, got lost, had to backtrack in very hot conditions, and eventually found the bar called 'Jack Daniels'. The bar was ok in a big barn sort of way, but the staff and locals were friendly. A bit scared to say anything else.

Craig; Fir Park was our next stop and after a wee bit of a run around we found it. Since there was no game on, we didn't bother checking out the park itself and settled for a beer in the social club. I wasn't sure the place was open but we were so thirsty we thought it was worth chancing our arm and wandered in.

What a nice place and all the staff we met were very polite and helpful. You've got to wonder though if they are still as cheery on a cold winter's day with a busload of half-cut supporters demanding a top-up before the game.

The lounge is very well decorated and comfortable. We thought the barmaid was very pleasant and the beer was perfectly chilled. These are two of the top ingredients for a good day out.

While sipping our beers we got chatting to a small group of regulars at the end of the bar. The conversation was all about the weather which, as you will no doubt agree, is not an unusual topic in any Scottish drinking den, at any time of the year. The

188

difference this time was that no one was actually complaining about the weather. We were all still in the denial stage of this strange weather phenomenon. That is to say no one wanted to be first to admit they were sick of the heat-wave and were getting nostalgic for a bit of light drizzle.

Chilling out in the supporter's club

John; Once inside 'The Jack Daniels', Craig ordered a pint and a glass of water. I knew right away he was not at his best, and indeed he said he had felt better. As I said earlier it was a very hot day and I managed to talk Craig into getting a taxi back to the Lum. With all the free drinks we had gotten today, there was money in the kitty. So 20 minutes later we were back in the 'Lum'. My Kate was out with friends so she had pleaded with us to get something inside us. She meant food, so we planned for fish and chips in the Lum. Craig was feeling better and we ordered two fish and chips, only to be told that it would be at least an hour. Only in Scotland! We didn't want to complain too loudly as it is our local. So we ended up with a liquid dinner and then walked up the road, fairly early, to our abodes.

Airdrie and Albion Rovers both have great pubs in the area. Motherwell did not seem to have as many good pubs near the ground, although I know there are great pubs in the town centre. I've drunk in many of them.

We had a great day out. We're making a habit of enjoying these days a bit too much. Mind you, at our age you might as well enjoy your days out as much as possible, 'cause you don't know how many you have left'. On that depressing note I will finish today's tirade (is that a real word?).

I am now not bothering too much about mentioning how much I spend, but sometimes I am. Today was not too bad although, it has to be said, Craig let the side down by his 'I'm no well' bit. He seemed to recover in the Lum though!

Craig; John had found another pub for us to visit in Motherwell. 'Jack Daniels' was the name of the place and according to John it was just up the road. This was either a case of wishful thinking or he is just mince at navigating. It took us ages to find the pub and I was absolutely knackered by the time we did. I am pretty sure I was in the early stages of heat exhaustion.

I was certainly not at my best when we arrived outside 'Jack Daniels' so maybe I wasn't the best person to give a critical description of the place but I thought it looked like a not very well designed council storage building. It was a bit better on the inside but not by much, in fact it looked like a large pool hall with a bar attached.

John was pretty shocked when I asked for a glass of water. This apparently shocked the barmaid as well. She obviously either thought I was kidding around or maybe I just look like a man who needs a regular dosage of lager. Whatever her reasoning she served the beer up before she handed over my water.

'Jack Daniels' is apparently a very popular place at the weekend for the younger drinker but there were only a few people in the bar when we were there. I was too far gone to be bothered talking to anyone and John thought they didn't look like the talkative types so we didn't find out what it was like in there on match days.

190

Going out into the sun again in search of one of John's nearby bus stops just didn't appeal to me and fortunately John didn't fancy that either so we decided to get a taxi back to East Kilbride. This went directly against our travelling ethos. We are supposed to be the cheap way around boys after all. But the clincher for John came when I pointed out that if we got a taxi we could be sitting at the bar in 'the Lum' in 20 minutes. By the time we got there I had fully recovered and was ready for a small refreshment before walking home.

Pubs we visited:

Fir Park Social Club;

Jack Daniel's;

How to get there by bus:

240X Buchanan St to ground

Annan

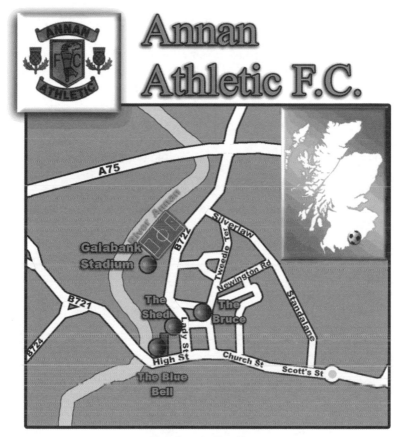

Galabank Stadium
Ground opened - 1953

John: Annan. It says in its web page that the nickname of the club is the 'Black and Golds' or 'The Galabankies', as Black and Gold are the team colors, I'm delighted that someone thought of a more original nickname, so 'The Galabankies' it is for me. As I've mentioned before, or after, depending on what order we put the teams in the book, there are some really crap nicknames that have taken little or no imagination to come up with.

Annan must be one of the newest teams to enter the league. They are certainly one of the most awkward to get to, unless you live in Annan of course. When I come to think about it, that is the whole idea of watching your local team, they're handy to get to. But back to today's story.

We had decided to go to the smaller clubs like Annan off-season, as it is the bars we are interested in. It was only the day before the trip that I discovered that there was a cup competition for the teams in the first, second and third division that was starting the very day we were going to Annan, and shucks, jings and help ma boab if Annan were not at home to Morton.

I had tried to book seats for us on the Dumfries bus, only to find that you could not book seats. It was first come first to get a seat. We were getting the bus at Hamilton which is handy from EK. I was a bit worried that as the bus starts at Glasgow, and with Morton playing at Annan, would there be hundreds of Morton fans filling the bus in Glasgow before we got a chance to get on in Hamilton. We had a back-up plan if the bus was full. We were going to go to Cumbernauld to check out the pubs there, where Clyde play, if that makes any sense. Let's hope we get on the bus.

I collected Craig at about 8.15am and we walked the few yards to the bus stop to get a 201 to Hamilton. We got our bus right away and it fairly belted down the road to Hamilton, getting us there before nine o'clock. We were first in the queue.

Right on time the X74 arrived with only a few passengers on board, all my worrying had been for nothing. We had our pick of seats and in brilliant sunshine our bus headed down the M74 to Dumfries. The only memorable thing to report was the fact that my trousers got soaked. I had lifted up my bag with all my notes and pieces to get stuff out. Just as I was to put it back on the floor I felt a wetness between my legs in the upper areas, but it was not warm as normal, it felt very cold.

Now I know you will think I am making this up, but this is dead gen. Irene had filled one of these plastic cartons you get your Chinese carryout in with ice. Now this carton was inside the poly bag containing Craig's pieces and other bits and bobs that Irene gives Craig. The carton was obviously going to leak, well obvious to the average minded person. The weather was roasting. You can work out the rest yourself, I was soaked. Thank god it was only water, so there was no smell.

194

It was glorious when we got off in Dumfries. Our first task was to go to the local Waterstones to sign the books they had. I had phoned to inquire if they needed any stock as we were going to be in the area, Fiona, the lady I spoke to checked and said no, but could you come in and sign the books we have. You couldn't say no, even if you wanted to. We had a nice time in the store and Fiona was great fun. She even promised to order hundreds of our next book, which we were working on that day.

Craig; Annan Athletic is the most southerly we will be visiting on our trek around Scotland's senior football teams. Actually it was touch and go whether we paid it a visit or not. It is just so difficult to get to by bus. But during a particularly heavy planning session in our HQ, that is to say The Lum, we decided to give it a go.

John took it upon himself to make all the travel arrangements, as usual, but got into a bit of a fankle when he discovered that there would actually be a football match taking place on the day of our visit. That combined with a music festival down by Kirkcudbright had him agitated. He phoned me in a panic at eleven o'clock the night before our trip.

He was certain that our bus would be bursting at the seams with football hooligans and hippies, leaving no room for us. Fortunately I managed to calm him down and we set off at 8.30 the next morning as planned.

The trip down to Dumfries passed without incident except of course for John wetting himself. I suppose I really should explain what happened.

As usual John had offered to carry my wee poly bag of food in his rucksack. Unfortunately it would appear that Irene had placed a small plastic box full of ice cubes in with my pieces. She later told me that she had been worried that because the weather was hot the butter in my pieces would go off. The home-made ice pack she had slipped into my bag was meant to stop that from happening.

195

Now it has to be said that Irene is exceptionally good at making lots of different things. Unfortunately cobbling together an efficient ice pack is not one of those things. John was the first to find this out. He was rummaging through his bag when he suddenly became aware that freezing cold water was leaking out of the bag and onto his lap.

It was bad enough that he looked as if he had been involved in a nasty and embarrassing accident but my hysterical laughter seemed to annoy him as well. That was cut short when I suddenly realised that all my food for the day had just been ruined.

To make matters worse John took the box out of his bag and placed it on the floor of the bus. Almost immediately it shot down to the front of the bus and we spent the rest of the trip worrying about pensioners disappearing under their seats as they stood on escaped ice cubes.

Happily we didn't see any skating senior citizens and we managed to get off the bus before anyone was injured. To avoid further embarrassment we kept to the back streets until John's trousers dried off.

I had been looking forward to visiting Annan since we began planning our trips around all the football grounds. It would be a long awaited return to a place I enjoyed visiting once before. It was about forty years since I had last stopped in the town and I was quite keen to see if there was anything still there that I remembered.

As our bus drove into the bus station I thought I recognised a building. I remembered being in a pub there on that last visit and when we walked back for a closer look I was happy to find it was still there. We decided that this pub, 'The Bruce', would be perfect as a last stop before we caught our bus back to Dumfries. For me that was for nostalgic reasons while John thought being able to see our bus stance from the pub window was a great idea.

John; Back down at the bus station, on the edge of the river, we had about a pint to spare before our bus was due, so we had a pint sitting outside in the sunshine watching for our bus. A great start to the day,

196

apart from the leg soaking. Our bus arrived on time and we had a lovely run through beautiful countryside into the wee town of Annan.

It was a 10 minute walk up the road to the park, which is lovely in a small way. It has a great social club bar and we were made to feel at home right away. The club secretary Allan Irvine filled us in on the history of the club and how it came to be in the football league. It is fantastic all the work that is carried out by volunteer supporters in the background to help keep clubs afloat. We had a great time in the club, but all too soon we had to leave to find somewhere else to drink. Halfway down the hill to our next stop Craig remembered he had left his jacket back in the club, so he offered me a great deal, he would watch the bag while I went back up the hill to get his jacket. I had no option but to agree as he is not great at rushing about and I would have felt guilty if I had let him go back himself.

Craig; Up at the stadium we were very impressed by how neat and tidy the place was. Inside the social club there were only about half a dozen people sitting around enjoying a drink. At a guess I would say that the hall could comfortably hold about a hundred to a hundred and twenty customers.

The décor could be said to be more functional than fashionable, but that is what you would expect with a supporters club after all. Apparently there is entertainment on at weekends.

We were served quickly by a young girl who seemed very pleasant. The beer was also quite pleasant and just what we needed after the long walk up from the bus station. It would have been a fair bit shorter if we hadn't listened to the directions offered to us by a local we stopped in the street. I'm still not sure if he was having a laugh at our expense or if he was genuinely crazy. Either way we managed to take the scenic route.

The club gradually filled up with Annan fans and it was good to see the club being so well supported.

While we were appreciating our beers the club secretary Alan Irvine came over for a chat. He told us that the team had a core support of about 400 to 500 fans who turn out for every game. It was very interesting to hear Alan talk about how Annan had come up from the amateur leagues to its present position in

197

the Scottish league. The club also has high hopes of progressing to higher divisions, eventually.

We were really enjoying our stay and decided that in order to do a proper assessment of the social club we should sample another pint. I am happy to report that it was just as good as the first one.

By the time we were polishing that one off the club was getting really busy, there were even some away fans coming in. We thought it was only fair to let some real supporters have our seats and since we needed to check out another three pubs in the next couple of hours it seemed like a good time to move on.

We had been told that there was a pub a mere five minute walk from the ground which was a favourite with the fans. Remembering our run-in with the crazy local from earlier on I decided not to get my hopes up.

John; The Jacket safely returned, we wandered in to our next bar, 'The Shed'. This was a sports bar with lots of big screen tellies, not the sort of place we normally frequent, but this was a great bar with a happy mix of old and young filling the place. The boss Len Roddie and the barmaids, a mother and daughter combination, Christine and Elaine, were great fun and Len insisted on getting us a round in. A great bloke. A regular, Willie who is stuck in a wheelchair because of illness, did not let this get him down and was great company. We could have stayed all day, but our need to let you all know of as many bars as possible made us say our goodbyes. We found our way to 'The Blue Bell Inn'. This is another great bar, an old fashioned bar which specializes in Real Ale. Ceilidh, the barmaid was great company and we had a lovely time there as well. Annan has great bars.

Craig; *The way it turned out it took us about fifteen minutes to reach 'The Shed'. Although I do have to admit that about ten of those minutes were spent going back to the social club for my jacket. Actually John had volunteered to go back for it for me. I think he suspected I might stop there for a quick pint.*

The Shed is a real sports bar and normally not the type of place we would frequent but this place was different. There was a

198

good age range of customers and I even spotted some women enjoying a drink in there.

The pub boss, Steven Keets, came round the bar to say hello and demanded that we take a drink from him. Normally we would never dream of accepting free drinks, but Steven was a nice guy and very insistent. So we abandoned our principles and wolfed down a nice cool beer. It actually does taste better when you get it for nothing.

The barmaid was a good laugh and chatted away to us until she saw me writing a few lines in my notebook. I think she might have thought I was from a certain government department. She claimed her name was Myrtle but I have it on good authority that her name was actually Christine. Every time I even touched my camera she let out a yelp and ran up to the other end of the bar.

While I was amusing myself by torturing 'Myrtle' with my camera John had got on the chat with another of the pub's customers. Willie, who had recently been confined to a wheelchair, was definitely up for a laugh. The pair of them had a great time swapping ancient football stories which, since I didn't have any to swap, gave me plenty of time to savour my beer in silence.

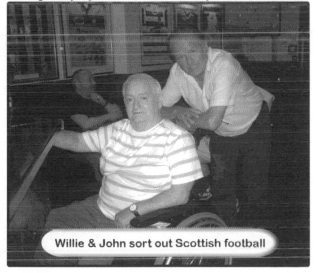

Willie & John sort out Scottish football

199

The next pub on our list was the Blue Bell and since I had checked this one out on my computer I knew we didn't have far to walk. I really should have asked a local how far away it was just to see what they came up with.

The Blue Bell is a really substantial sandstone building right on the edge of the town. We actually had a bit of trouble finding the door in. I put this down to bad design rather than overindulgence, but I could be wrong.

The bar is up five or six stairs from street level and is quite old-fashioned as you would expect from such an old building. There was a reasonable crowd in the place but no sign of any football fans.

We were served straight away by a very nice young lady who told us her name was Ceilidh. I immediately thought she was kidding me on, just like the barmaid in the last pub, but she said that her mother was a big fan of Scottish Country dancing.

She told us that the Blue Bell was a real ale pub and was very popular with football fan, particularly away supporters. When you consider how far any away supporter has to travel to get to Annan added to the fact that this is the first pub they would see coming into town, I can understand why this is the case.

Ceilidh, like the girl in the last pub, asked me not to take her picture. I've never been in such a camera shy town. Usually people will trample over each other to get their faces in front of the camera. John thought that maybe everyone in Annan was on the social and working on the side. My favourite theory was that Annan had become the dumping ground for a police witness relocation scheme.

John; The day was made complete for Craig as he found a bar, 'The Bruce', just round the corner from the bus station. He had been there as a boy. I will let Craig fill you in with the details of the bar and its owner. Needless to say, it was another great bar.

Annan is a grand wee town with great bars, people and supporters. Well worth a visit.

Our trip home was uneventful and dry. We had another pint in Dumfries as we waited for our bus, a pint in Hamilton as we waited for our next bus, and a pint for luck in 'The Lum' before staggering home. Another memorable day out in a great wee town!

My spends today were average, about £30-£40. The pints on the way home from Annan didn't help, and we would have saved about £10 if we hadn't had to wait for buses. Well, you can't wait at the bus stop, can you!

Craig; Our last pub of the day was of course The Bruce. I had been looking forward to having a pint in it for years. In fact I wasn't sure if it still existed.

The last time I had a pint in this pub I was about eighteen years old. I had been hitchhiking and ended up in Annan for the night. I walked around the town I came across a pub and picture house just off the high street. The funny thing about it was the whole complex was made of wood. It actually looked like part of a street scene in a western.

Barrie and Gordon Clark

The Bruce adjoins Annan's bus station so it was already scoring brownie points before we even got into it. Everything was still the same shape but it was now modern and brick built.

201

Unfortunately the old cinema has long since gone and had been replaced with a Costcutter store.

I was really wanting to talk to someone about the old buildings as I was beginning to think that maybe I had imagined the whole thing. Out on the pub veranda I spoke to an older couple. I asked them if they were locals and the man said yes in fact he had lived in Annan all his life. Being 85 years old I think he really does qualify as a local.

It turned out that the man I was talking to, Gordon Clark, was the owner of all the buildings in the complex. He told me that the original wooden buildings had been built by the American Army during the First World War. Gordon bought the buildings and turned them into a bar and cinema. Instead of selling up when the buildings got into a bit of a state due to old age, Gordon replaced them, even keeping the original layout. I could have stayed on reminiscing with a Gordon but it was time for us to return home.

Pubs we visited:

Annan Social Club;

The Shed;

The Blue Bell Inn;

The Bruce;

How to get there by bus:

X74 Glasgow to Dumfries
No.79 Dumfries to Annan

Stirling

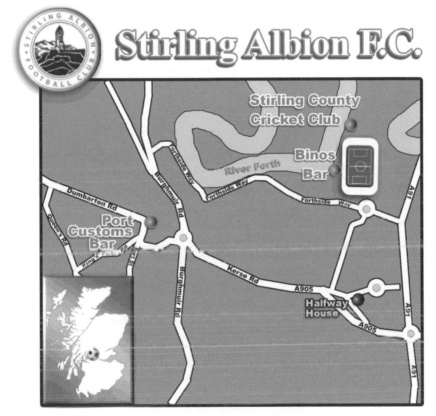

Forthbank Stadium
Ground opened - 1993

John; Today's plan was to visit Stirling Albion, check out a couple of pubs and then head to Perth to visit St. Johnstone, who were playing Hearts today, or so I thought.

In our now very professional manner of doing trips, I had booked us bus tickets, and printed out maps of the area around the grounds. How professional is that! I never thought of double checking to find out who was playing who today.

We had our usual start to the day. I got Craig at 8.15am and we caught the No. 18 into George Square and tramped up the hill to the bus station. It was only when I became old that I realized there was a hill from George Square up to the bus station, and it seems to be getting steeper each time I go up it. Aye, it's true what they say, old age never comes alone, even if you are alone when it comes!

I had the munches as I had been away sea fishing the day before and the day had turned into night before I did the sensible thing and get to bed. There's no stopping me. So with a Bounty Bar, Quavers and a Coke purchased, as well as my right wing rag, as Craig calls it, we got on our coach, the M8, for our run up to Stirling, our supposed first port of call for the day.

As we settled into our seats, about 20 Chinese people got on. What a racket they make. God knows what it must be like in China if they all shout and bawl like the ones on the bus did. It's like the way us Scots carry on after a good bevy. We wondered if it was the Chinese New Year in Stirling or something, probably something.

On the bus Craig suggested I look at the paper and find out if Stirling Albion had a game today. I had not checked as we were visiting in the late morning before going on to Perth to visit St. Johnstone. The paper gave us good and bad news. Yes, Stirling Albion had a game against Hamilton, which meant there would be some officials and supporters who we could talk to, but the shocker was that St. Johnstone were playing Hearts on Sunday. This was Saturday. Craig gave me some abuse. At least it cheered him up. We decided to carry on with our plans as it is the pubs that are important, not the games.

We arrived in Stirling and all the Chinese people got off along with us. One of them asked me where they could get a number 67. Craig anticipated my 'is that not Sweet and Sour Chicken' answer and pulled me away before I caused an incident. He's no fun. Our next bus, the P1, was at the next stance and we got on right away and set off on the eight minute journey to the ground. The lack of Chinese on the bus made for a very quiet journey.

Craig; Our trip to Stirling and Perth didn't go to plan; in fact 50% of it never actually happened. There were two main reasons for that and both of them involved John. When he wrote out the schedule for today's trip he was under the impression that

St Johnstone were playing at home that week. As it happens they were but unfortunately they wouldn't actually be doing it for a further 24 hours. The game had been changed to a Sunday kick-off. The cheek of these people changing fixtures without alerting John! Ever adaptable we decided to visit Perth anyway but just concentrate on the town's pubs.

That visit still didn't happen though and for what might be described as a very fishy reason. The day before our trip John had gone on a trip of his own. He had been on a sea fishing trip on the east coast. I don't think it was all the bobbing around on the ocean wave that made him a bit fragile the next day, it was more likely to be the four or five hours in the pub afterwards. It is of course possible that it could have been a combination of these factors, but whatever the cause John looked well below par and unlikely to complete today's mission.

We got our usual number 18 First Bus down to Glasgow and the journey passed in almost total silence. Every passenger upstairs was sitting staring at their phone, It looked really weird. John for his part wasn't staring at anything I seriously doubt that he had regained the ability to focus never mind stare.

We were first on to the Citylink M9 at Buchanan Street bus station so we got a good look at our fellow passengers as they came on board. Strangely most of them appeared to be Chinese and they all seemed to know each other. As soon as the coach moved out of the station they began to shout loudly and kept it up for the entire length of the trip.

Obviously I have no idea what they were shouting about but I did wonder if they were just trying to get their own back on us. Like most men I remember in my youth staggering into the odd Chinese restaurant and acting like a complete prat by shouting my order slowly to my waiter. Revenge, as they say is sweet, not sour.

We caught a bus up to the park almost immediately after we got to Stirling bus station. It takes all of eight minutes for the journey and that includes three or four minutes doubling back on our own tracks. We were very impressed with the location of

205

Forthbank Stadium. It is part of a large sports complex which has tennis courts, five-a-side pitches and a cricket club.

John; We got off the bus at the stadium which is in the middle of a giant sporting complex, with all sorts of outdoor and indoor activities. It is fantastic. The Stadium looked nice so we went in the main door to be met by two very friendly and helpful girls. We told them what our mission was and they thought it was a great idea. One of them, Anne Irvine, showed us round the ground and on to the park which was great. When we came back to the reception, the Chairman David McFarlane and his wife Margaret met us and took us upstairs to show us the boardroom and the bar that is used by supporters before the game. Now this was more like it. The bar is called 'Binos' which is also the nickname of the club, and a great, and imaginative nickname it is, unlike some other clubs. They offered us a drink, but unbelievably we said no, that we would like to visit a couple of bars in the area and then come back.

They suggested two places, 'The Halfway Bar' and the local Cricket Club just behind the East Stand. We followed their instructions and eventually found 'The Halfway Bar'. It had been shut for two years! It was raining now as we walked a roundabout way to the Cricket Club; we passed about six roundabouts! The roundabout route was Craig's idea.

Craig; *The girl at the stadium reception desk, Elaine, was very helpful and along with Anne Irvine, who is either the cleaner or the stadium guide, or both, managed to arrange a mini tour of the stadium for us. We even got out to the pitch for a wee photo shoot. Then the main man himself David McFarlane arrived and showed us around the boardroom and the bar. David and his wife Margaret keep Forthbank Stadium running like clockwork.*

We were very impressed with the bar set up. That probably won't come as a great surprise to most of our readers, but this bar is different. It was built to fold away when not in use. The units of the bar are hinged and the fridges are on casters, it's brilliant. If I had a wee bit more room and an awful lot more money, not to mention written permission from Irene, I would like something similar for our living room.

It was a wee bit too early for a drink even for us so we decided to walk back into town to find a pub we had been told about. The Halfway is a favourite with both home and away supporters, or so we were told by Elaine.

All I can say is if it had been so popular you would have thought someone would have noticed a marked decline in attendance up at the park when the punters stopped going to this pub. The Halfway was so popular that it shut two years ago.

Our problem was that we didn't find out about the closure until we had trekked the mile and a half down the road. John was beside himself with rage. I was too knackered to do much beyond sulk, quite a lot.

Before we found out about it being a wild goose chase John had taken it upon himself to be our path-finder. Actually he saw an overgrown path through the trees and tried to convince me that it was probably a good short cut to the pub. Needless to say I refused point blank to follow him through the bushes and insisted we take the main road round.

Looking back on it he was probably right. At least we would have found out a lot quicker that we were heading away from any chance of a beer and not towards it.

Just to take his mind off our sad situation I pretended to get us lost on the way back up to the stadium. I did a really good job of it too. Shouting and swearing at me fairly took his mind off our troubles. By the time we caught sight of the stadium he was back to his usual cheerful self.

John; Eventually, hidden behind trees, we found 'Stirling Cricket Club', and in we went. At first I thought it was a funny place for some of Glasgow's jakies to be hanging about, but it was just some of the Cricket team in their whites' hanging about waiting for the rain to go off so they could get their game started.

At first we got the impression that this place was going to be a disaster, again. How wrong we were. The girls working behind the bar, Catherine and a young girl called Laura were great fun. They were having a lot of trouble with the draught beer and eventually we ended up

207

with two cans of Red Stripe which were great. The people in the bar, some of them the cricketers were great company and we even met Donald Morton, the Deputy Editor of The Stirling Observer. A great guy, especially as we will be looking for all the publicity we can get for the book we were there working on. I'm sure it will now be front page news in Stirling! Who am I kidding? When the girls got the pumps working they gave us a pint each on the house. What lovely people.

Time was racing by and we were still in the Cricket Club at the time we should have been leaving Stirling. Who cares. We eventually said our goodbyes to the Cricket Club and wished them all the best for today's game. It was brightening up and it looked as if the game would be on.

Catherine and Laura at the SCCC

Craig; Eventually we made our way round to the cricket club, more by accident than design. Stirling County Cricket Club had a bar and we were fairly sure it was open. Although there were five or six people sitting around the lounge we were the first customers at the bar. All the others in the bar were watching a cricket match on the telly while they waited to go out and play a match, so it was soft drinks only for them.

The girls behind the bar were having trouble with the draught beer and so I decided that bold action was required. Thinking quickly I ordered cans of lager instead. To be a successful pub reviewer you have to be adaptable.

208

Our barmaids, Catherine and Lorna, were a great laugh and helped us get over our earlier disappointment.

Cricket is just one of the many sports I don't particularly like but after a couple of beers it didn't annoy me quite as much. Another half dozen and I might even watch a bit of it.

We asked Catherine what it was like in the club when Rangers played Stirling Albion last season. She said the fans were queued out of the doors. Apparently the noise of the supporters was unbelievable, but knowing what the bar receipts were likely to be made things more bearable.

I hate to think what the scenes were like down on Kerse Road when several hundred angry blue-noses found out the fans' favourite pub, The Half Way, had shut its doors for good.

John; We wandered back over to Stirling's Football club and were shown up to the bar which was starting to fill with supporters. The bar, which is used as a conference room during the week is in a great position. Huge windows give a good view over the park, but they are not allowed to use the bar when the match is on. There would be a huge potential revenue stream if they were allowed to charge people for watching the game in comfort and having a drink at the same time. I think some of our laws about banning drink are crazy, mind you, so are most of our politicians.

Time was slipping past us we talked to the supporters, who, like in most clubs, are working in the background raising money to help keep their clubs afloat. By this time Craig and I were afloat from the pints we were drinking. We were only doing this to help raise money for the club! I think we were both thinking the same thing by this time, so I said to Craig, 'How do you fancy doing Perth another time'? 'If that's what you want', he replied, trying to kid me he was all for still going to Perth, he could hardly walk by this time, so we decided to stay in Stirling and enjoy the company. Eventually, we had to leave, so after saying goodbye to the barmaid, who was a great laugh, and the supporters, we walked up to Morrisons car park to catch the shuttle bus to take us the eight minute run back to Stirling Bus Station.

Now even though we had had a good few pints and would have preferred to go straight home, we are working on the book and so forced ourselves to find a pub near the Bus Station for more research!

Craig; *Back round at the stadium we gave Elaine a bit of a hard time for sending us to a shut pub. She was mortified and we let her stew for a while before we forgave her.*

Our new pal David McFarlane met us at the front desk and took us up to the Binos Bar. He must have noticed how knackered we were after all our wanderings as he took us up in the lift.

In the bar we were introduced to Lynne, who was serving that day. The bar is run by the fans and all the profits go to the club. As yet there is no draught beer to be had but I was getting used to drinking cans anyway so I didn't mind.

There were a few customers in the bar and we got chatting to them. They were a great bunch of guys and, apart from an irrational dislike of Auchinleck Talbot, we got along very well.

It was about this time that I noticed John was beginning to wilt a bit. There was no real chance that we were going to manage a trip to Perth.

Having a ball in 'Binos'

We needed to make an executive decision on the matter and we did so by ordering another couple of cans.

By the time we reached the city centre John had perked up a bit and insisted on having a quick pint of draught beer. That's how we ended up going into The Port Customs, a very nice pub just outside the main shopping centre.

John; The bar we found was 'The Port Customs', I think, so in we went. This is a classic man's bar with a wide range of customers and the owner and his wife, Gary and Donna McGregor were a lovely couple and great company, as was Harry Gillespie, a local worthy who filled us in with local gossip. Donna and Gary insisted on getting us a round up. This was turning into one of our best days.

I've no idea what time it was when we said our goodbyes and headed back the few yards to the Bus Station. We slept most of the journey home, walked straight down to Central Station and got the train to EK. We were thirsty by then so a couple of pints in 'The Monty' in the village were needed. Craig tried to call Irene to pick us up, but got no answer, so we got a taxi up the road. Walking was out of the question.

So ended a great day out at Stirling Albion. St. Johnstone will have to wait. Although we had a wheen of drink, a lot of it was free and I don't think I spent much, about £30.

Donna and Gary share a joke with Harry who's got into the habit of visiting 'The Customs'

Craig; The Port is a really neat and tidy pub with a fine long bar for the weary traveller to rest against. There was a good mixture of customers in while we were there but unfortunately didn't seem to be any football fans present.

After we were served I asked the barmaid if they ever got much trade from passing football supporters. She told me that, as far as she knew, the Port didn't see much in the way of football custom. This surprised me as Forthbank Stadium is only an eight minute bus ride away, or a twenty minute walk for the thirsty fan.

Just before we were about to leave, Gary, the owner, plonked down another couple of pints in front of us. We protested loudly of course but he insisted. Another pint was the last thing either of us needed but it would have been the height of bad manners to refuse such a generous gift. Besides it guaranteed me a quiet journey back to Glasgow as John would be asleep in no time.

Once we got back to Glasgow we played it safe and made straight for the train station. This took quite a bit of effort as you can imagine. Being traditionalists we had to fight our instincts and not turn into Drury Street, the home of the famous Horse Shoe Bar.

By the time we arrived back in East Kilbride John was claiming that he was now stone cold sober and therefore needed another couple of pints. I didn't believe the first part of his statement but I couldn't fault the logic of the second part so we nicked into the Monty to round off the day.

John; The Stirling Albion club is brilliant, as is the Cricket Club. We even came up with the idea of visiting every Cricket Club in Scotland in a future book, so we must have had a good few by then. 'The Port' near the bus station is also a great bar.

Pubs we visited:

S.C.C.C.;

Binos;

Port Customs Bar;

How to get there by bus:

M8 Scottish Citylink
Buchannan St. to Stirling Bus Station
P1 Local service to Ground

Greenock

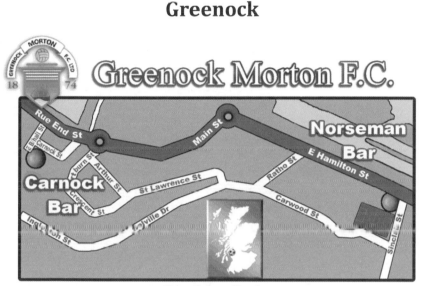

Cappielow Park
Ground opened - 1879

John: Morton, Nickname 'The Ton', better than 'The Mor', but not a lot. As I've said before, clubs and supporters should put more thought into their nicknames. Now I don't like slagging off nicknames without being able to come up with a better, or at least a more original one. So I have given it a minute's thought and here are a couple of beauties; 'The Clydesiders' as they are the only senior club on the banks of the Clyde, or what about 'The Nockrockers', that's a more obvious one, but great?

Greenock is one of these towns that has a bit of a reputation for being a tough area. I'm sure it is no worse than any other town and I hope today we will prove that the bars in Greenock are as friendly as anywhere else.

213

A fact that you might find interesting is that my wife Kate's sister Margaret was one of the first lady Policemen (not Policewomen) and she lived and worked in Greenock for years and said the people were great, not only that, but her late husband Robert liked nothing better than to regale us with his particular favourite song at family gatherings. It was called 'The Green Oak Tree'. I can only remember the last line of the chorus which went;

''and I'm proud to be a member of the Green Oak Tree''
I can't write music to let you all join in the tune, but the beat went;
(dum-de-dum-de-dum-de-dum-de-dum-de-dum-dum-dum)

Note; Green Oak means Greenock - explanation for the dum de dummies reading this!

But now back to the realities of today's trip. If I had a pound for every time we got the old no. 18 into Glasgow, I'd have a good few quid. But today was different, because the 18 does not go into the bus station in Glasgow. We have a choice of it or the number 6, which until recently was the 66. This bus goes a different way into Glasgow but ultimately drops you off at the same place, so we had a choice, and the no. 6 arrived first, so no more pounds in the kitty today.

We had decided that as our next bus would not be busy (I decided that), we would not walk up to the bus station, but get off in St. Vincent Street at the same stop that our next bus visited. I knew which stop it was. Unfortunately our bus did not stop there but shot straight past it and was about to turn into Hope Street when I looked back in a slight panic and saw our next bus, the McGills bone shaking number 906 to Largs, stopped at the traffic lights before the stop. Now this was an earlier bus than the one planned, but I still thought it would be better to catch it and get to Greenock a pint earlier, but obviously this was not going to happen, or was it? As we got off in Hope Street, we heard the sound of an Orange band which was marching down Renfield Street.

Now, although this was still early morning, my mind was alert and I immediately realized that if the band got to the corner the 906 was at, the bus would have to wait, and that's what happened. By the time the band had passed we had got to the stop and the bus pulled up at the same second. It just goes to show that God is a Prod!!

Craig; *It seems like ages since we talked about going to Greenock, the home of Morton FC. But the fact is John had taken*

214

charge of the planning side of all our little adventures and so it was all up to him when we visited the various football grounds.

I'm not entirely convinced that turning out as a ball boy for Partick Thistle, many many decades ago, gives him the proper credentials to plan all our trips round every Scottish league team. But he does love his spread sheets so I just go along with things to humour him.

It should come as no surprise then that he buggered up our trip to Greenock. Originally Morton was the last team on our long list of places to be visited. But, due to what I will generously call a technical hitch, we had to move it up our schedule.

The journey down to Glasgow was uneventful. It was only when we arrived there that things got interesting. John, the seasoned traveller, insisted that we should wait on the bus until the second stop past George Square. The only problem with that is, there isn't a second stop. We went wheeching up Hope Street for what seemed like half a mile or so.

Even before we eventually got off the bus I could hear music being played. Actually it sounded to me as if someone was strangling a cat. It turned out to be bagpipes being played, badly.

As we made our way back down to the road we should have been on it became clear that the Orange Lodge was out for a walk. The nearer we got to the source of the music the stranger John's walking style got.

I was certain that not only was he keeping time with the music but he also had a definite swagger going on. My own theory on his bizarre walking style is simply this: his Govan DNA was kicking in.

John; The bus fairly belted down to Greenock, and in no time at all, five past eleven, we were getting off at our supposed first port of call, 'The Norseman'. From the outside, this pub is the most uninviting place I have ever seen, and it was shut. Metal shutters covered every potential entrance, it was scary. Craig thought he was back in Auchinleck!

The web page had told us that this was the only pub near the ground, so a sober day might have been on the cards. Actually, I had

215

been warned by her indoors to try and stay sober and be home early as Craig and I and the wives were going out to a wedding reception sort of thing that night, and I had promised her I would stay sober-ish!

Cappielow was right behind the shut bar so we wandered up to have a look round. Again, metal shutters were everywhere and it was only when we got to the side of the main stand that there was an entrance into the ground. This was being used by early morning deliveries of pies and things. We wandered in and got straight on to the park, which looked in great condition, and as flat as a pancake. So far, this was the only thing in Greenock that looked in great shape. The ground is very old fashioned, but I loved the set up of it This is one of the most atmospheric grounds I have seen, and I've seen a few.

No pints had been supped, and Craig was getting restless, so we went back down to find 'The Norseman' still shut. Not to be beaten, we had a reserve plan. A local bus took us towards the metropolis of Greenock. Now I knew, from driving through this area on my way to catch the Rothesay ferry at Wemyss Bay, that there was a pub up beside the Fire Station, and there was. We got off outside Morrisons Supermarket, cut across the car park and over a wall at the back. Now this wall was not high for a young person, but I got a laugh watching Craig struggle to get his leg over!

Craig; *The Mc Gill's 901 dropped us off almost directly outside the Norseman Bar in Greenock. At any other time we would have been delighted by this happy accident, but not today.*

For one thing, it was far too early to get a pint, being only twenty to eleven. Another drawback to our enjoyment was the fact that we could find no way into the bar anyway.

We cut our losses and walked the few yards up to the football stadium. It was more or less shut as well. We did manage to find a way onto the pitch so that John could pretend to be sporty.

Our only option after that was to catch a bus further into town and search for an open pub. We found a great one. Although from the outside it didn't look too promising

John; From a distance of about 20 yards, the 'Carnock Bar' looked pretty drab and shut, but it wasn't, it was open, so in we went. Inside, the place was very nice, just the sort of place we like, but better still, the barmaid 'Big Bird' Brenda was brilliant company and a great advert for how a bar should be run. She even ended up giving us pub tee shirts. Magic!

As it was still early there were only a few locals in, but they were all great company, if not a bit mad, in a good way. Jim McShane filled us in with stories of the bar and all the crazy and great people from the area. Jim, I would need a complete book to tell the half of your stories. Names like Joe Harper, Andy Ritchie, and a woman they called Harry Rednapp all rolled off his tongue. He showed us a brass plaque on the bar in memory of Chick, a regular who passed away all too soon. Jim even insisted on getting us a drink. What a guy. My only worry is that Jim, and the owner, who we only met as we were leaving said that they would want royalties every time we mentioned the bar's name, so Jim, Carnock, Carnock, Carnock, Carnock, Carnock, that's about a fiver I owe you.

'The Carnock' (I've said it again) is up behind the Fire Station and is a bar well worth a visit.

With a wide selection of handshakes, we said farewell to 'The Carnock', walked down to the front street and got on a wee local bus which took us up the back streets and dropped us off just behind Cappielow. We went in to the entrance of the ground and spoke to one of the officials who told us there was no paying bar in the ground, just hospitality. But he told us in a friendly way so we were well pleased with the ground staff.

Craig; In fact The Carnock Bar looked derelict to be truthful, but inside it is a fine traditional Scottish pub

There were fewer than ten customers in the bar, and that included us. We were served straight away by a very friendly young lady. I say young because she told me to say that. Brenda, also known as big Brenda, or Big Bird, was very definitely up for a laugh.

When she found out what we were up to she demanded that we put her age down as twenty eight. Obviously I am too much of a gentleman to even guess at her real age but it surely can't be an awful lot more than that. If that doesn't get me a free pint the next time I'm in the Carnock I will be very surprised, not to say huffy.

217

Her pal, who was sitting next to me at the bar, told Brenda to tell us the story about how she dealt with a customer who was bothering her recently. Apparently he had spotted a tattoo Brenda had on her arm. He claimed she wasn't entitled to have the tattoo as it was only army personnell who should have it. She told him she had recently had a sex change operation and used to be an army sergeant. The chap stopped bothering her.

Big Bird Brenda ruffles feathers at The Carnock

Then we got talking to another customer, Jim McShane. Jim is a shipyard worker and life-long Morton supporter. He told us the story behind the brass plaque which was attached to the bar where I was standing. It was in memory of one of the Carnock's regulars, Chick, who had died recently. Apparently the bloke was only 51 and was a well thought-of friend to many in the pub.

We both thought that putting plaques up like this was a great idea. John kind of wasted the moment however when he said that when I go somebody is going to have to get a couple of hundred made and post them all round Scotland. It is very fortunate that I have a very thick skin. I decided to wait a while before I extract my revenge on John, although I will of course get him back for it.

We asked Jim about other pubs nearby which were used by football fans. He told us that there were quite a few good bars not

*too far away which were favourites with Morton fans. He spoke
about one in particular which he said we would be wise to avoid.
Apparently it is the one the jakies end up in after being barred
from all the other pubs in Greenock.*

*Between us we decided that it should change its name to The
Last Chance Saloon given that it was full of cowboys. Its real
name shall remain secret, at least until we can actually pay it a
visit.*

*Eventually we made our way round to the bus stop and
waited for our bus to take us back up to the Norseman.*

*John was still checking the timetables when a bus stopped
behind him. He shouted to me that this was our bus and jumped
onto it. The bus travelled about twenty yards before turning off the
main road.*

*We were bumped around a housing scheme with John
getting more and more agitated. He obviously knew I would make
his life hell if our bus didn't end up at the football park.*

*The woman sitting in front of us took pity on him and told us
which bus stop to get off at and how to get from there to the park.
He breathed easily once more.*

*We were fairly certain that Cappielow didn't have a social
club attached to it but we felt we had to ask anyway. The security
guys were friendly which I have to say was quite surprising, but
they confirmed that there was no bar in the stadium*

*They told us the nearest bar was the Norseman but added
that we should keep our hands on our money at all times if we
went in there. To be honest we got that impression from just
looking at the place from the outside.*

John; It was only a few yards down to 'The Norseman' and one
of the metal shutters was up. We assumed this was the entrance and we
went in and up one of the most depressing set of stairs you have ever
seen, and the smell was just as bad. Needless to say it was with a wee bit
of trepidation that we held our noses and went up the stairs and into an
unusual looking big bar. It's hard to explain the bar, it looked as if it had
been laid out for god knows what. The bar was completely stainless

219

steel. Our first impression was, why are we here, but after about an hour and a half we didn't want to leave the place.

This was another case of 'it's the people who make the bar'. And the décor and layout of the place started to grow on us as soon as we settled at the bar. The owner said his name was Maxwell Park; I asked him if he was taking the piss, but he assured me that it really was. He was a great bloke with fantastic hearing. He was in the back shop, which he said was a kitchen! When I said something to Craig in a whisper, did he no hear every word. Thank God I was being nice about the place.

Big Max parks himself behind the bar in The Norseman

There are lovely views of the Clyde out of the picture windows. Maxwell said you could see the Dumbarton Rock and even the Erskine Bridge from the window. He took me over to let me see. All I can say is that his eyesight must be as good as his hearing. I saw nothing. Maggie, the Dragon Lady and her young assistant Cheryl were good company and we had a great time with them and the few locals who were in. Maxwell told us the place was quieter for a match day Saturday than it used to be. This recession is hitting everybody. I hope the locals support 'The Norseman', because even though it will never win any prizes for its looks, outside or in, it is a great bar run by a great guy with a funny name.

We had had a few more rounds than we had planned, but we knew the two hours it would take us to get back to EK would remove the alcohol from our system

'The Norseman' is definitely a surprise of a bar and it is also well worth a visit.

Craig; The Norseman was a bit grotty, especially the entrance. But as soon as we stepped into the bar I knew that I was going to like it in the Norseman. I do have to admit that the stainless steel bar took a bit of believing. Why would anyone build a stainless steel bar the whole length of the building?

My first thoughts were that it was there to make it easier to hose the blood off after the fighting. Unfortunately I said as much to John. That wouldn't have been so bad had it not been for the fact that the barman had some sort of super hearing. Fortunately he took it in good part.

The barman, who turned out to be the owner as well, told us that his name was Maxwell Park. I thought he was taking the piss and told him so. For some reason I thought Maxwell Park was a sports field in Kilmarnock. Not for the first time I was wrong.

Max told us that his bar was the closest bar to any senior ground in Scotland and I saw no reason to disbelieve him. The pub is open seven days a week and although not as busy as it used to be in still a favourite of the fans.

Billy McNeil Andy Goram and Stuart Cosgrove are just three of the famous people to visit Max's pub. And the fight scene from 'Just a Boy's Game', the BBC play was filmed there.

Maggie the barmaid came in and we chatted to her for a wee while. She was interested to hear about our book and when I suggested taking her picture to put in it she asked if she should pull up her top for it.

I don't know if she was kidding but John nearly swallowed his tongue when she said it. Unfortunately for all would-be glamour photographers Maggie is leaving the Norseman soon to take up a job as a nurse.

We also got to talk to quite a few of the pub's customers and despite all the warnings we got about the pub being rough they all turned out to be great guys.

Just after we came out of the Norseman I checked my pockets and, believe it or not, I found that I still had money. So there!

John; After more fond farewells we covered our noses again, went down the stairs, across the road and our 906 arrived soon after to take us back up the road to Glasgow. I slept most of the way and wakened refreshed for a night out and more bevy.

This was one of the cheapest days out we have had. Our £40 kitty had money in it when we got home.

Pubs we visited:

The Norseman;

Carnock Bar;

How to get there by bus:

906 McGills - Buchanan St. bus station

Stranraer

Stair Park
Ground opened - 1907

John: Another club with a rap nickname. When will clubs learn? They play in blue shirts and their nickname is 'The Blues', I wonder if they paid an advertising agency good money to come up with 'The Blues'. How about 'The Ferry Men' or the 'Roll On Boys'.

Stranraer should organise a competition to come up with a good nickname. The winner could get a return trip to Larne. Second prize could be a return trip with a week's bed and breakfast thrown in!

The pressure of doing all the clubs on a Saturday is mounting, so this was one of the clubs we did midweek, a Thursday to be exact. We have been to Stranraer about three times in the past and have always had a good time, apart from missing buses and Craig not fulfilling his life ambition to visit Portpatrick. But the table dancing made up for these disappointments.

I had a friend at school who was the centre half and captain of Stranraer for a while. His name was John Heap, I wonder if he is remembered by anyone in Stranraer.

Getting to Stranraer on the bus is a problem. The morning City link bus is always full of people going to catch the ferry to Ireland, and you can't book Stagecoach, so it's a bit of a lottery. Mind you, so is life. Craig and I took the bull by the horns, lived on the edge, and off we went without booking.

We had a bit of luck the day before the trip. Waterstones in Ayr, where we were passing through, called and asked for about 15 books. This meant we could deliver on the way to Stranraer for nothing. A result!

While we were waiting for the X16 to take us to Ayr, I nicked in to the newsagent to buy my right wing Tory 'Mail'. I thought it was very heavy. It wasn't till I opened it at the bus stop that another one fell out, I'd bought one, but stolen another. It was too late to return it as the bus was approaching, so Craig was able to read the whole paper and begin to appreciate that hanging is the only answer to petty crime and the unemployed!

The older you are, the bumpier these wee single deckers seem to get. Craig seldom complains, but I know he's not comfy. The run to Ayr was uneventful and we got off just before the bus station and nicked up the high street and delivered the books. This was about 10.30am and our next bus was at 11.20am. Now normal people would just go for a wander or a coffee, but not the true bevy merchant. We had been to Ayr before and knew that many of the pubs opened at ten to cater for the fishing industry that ended about 30 year ago. Old habits die hard. Craig insisted we have a quick one, so we did. I tried to complain, but it was difficult as I thought it was a great idea.

A quick one later we were at the bus station and on the Stagecoach number 25 to Stranraer. Now when I was checking the timetables, (you can't book Stagecoach, or I can't), the journey time from Ayr was two hours. I never gave a thought to the reason for the two hours. The wee shaky bus went through every village and back street on the route as well as most of the countryside in Ayrshire. This, linked to a family of a mum and three weans, the older two of whom never shut up and a baby who roared the whole journey, made for a hell of a trip that felt like six hours. Craig was not happy at all. To cap it all the bus was about a quarter of an hour late arriving so our time in Stranraer was only about two hours.

Craig; *I really think I'm beginning to lose it. The old memory is not performing at anything like an acceptable level. If it was I would have remembered how bad the journey down to Stranraer was and have come up with a good excuse not to go there. As it was, the true horror of the journey only hit me when I saw the state of the bus we would be travelling on from Ayr to Stranraer. It was like a biscuit tin on wheels, I had been expecting a luxury couch.*

The rattletrap of a bus must have covered most of south Ayrshire and I'm pretty sure most of it has been recently cobbled for the occasion. It certainly felt like it. I would strongly advise anyone who has had a hip replacement or who suspects they might be needing one soon, not to take a bus to Stranraer. Actually I would give the same advice to any one who likes a bit of peace and quiet. I was wishing I had been wearing ear defenders on our trip.

Things had gone quite well, initially. We had cleverly worked out a schedule which allowed us to miss out an hour long trip into Glasgow to catch our bus to Stranraer. And of course we had a wee bit of business to take care of.

We had books to deliver in Ayr which turned out to be a bit of a godsend. I really needed to stretch my legs after the trip down from East Kilbride. This was a particularly bad omen as the on-going journey to Stranraer would be twice as long and we would be travelling on roads which wouldn't be allowed in any self-

respecting third world country. I decided that what we needed was a wee bit of anaesthetic, in pint form obviously.

The last time we had been in Ayr we had been to a pub beside the River Ayr. The Black Bull on River Street is one of the early opening bars in the town and it had a fair number of customers even at twenty past ten in the morning. We really should have been there a bit earlier but John had taken charge of the navigation. I knew we were in trouble when he led the way through an old graveyard.

After a pint of very acceptable Tennent's Lager it was time to face the dreaded Stranraer bus. As soon as we ventured off the main road I knew my poor old spine was in for a pummelling. I had to keep checking to see if we were actually trundling over cobble stones. The scenery was fantastic but I was having trouble focusing on it because of constant the vibrations of the bus.

Things improved a fair bit as we approached Girvan, and then they got a whole lot worse.

A young woman and her three extravagantly named weans got on the bus in Girvan and turned what was merely an extremely uncomfortable trip into a living nightmare. We got to know the names of the kids very quickly as their maw kept roaring them out in a vain attempt to control them.

They were climbing over, and occasionally under, the seats, they rolled around the floor and they would head in different directions when their mother could be bothered getting up off her backside to stop them from killing themselves. It was like watching someone trying to herd cats.

As if it wasn't bad enough that the bus had to stop in every town, village and hamlet in South Ayrshire and Galloway, we also managed to get caught up in some major road works, although there was precious little sign of any work being done.

John; Google map to the fore, Craig directed us in the direction of the bars closest to Stair Park. The first one he wanted to visit was 'The Ruddicott Hotel'. Craig had checked it out on Google Street View.

226

That's the wee yellow man on the screen. Google cannot tell you that bars are shut, and this one was.

Not to worry, we doubled back and into 'The Pub'. The pub was called 'The Pub'. Imagination runs amok in Stranraer. It was a fine wee pub though and we had a great time talking to the barmaid Sylvia and a couple of regulars. One of them, Davy was a long time Stranraer supporter and filled us in with stories of the great players of the past.

I was delighted, and Craig shocked, when the first player, and ex-manager of the club he spoke about was John Heap, the guy I went to school with. Well him and a lot of other guys as well, but no girls! He said John was one of the greats; I was chuffed. Glory by association. He said it was a nightmare being a supporter who went to away games. Every match is an epic journey. He told stories of sleeping in cars, all to watch Stranraer playing away. That's what being a supporter, or nut case, is about, loyalty. Davy even went out to his car, or he may have lived upstairs, and brought in a programme from 1976 for a game against East Fife. By the way, pensioners get 15% off their drinks during the day, midweek. We didn't get the discount off our first drink as Sylvia said she thought we were too young. That's right, she was full of shit.

Sylvia serves up the beer and the cheer in The Pub

Craig; We wasted no time once the bus arrived in Stranraer and made straight for the pub nearest the stadium. The Ruddicot

227

Hotel was first on our list and I have to say I was really looking forward to that first pint.

It was more than a little disappointing then to discover that the hotel was shut. I got the impression that it was still operating as a hotel but that maybe the bar was only open in the evenings or at weekends. Under the circumstances I thought I managed to control my emotions rather well.

Stranraer was fast becoming my least favourite place in Scotland. But there was no time to waste moping around the back streets of the town so we implemented plan B and scurried along the road to our second choice, The Pub. I wonder how long it took them to come up with that name?

They say you should never go on first impressions but personally I've always found that you would be daft not to, up until now that is.

Although The Pub looked a bit dark and dingy from the outside it was really good once we got inside. Strangely this disappointed me quite a bit. The reason being that I had been looking forward to finding a nice wee grotty pub we could slag off.

There has been a certain lack of mankyness about all of the pubs we have been visiting lately. We have often been accused of being a pair of grumpy old buggers because of some of the comments we have made about a few places we have had the misfortune to find ourselves in. Actually grumpy and buggers are two of the tamer descriptions which have been attached to our names.

Anyway I have been concerned lately that we might be going soft. If we don't find a right midden of a place soon we will lose our edge.

The Pub was no help in that respect as it turned out to be a great wee bar. There were only two other customers but we were soon all chatting.

Once again I pretended to know a lot about football and once again I was very quickly shot down. I said something about

228

Stranraer doing quite well in the third division only to be ridiculed for not knowing they were now in division one.

The guys told me that the leagues had been changed and now make even less sense than ever. How can you have four divisions where the lowest one is the second? It sounds like something out of Orwell's '1984'.

Since we were enjoying the company, and the beer, it was decided that we should have another drink in the Pub. Sylvia, our barmaid, told me she used to work on the Irish ferry and had seen a fair bit of trouble between certain groups of football supporters. In an effort to stop some of their nonsense the ferry company once decided that all team colours should be banned on board their boats. All bar staff were told by their manager 'No colours in the bar'.

Unfortunately a friend of Sylvia's, who also worked behind the bar, was not really on the same page as everyone else and nearly caused an international incident.

When a black man wandered into the bar she refused to serve him and told him he had to leave. As you can imagine there were consequences.

Since we had missed out on a visit to the Hotel we asked Sylvia if she could recommend another pub close to Stair Park. It turned out that the Royal Hotel was the next nearest.

John; Sylvia told us that 'The Royal Hotel' bar was good, and as it was the next one we had planned to visit we said our fond farewells and wandered the few yards and into a busy bar with a good atmosphere. The barman James, who is called 'Crow' (suppose he wanted to be a high flier) was great company and we had a pleasant time chatting to him and Phil, a regular. A friend of Crow's, Craig Park, was in the middle of a sponsored walk from Glasgow to Stranraer to raise money for 'Help for Heroes', a great charity. My Craig reckoned they'd do the walk quicker than our bus did this morning.

Craig; *We really should have clocked The Royal ourselves as we had walked past it to get to the Pub. I think Sylvia was just sparing our feelings by not pointing that out.*

229

The Royal Hotel is a fairly traditional building and I think the actual bar might be original. Some of the customers could have been as well.

We got chatting to the barman and a couple of his customers about the state of Scottish football and I think we were more or less all in agreement that things were looking pretty terminal, so nothing new there then!

Some of the old boys up the other end of the bar even asked if they could buy a couple of books from us but we were carrying so much in the way of food that we hadn't packed any.

Before we knew it our time in Stranraer was up and we had several hours sitting in a rickety uncomfortable bus to look forward to. I could hardly wait!

John; As our time was limited we said our goodbyes and wandered out into the rain and found our way back down to the front and waited for our bus back to Ayr. Unlike the journey down, the return trip shot in, sleeping for two hours will do that.

Awakening refreshed in Ayr, with forty minutes to kill, it was along to 'Bridges Bar', an old favourite, for a couple of quick ones before heading back to the bus station.

On our return to East Kilbride, we managed to get off the bus before the bus station. Now this stop is only a couple of hundred yards from 'The Lum', so it seemed daft not to go in for another quick one.

So ended a long day, about 12 hours door to door, with only two of them being in Stranraer, but such is our determination to produce an encyclopedic book on pubs near grounds, that we do this without complaint, except for Craig, who moans all the time, but mainly about crying weans.

Our kitty of £20 each was enough for the day. This must be the cheapest day out we've ever had. Mind you, we had about eight rounds, so that's cheap drink! By the way, Kate has suggested I go on a diet, so I'm cutting back on food and trying to exercise. She has told me that all I have to do is cut back on the drink. After 43 years married she has no idea! Having said that, I've decided that instead of drinking pints, I'm going to drink Vodka and Soda, which I did today. Iv'e checked it out and found that it has much less calories than pints do, so I'll give it a go.

230

Craig; On the bus again we congratulated ourselves for finding two really good pubs. But I told John that I was worried our wee pubs might be a bit overwhelmed when Rangers came down to play Stranraer the following Saturday. They have a huge travelling support, many of whom like the occasional beer before the game. John agreed, I think, saying it would be "like an aquarium full of seagulls." Before I got the chance to ask him what the hell he was talking about he slipped into his usual travelling coma and I was left with a mental image that I could not get out of my head.

John wasn't a bit bothered by the journey home. As far as he was concerned the trip only lasted about twenty minutes, with a short interval in the middle for refreshments in Ayr.

By the time we got back to East Kilbride I was a physical wreck and needed a couple of pints in The Lum to rectify that situation.

The pubs in Stranraer had been great and I would recommend them to everyone who enjoys good beer in good surroundings, though you might want to make the journey by train.

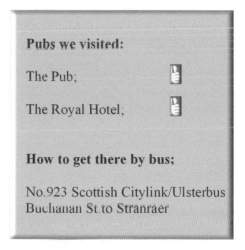

Pubs we visited:

The Pub;

The Royal Hotel;

How to get there by bus;

No.923 Scottish Citylink/Ulsterbus
Buchanan St.to Stranraer

St. Mirren

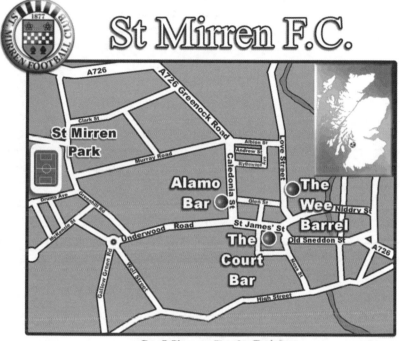

St. Mirren Park, Paisley
Ground opened - 2009

John: As you know by now I like a club with a good nickname, and 'The Buddies' fits the bill, but what inspired person came up with the name St. Mirren Park for the new stadium! What's that all about? As I said before, I don't slag names willy nilly without coming up with a better one. This is my first stadium attempt, so my inexperience may show. However, I think that 'The Saint's Stadium', 'The Buddies Barn' or even 'Mirren Mansions' would be an improvement.

It was a miserable morning. Just last week Craig had said how we had been getting great weather for our trips. Sod's law takes over. Because of the rain and the position of Paisley in regards to EK, we decided to get the train the whole way. This is the first time in four books we have done a trip without using the bus. Having said that, we did. The wee orange M1 picked us up at the Murray Road and took us along to Hairmyres Station where we got returns to Paisley Gilmour Street for only £2.50 each. Now I hear you saying that we should be taking the bus, but come on, give us a break, this meant that we could get to Paisley without getting wet waiting for a bus in Glasgow. So we did!

Lashing rain met us as we left the dryness of Paisley Gilmour Street Station. Now the Love Street area in Paisley has never won any awards that I know of for being the prettiest area in Scotland, and pouring rain sure doesn't help. It was miserable. This wasn't helped by the fact that because of the quick trains it was still only ten to eleven. Now ten minutes is not a long time to put in normally, but by the time we had wandered down Love Street to see the remains of where the old stadium had been we were miserable.

Craig; *They say that a little bit of sunshine can make even the grimmest place look welcoming. It is a real pity then that the rain was stoating down on the day we decided to visit Paisley. If ever a place could use a bit of assistance in the looks department that place is Paisley.*

If ever any would be author fancies setting their risqué novel in a large Scottish town I would suggest Paisley. It could be called 'Fifty shades of dreich'

We didn't see very much of the scenery on the way down to the town as the windows of the train were all steamed up.

I usually have very little good to say about Scotrail staff but for once I have to give praise where praise is due. The conductor on our train down to Glasgow went out of his way to find us cheap tickets for our journey.

All of these feelings of gratitude disappeared when I couldn't get my tickets to work in those dammed machines at Central Station.

I had checked out a couple of likely looking pubs on the internet, so as soon as we got off the train at Paisley Gilmour Street I knew exactly which way to go. John's admiration for my pub finding skills was obvious, so much so that he felt he didn't have to say a word.

We were a bit earlier than planned and since Paisley has never had a fishing fleet there were no early opening pubs to visit. To kill a bit of time we took a walk up Love Street to where St Mirren's old stadium used to be.

That took a good five minutes before we got bored with it and made our way back down to The Wee Barrel. It had just opened so we were its first customers of the day. The place fair reeked of nostalgia and bleach, so John was in his element.

John; Fortunately our first port of call, 'The Wee Barrel' opened sharp at eleven and we were first in. Even the smell of bleach was welcome. This is an old pub. The barmaid Donna said she thought it was the oldest pub in Paisley which is in the same place as when it opened, many years ago. Although it was early and miserable outside, we had a great time chatting to Donna, who filled us in with facts about the place including famous customers, including Rod Stewart. This is a very atmospheric pub and well worth a visit. Although it is not as close to the new stadium as it was to Love Street, it is only a wee five minute or so walk to the new park.

Craig; *Since we were The Wee Barrel's only customers the barmaid, Donna, had plenty of time to chat to us. She told us that The Wee Barrel was the oldest pub in Paisley and looking around the place I could only agree with her.*

The pub was a wee bit threadbare and in normal circumstances a lick or two of paint might be called for. Fortunately the pub's owner is either a bit of a skinflint or a man of vision. Any major decoration would cost an awful lot of money and just ruin the whole atmosphere of the place.

Donna told us that the pub had lost a lot of trade since St Mirren had shifted to their new ground. The old stadium was only a hundred yards or so from the front door of the pub. Luckily, there is still enough trade from local drinkers to keep the old place going.

We had another drink in there, not just because we liked the feel of the place and the good company, provided by Donna, but also because we needed to dry out our clothes. Scottish summer had returned with a vengeance and we had been soaked to the skin.

Donna knows a good book when she sees one

John; Donna gave us instructions to our next pub, 'The Alamo'. Craig had checked it out on the web and said we must visit it, and glad I am we did. This is a country and western bar full of memorabilia and great people. Alex, the barmaid made us very welcome and a regular couple Jim and Moira Cat (Cat is a handle, thought I'd explain that for our non country and western readers) filled us in with details of all the other mad people and clubs that come to the pub. The best one was 'The Wee Spookie Club'. Nobody seemingly knows what exactly they are, but sometimes they bring in Steamed Sausages and Mashed Potatoes and sell them to the locals, who are too frightened to say no. Not much you can add to that story.

'The Alamo' is a must to visit if you are in the Paisley area, even if you're not going to a match. It's also only a wee walk to the new park.

Craig; *I had found another pub on the net that I liked the look of. The Alamo Bar looked completely mad and therefore well worth a visit.*

There is however one great problem with checking things out on the internet and that is you can never be sure when the pictures on it were taken. It wouldn't be the first time that we have turned up to visit a really nice looking bar only to find a building site there instead.

So just to avoid any disappointment, not to mention a bit of caustic ridicule from John, I asked Donna if the Alamo was still in business. She told us that it was still there and that it was a really good pub to visit. She was right.

I have never seen a pub with a window display before, and what a display it was. There were American Indian figurines, model stagecoaches and a whole lot more: completely mad!

Inside was even better. The walls were almost entirely covered with western memorabilia. There were guns and gun belts, bows and arrows and loads of mocked- up wanted posters.

It is the nearest thing to a theme pub we have been in so far on our travels. As soon as we sat down at the bar some of the customers came over and started talking to us.

Jim and Moira were a great laugh and told us a few tales about the pub. Apparently the pub owner and some of the regulars go over to Texas every year or so to visit the Alamo. The boss even has a small private museum in the pub dedicated to all things western.

Alex, our barmaid, showed us the lounge which is used for Karaoke at weekends and also leased to other local groups. Apparently there is a motorbike club, not a gang it was stressed, which meets there regularly. The regulars seem to get on with them quite well, which is more than can be said about the spiritualist group who also use the back lounge. The Wee Spooky Group sounds like the kind of club you might want to steer clear of. A lot of the locals certainly do.

Moira also told us about the recent visit to the pub of a group of German line dance enthusiasts. In fact there were so many of them that they ended up dancing in the street.

237

What amazes me is that nobody in the area seemed to think that 30 large Germans marching up and down the Greenock Road was in any way odd.

While we were having a good laugh with Alex, Moira and Jim some actual football supporters came into the bar. It was about 1.30pm and there were small groups of both home and away fans wandering in looking for refreshments. This was a great relief for John who by this time was beginning to think he had got it wrong again, picking a day when the team was playing away from home.

Alex, Moira (Cat) and Jim in The Alamo

We had a couple of drinks in the Alamo and could quite easily have stayed on but we had a job to do, so we sadly made the decision to move on out into the driving rain once more.

John; The last bar in Paisley we visited was 'The Court Bar'. This is another bar frequented by fans on match day. It was not as atmospheric a bar as 'The Wee Barrel', or as crazy as 'The Alamo', but having said that, it was a nice, but more modern bar and the barman Mick was good company. He even remembered reading about us in 'The Evening Times'. That alone got him into our good books. This is another

238

handy bar for the ground and although not a memorable as the first two is also worth a pint or two before or after the game.

Before we left Paisley, Craig insisted we go back to 'The Wee Barrell' to have a final drink and see it with a few more customers in it. Another pint, and Vodka and Soda for me was downed before we left, in sunshine, for our journey back to East Kilbride.

Craig; The guys in the Alamo had suggested that we should check out The Court Bar as it was also a favourite with the fans. I had one look at it and decided that it wasn't going to be a favourite with me.

Don't get me wrong; there is nothing particularly bad about The Court Bar, it just didn't have the character or the atmosphere of the other two pubs we had visited in Paisley. In fact this pub is more like one of those big corporate efforts, all high ceilings and brass rails.

Of course The Court is probably bigger than both the other two pubs put together and would therefore probably suit supporters club buses.

The beer was good and the service was efficient, so if the aforementioned supporters are not too bothered about ambience and good pub patter this bar will do fine.

John; We walked up from the station in the village and decided that as it was so nice now, we would sit outside 'The Monty' and have a quick one. To cut a long story short, company developed. We even sold a couple of books with promises of more and we had a good few before we had to get a taxi home. The reason for the taxi is that we would have had trouble walking. I have no idea why we do this, but it's great at the time.

No idea how much today cost, but I remember the pubs in Paisley being very reasonable and so I think about £30 would have covered it, plus a taxi. Hope we sell more books!

Craig; To round off our day out in Paisley we wandered back round to The Wee Barrel, just to check if any more fans had found their way in for a 'wee swally'.

They hadn't. But there was still plenty of time before kick-off for the hordes to descend. While we waited for this to happen we felt obliged to have another wee drink. I think Donna appreciated the gesture.

Back up in East Kilbride we made the mistake of going to the Monty for one last beer, the fact that I can write no more about what happened next should speak volumes.

Pubs we visited:

The Wee Barrel;

The Alamo;

The Court Bar;

How to get there by bus:

No.9 Buchcnan St, bus station to ground

Clyde

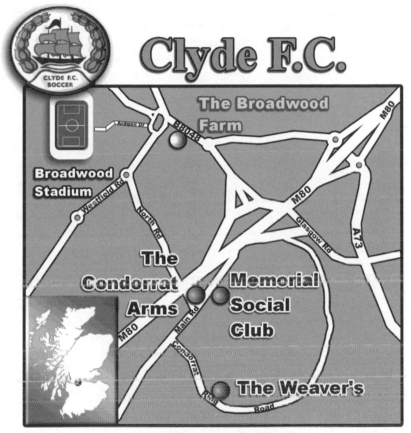

Broadwood Stadium
Ground opened - 1995

John; Clyde, 'The Bully Wee', one of the great nicknames. I've no idea how the name came into being, but it is not as important as the fact that it's a bumper.

In the old days Clyde played at Shawfield Stadium, a great and very atmospheric stadium. It's became better known as a greyhound stadium although to be honest, I've no idea if they do any dogs there nowadays, I'll have to check. It's funny to think that in the old days

241

Clyde got the runaround at Shawfield and then the greyhounds got the runaround! There were great pubs around Shawfield in the old days. Today we are going to find out what the ones are like around the present stadium in Cumbernauld. I'm not confident, being an East Kilbride man.

Getting to Cumbernauld is fairly easy from EK, the 18 into Glasgow, walk to the Bus Station and then get the X3 which takes about 40 minutes to get to the roundabout just beside Broadwood. All this went without a hitch. We got off the bus at a big roundabout, just like the ones in EK, and walked the couple of hundred yards down the road to the stadium.

I noticed a big door opened at the end of the grandstand and wandered in to have a look at the ground from the inside. The park was full of youngsters of various ages being trained on something or other, might even have been football. The grass itself was artificial. There seems to be quite a few of the smaller teams that have artificial grass. The idea of using the park for various athletic types of things is great and good luck to them all.

Craig; John announced that he was extremely confident about today's journey to and around Cumbernauld. The home of Clyde FC. Every time he comes out with statements like this I get worried, and with good reason. I have lost count of the number of times we have found ourselves totally lost and, worse still, nowhere near a pub.

So it was with an uneasy feeling that we set off towards the Scottish capital of dodgy architecture; Cumbernauld. I have no idea why Clyde play their football in Cumbernauld, in fact I didn't even know that Cumbernauld had a senior football team at all. As it turns out quite a large number of its citizens seem to be a bit in the dark about that as well.

The bus from Glasgow to Cumbernauld was of the small rickety variety and did very little to help the condition of my spine. The only thing that kept me going was the thought that very soon I would be enjoying some natural anaesthetic: an extra cold pint of Tennent's Lager.

John had printed out a large scale map of the area we would be visiting and spent much of the journey staring at it. But it was only when he started turning it round to view it from other angles that I began to think we may be in for some trouble.

You could have knocked me down with a feather when we found the stadium almost as soon as we got off the bus. John looked a bit shaky on his feet as well it has to be said. After a quick scout around the stadium we decided that we had earned ourselves a wee drink. That's when the problems started.

John; We wandered back up to the roundabout. The website had told us that there was a Brewers Fayre type pub/restaurant at the roundabout. We looked about but couldn't find it. We went under the roundabout to the bus stop and asked a couple of wee women who told us the way. They told us to go back under the roundabout and keep turning left. Obviously we missed one of the left turns cause we never even got a glimpse of the place. The bushes and trees are so dense that if you are not up against the place you will never see it. Like similar places in EK, they are designed for people arriving by car, not walking.

This was a disappointment, but not a disaster as we don't like these types of places with the carpets, the kids and women all over the place. No offence meant to the carpets!

I had printed out a map of the area and even though we were lost, I knew where we were, if you know what I mean. We decided to carry on and walk down into the village of Condorrat, which is only a 10 or possibly a 20 minute walk from the ground if Craig is with you, which he was. So 20 minutes later we were in this nice wee village. The computer had told us that as soon as you went into the village, 'The Masonic Arms' pub was on the left. It was, but it was 'The Condorrat Arms', and had been for seven years. Who cares, the name of a pub is not important.

Sammy, the lovely barmaid was great company, and she and Allan, who commutes from Rutherglen to be with his girlfriend filled us in with the pub's background. When I asked why the pub had changed its name, they said it was because Celtic supporters frequent the pub and didn't like the name. It didn't matter to us what it was called. It's a great wee pub and handy for the ground. Not as handy as the Brewers Fayre one, but it's easy to find and more like the type of pub supporters would want to visit. The pub had also won the Sunday Mail pub of the year a few years ago, so there you go.

Sammy and Allan keep us laughing in The Condorrat

Craig; We had been told that there was a pub just off one of the town's roundabouts near the park. It was one of those big brewery owned places called The Broadwood Farm. Not being too fussy we headed there for our first refreshment of the day anyway. The only problem was we could not find it.

In a desperate search which seemed to go on forever but in reality only took 20 minutes we never so much as caught a glimpse of the pub.

Finding ourselves on the outskirts of the village of Condorrat we abandoned all hope of finding the brewery owned pub, which we had by this time decided was probably rotten anyway, and made for the Masonic Arms. That proved a little more difficult than it should have. Without telling anyone, well us anyway, the pub had changed its name to The Condorrat.

This is a good old-fashioned solidly built pub. It could do with a bit of money spent on it as it has seen better days but that being said it is still a very nice place to sample a beer or two on a hot sunny morning. It seems that not very many Clyde supporters drink in this pub on match days and I don't imagine too many visiting fans ever find their way in there either.

We asked the barmaid if there was another pub in town which maybe football fans frequented before the game. She told us that our best bet would be the Brewery owned pub outside town. As you can imagine we were less than pleased to hear this.

Apparently this phantom pub is built in a depression meaning it is hard to see. Talking about hard to see it seems that another place we would be visiting, the Memorial Social Club, just across the road from the Mason's, is hidden round the back of the building. I was beginning to think that the publicans of the town were not too keen on outsiders drinking in their bars.

John; As you know, this encyclopedic masterpiece demands that we visit at least two or three pubs to give our readers a choice, so we asked if there was another decent pub in the village. They directed us across the road and up a wee alley to 'The Condorrat Social Club'. We wondered if we would have to be signed in or have a special handshake, but there was no problem. In we went to a very nice club with snooker and pool tables as well as a nice bar. Catrina, the manager and her assistant Maureen,who was 65 today were great company. Maureen said her husband is a really nice man who even let her work on her big day. What a guy!. At this time of day the bar was quiet but I could imagine it having a good atmosphere when busy. The girls told us that if we were looking for somewhere else to visit, 'The Weavers' was just down the road. She mentioned about three left turns and a right, I had no idea how to get there other than to ask someone on the way.

Five minutes later we were lost so I asked a guy who was roughcasting a house in a wee estate where the pub was. He answered very politely in perfect English that he didn't speak English. I really admire the attempts of our imported countrymen to learn our language, or at least enough to get rid of you.

We soon found a couple of local natives who pointed to the pub. It was just down the road opposite the Vets. 'The Weavers' is a terrible looking place from the outside, really crap, but inside it is very nice and again the barmaid, Tricia Riggens, who has the tenancy of the place was great. We had a good time with her and the locals. One of them, Gordon was terrific company and after a great time with them, showed us how to get out of the place and to a bus stop. Can't begin to tell you how

245

important this was as this pub, like almost all the places we found, or didn't, can be very hard to find, especially this one.

Craig; Over at the Memorial Club we chatted to a couple of the volunteer barmaids who told us that they often get a lot of football supporters in the club on match days. However we obviously had our wires crossed as they were talking about Rangers and Celtic not Clyde. Apparently the club runs buses to all home and away games of the big two teams.

Catrina and Maureen make us welcome at the Social Club

I made a mental note to check the Sunday papers to see if anyone ever turns up to watch their local team. The club looks like a nice place to spend an afternoon. It is well equipped and prices are very reasonable.

Still looking for our first real supporters pub we asked the barmaid if there was another pub we could check out. Her directions to the Weaver's turned out to be more complicated than we thought. Or maybe it's just that we get easily confused after only a few drinks, even the one of us who had been bumming about the wonderful map he had produced without any help from the other one. Whatever the cause the result was inevitable, we got lost.

Eventually we did find it. I would like to say we did so by using our natural, inbuilt navigation system, a skill only a few men of experience possess. Or perhaps by using John's wonky map, but actually we stumbled on it by accident.

To be honest it would be easy to miss as it doesn't really look like a pub at all. I had been expecting a quaint stone-built thatched cottage type of the building, where generations of weavers had once plied their trade. What we got was a recently built stubby looking industrial unit.

Fortunately it looked a lot better inside. We got chatting to the barmaid, tricia, and told her we were surprised to find a building like the Weaver's on the edge of a housing estate. She told us that we would have been even more surprised if we had gone into an almost identical building in the town as it was a Church. According to Tticia the same plans had been used for both, possibly to save cash.

Tricia hears a lot of yarns at The Weaver's

The mind boggles at the potential for John to make a complete arse of himself if we had walked into the wrong one. Especially after a number of refreshments!

Once again we were told that not very many Clyde supporters find their way to this pub on match days. This did not really surprise us especially given the fact that, like all of the other pubs in the area, the Weaver's is so well camouflaged.

A customer we talked to said that there was little interest in Clyde with most football fans choosing to support either Rangers or Celtic. In fact he claimed that the Masons Arms had been forced to change its name when it became a Celtic pub.

We had to admit defeat in our efforts to find Clyde supporters. Despite visiting three rather large pubs we had failed to meet a single Clyde supporter, it was time to go home. The journey home was uneventful, bone jarring but uneventful.

John; Our bus back to Glasgow, the X5, turned up and looked as if it would get to Glasgow in no time at all when we started to hear a peeping noise. Minutes later the driver stopped the bus and announced that it was overheating and another bus would have to come out from Glasgow and pick us up. I thought he was over reacting as we were only two or three miles from the bus station. He phoned someone who had the same opinion as me, so the driver got back into his cab, probably robbed of an hour's overtime, and we got into Glasgow no problem at all. The train back to Hairmyres, the 201 bus to 'The Lum' and a couple of pints later we were home, and it was only about half five. Are we starting to get sensible?

The three pubs we visited were all handy for the ground, if you can find them, and are all worth a visit. I had change left out of £20, this is definitely our cheapest visit yet.

Pubs we visited:	
The Condorrat Arms;	🍺
The Memorial Social Club;	🍺
The Weavers;	🍺
How to get there by bus:	
X3 Buchanan St. to ground	

248

Ross County

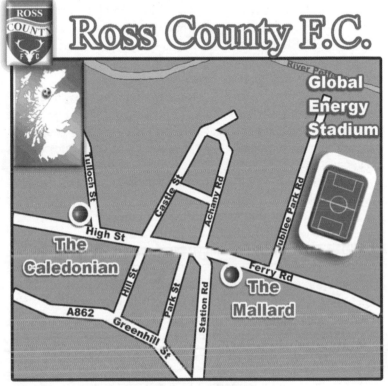

Global Energy Stadium
(formerly known as Victoria Park)
Ground opened - 1929

John: This was going to be an epic. To visit every ground in Scotland, one at a time on a Saturday match day would have taken years, and this book just had to be written before senile dementia took hold of me.

The main problem with these four clubs is that they are nowhere near EK, or most populated places for that matter. But the pubs around them had to be visited so this encyclopedia of bars could be complete. So to the north we went.

As you can imagine, visiting these places, getting drunk, sobering up and moving on to the next in one day would be impossible, even for experienced bevy merchants like Craig and me. So a two day trip it was, with an overnight stop.

We decided that as Aberdeen was the big club, we would get to them on a match day Saturday, so what we planned to do was to visit Ross County and Elgin on the Friday, stay overnight in Elgin, and do Peterhead on the Saturday morning before finishing up in Aberdeen on Saturday afternoon. It's not easy being us.

I did all the travel and digs planning. The buses were no problem and the fact that we could book the legendary 'Gold Bus' up to Inverness and back from Aberdeen helps make the travel a pleasure. The problem I had was getting accommodation in Elgin. I tried several sites on the web with no success.

Some of these web sites are unbelievable, and it's not me, I've book flights on Ryanair! You key in Elgin and the date you're staying and the web comes up with about a dozen places. In small type hidden away on the page it tells you it's 20 miles from Elgin. What's that all about? All I can say is that Elgin must be a popular place.

I then came up with a great idea. The bus we had thought of getting on the Saturday morning from Elgin to Peterhead, via Aberdeen takes ages, but it passes through lots of wee places with B & B's, so I picked a place called Inverurie, which was on the bus route and managed to get us a place to stay. How clever is that? This also meant that in the morning, it would be easier and quicker to get to Peterhead. It was all coming together.

It was a reasonable morning when I collected Craig at 7.15am. As usual we had phoned any Waterstones in the places we were going to be near in case they wanted any books. We were delighted when the Aberdeen store said they would take 20 of our books. The bad part was that we had to hump them everywhere with us as Aberdeen was our last port of call, and they're heavy, so we took 10 each in our bags.

There were no major incidents on our trip into Glasgow on the 18 and the run up to Inverness on the 9.00am Gold Bus was great, free tea, scones and shortbread. My only gripe was that Craig told the wee man serving us that he didn't want shortbread. I would have taken his bit. He never thinks.

Craig; *It seems to be turning into a bit of a tradition for us to have at least one overnight stay when we are going around the country checking out the pubs and clubs of Scotland. Although it may sound like an excuse for two auld guys to be let off the leash it never quite works out that way. For a start we are usually far too tired to get up to any nonsense.*

This time around we would be visiting four senior clubs in the two days of our tour. A couple of them in the Premier league and the other two well down the divisions. Given the reorganisation taking place right now I have no idea whereabouts in the league structure they actually are.

That's just another demonstration of my knowledge of Scottish football, the fact that I can't be bothered finding out tells you that my position is unlikely to change any time soon.

As always our trip began at an ungodly hour and most of the travelling justly deserves to be skirted over. Suffice it to say we reached Dingwall with just enough time to visit the stadium and two nearby pubs, the perfect set-up in fact. Not long enough to cause any trouble, but long enough to get a feel of the place.

John; We thought we would miss our bus to Dingwall, the Stagecoach number 27, as we arrived a minute or so after its departure time, but it was running a bit late as well, so we got it and enjoyed the half hour journey up to the home of Ross County, our first official stop.

Ross Countyl has two nicknames, 'The Staggies' and 'The County', no points for guessing I'm calling them the latter (that's 'The Staggies' for you daft readers).

The sun was splitting the coconuts as we wandered down the main street to find a bar. We found one on each side of the road. The first one we tried, 'The Commercial', was shut. Thankfully, the one across the road, 'The Caledonian Bar' was open, so in we went. It was an old traditional bar, the kind we like, and the barman, Kenny Mackay was friendly in a reserved highland sort of way. It's likely he's related to me as my ancestors come from this area. Both my parents were Mackays before they were married. Means nothing, it's just a common name in this area. As I've said before, the graveyards in this area are full of deid Mackays.

251

Unfortunately, we did not have a huge amount of time in Dingwall, so after we had signed a couple of our leaflets which advertise our three books for a couple of locals, and honest, they asked us to do it, we said our farewells to a nice wee bar and headed up the road to have a look at the ground. We had checked out the area on Google and had maps of all the places we were visiting. The park was very nice in an old fashioned sort of way. Craig took a photo and we were on our way to the second pub we planned to visit, 'The Mallard'.

On the way I managed to create an embarrassing moment for a woman jogger. Craig, I know, will fill you in with what happened, but enough to say I still haven't mastered the metric system.

'The Mallard' is attached to the train station and at one time was part of it, a waiting room or something. It is a nice wee bar. A strange thing is that on one side of it there are about half a dozen alcoves and each one has its own big flat screen telly. This country is full of these things. Nobody in the bar was watching the bloody things. I believe young people in this country would explode if there was no background noise or tellies.

Having said all that, it was a nice bar and the barmaid, Cara Coburn, a lovely local girl who is also studying at Aberdeen University was good company and we were, as usual, sorry to leave for our next bus, another number 27 to take us back to Inverness.

Craig; We decided that since our bus had stopped a couple of hundred yards away from our first targeted pub we might as well just have a couple of beers there. The Caledonian was probably quite fashionable with the crofting set back in the 1920s. It is a style which I might be describe as farmhouse chic.

Don't get me wrong I loved it, but I would imagine some people might think it could do with a bit of modernisation. But as I'm sure John will agree we need to preserve pubs like The Caledonian, it is a heritage thing.

We were served by an older gentleman, not older than John of course, just an older man. It turned out that, like John, he belonged to the Mackay clan. John was delighted; I wasn't surprised. The North West is rife with Mackays, they're everywhere.

John suggested to our barman that they might be related. I suggested that everyone in the area might be related. And maybe in a way that wider society might frown upon.

Anyway the beer was good, the price good and the pub was well used by both home and visiting football fans on match days.

We talked to some locals and got the impression that Dingwall was a nice close community which also enjoys the company of travelling supporters and the occasional pub reviewers. Far too soon we had to move on as time was not on our side.

Although there was no game on we felt we should still visit Ross County's stadium. The Global Energy Stadium is a lot smaller than its strange name would suggest but is a tidy looking ground and is well positioned.

We ducked into The Mallard to meet Cara

Not more than a few hundred yards from the stadium was our next and last stop in Dingwall, The Mallard. Before we could get there however John managed to put his foot in things. A young girl was jogging along the road towards us. Before I could stop him, John decided to pass the time of day with her. Trying to be encouraging he said "keep it up, only another ten kilos to go". He obviously meant kilometres but going by the look on the girls face she didn't know this. All she would know is that a very strange old man thought she was a stone and a half over weight.

Since she was only about seven stones soaking wet I imagine John's remark may well have triggered an unfortunate bout of anorexia. The poor wee thing is probably still crying.

I managed to hustle him into The Mallard before the wee lassie's dad came looking for the bad man who had traumatised his daughter. I realise that the idea of hustling John into a pub sounds like an unlikely occurrence since, in the normal times, keeping him out of one is like defying gravity.

The Mallard is in a building which looked like it may have been the railway waiting-room a good few years back but inside it was very much a 21st-century pub. There were more flat screen televisions in there than in our local Curry's store.

The barmaid told us that the pub gets quite a good crowd on match days with lots of home and away supporters coming in for a drink. We really enjoyed our short stay in the Mallard. The only improvement I could suggest is to get somebody to take the plug off the jukebox as apparently it only has loud heavy metal records in it.

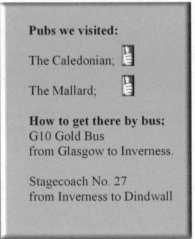

Pubs we visited:

The Caledonian;

The Mallard;

How to get there by bus;
G10 Gold Bus
from Glasgow to Inverness.

Stagecoach No. 27
from Inverness to Dindwall

Elgin City

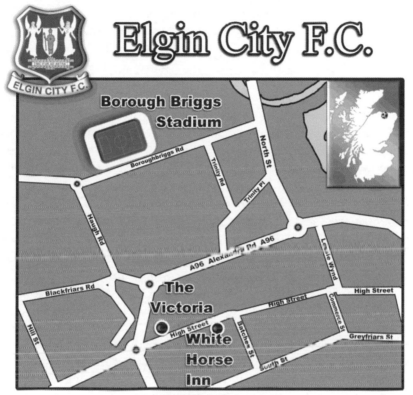

Borough Briggs
Ground opened - 1921

John; Returning from Dingwall to Inverness, we had time for a quick one before catching our next bus, the Stagecoach number 35 to Elgin. This bus took about one and a half hours to get to there. This is because, like most routes in Scotland, the bus detours through every wee housing estate on the way, even into a shopping centre. We call these detours LBD's (lazy bugger detours), and bugger was not our first choice. Could the bus not just stop on the main road and the locals walk the hundred yards or so down to get the bus. No wonder there are so many fat people in Scotland, between the no walking anywhere and the telly watching, we are loosing the use of our legs. Am I allowed to say fat nowadays, I don't know, if not they're obese, ok. The other good thing is the journey times would be halved and the buses would not use all the petrol they do, so it's a win-win situation. I should be an advisor to bus companies.

Having said all that, if it wasn't for the detours, we would never have passed through a wee town called 'Lochtodmoss'. What a great name. Just as we passed through it, or it might have been just before, I looked out of the window as we passed a huge Campbells soup factory, it seemed so out of place. In my excitement at seeing such a big place, I shouted to Craig, 'cock a lookie at that factory, it's huge'! You had to be there.

Craig; *I had been drawing up a map of Elgin for this book just before we set out on this trip, therefore I had a pretty good idea of the layout of the town. For some reason I forgot to tell John about this and when I led him straight to the football stadium he was visibly impressed with my direction finding.*

John; It was a lovely late afternoon when we got off the bus in Elgin. We made our way down to the park and as I saw an open door, in we went. We were met by a great guy called Cecil Jack, who is one of the directors of the club. He showed us the park, which I noticed right away is huge. Cecil told us he believes it is the second biggest park in Scotland, and a beauty it is. We were shown the dressing rooms and board room. It's a very smart club. Elgin were the last club to win a trophy called 'The Giant Killers Cup'. It is a huge trophy. Cecil says there is very little information about the history of the cup. It's nice anyway.

One thing I forgot to ask Cecil was who came up with the nickname 'Black & Whites'. They play in Black & White for goodness sake, could someone, like me, not think of a more original one, so here goes, 'The Elgalonies'. Now that's a bumper.

Craig; *Cecil Jack, one of the club directors, gave as a tour of the stadium showing us the boardroom and hospitality area as well as the dressing rooms. He told us the away dressing room was* *painted in black and white stripes just to psyche out the opposition.*

It was really nice to have a look around but we needed to move on in search of a decent nearby boozer.

John; We had been in Elgin before and knew all the bars were just up the road in the High Street, so we had a wander along and into 'The Victoria'. It was about half past five on a Friday night so the bars were busy. The problem with this one was the noise. Some nutcase with no taste in music was playing the jukebox, if that's what they're called nowadays, and it was blaring. There was nothing really wrong with the pub, just the noise, so we had just the one and left to find some sanity.

We left to find a quieter bar, and 'The White Horse', just across the road filled the bill. Again it was an old fashioned bar, but not as loud. Julia, the barmaid, who said it as it is, was great, and Gavin, a local worthy kept us amused with their tales.

There was a bar just up the road called 'Zed Bar' and we stuck our heads in the door, but it was not our scene, though it would be great for younger supporters. Noise, tellies and cheap drink.

That was our time in Elgin finished and we made our way to the bus station where we got the Stagecoach number 10B to our overnight accommodation in Inverurie. I don't have the room or memory to tell you all of what we got up to before going to bed, but drink was consumed.

Craig; *The Victoria fulfilled all of these requirements but that's about all. It is a traditional old guy's pub with booths along one side. This rather cuts down on the standing room. The beer was good and the price was just about right, however the noise was incredible, and not in the good sense of that word.*

Some moron was playing very loud and not very good early rock 'n' roll on the jukebox. Either everyone up in the north is stone deaf or all of the pubs up there bought cheap jukeboxes with no volume controls. We didn't get a chance to talk to anyone in the bar, but since the music was so loud there would have been little point.

Along at the White Horse it was much quieter, maybe some music lover had cut the plug off the jukebox. It is a good size pub and quite comfortable. We spent some time in there as it had been decided that it would make a good two pint stop. While we were propping up the bar we got chatting to the only other customer and the barmaid Julia.

Julia keeps The White Horse running smoothly

She was great company and told us a few stories about the good folk of Elgin. That being said I don't think she would put up with any nonsense from someone daft enough to step out of line. I know a few pubs that would benefit from a barmaid liked her.

It came up in conversation that Julia had been awarded a medal by the Humane Society a few years back for saving the life of a little boy who had fallen into the harbour in Lossiemouth.

There is quite a sad story attached to what happened that day but it is probably best left unsaid. To cheer ourselves up we bought another round. We are nothing if not predictable.

Like the other pub, The White Horse gets a good turn when Elgin City is playing at home.

As we were making our way back to the bus stop we had a quick look at a pub called Zed, but since we were both over 16 we felt we would not fit in.

Never having been to Inverurie before, we were a bit anxious about when to get off the bus. Luckily our bus driver could recognise a pair of lost souls when he saw them. He told us when we should get off for our digs

We spent the night in the Kintore Arms Hotel. I would definitely recommend it if you ever find yourself in the area for a wee holiday. There is a good selection of pubs in the town and at least one very good chip shop.

Pubs we visited:

The Victoria;

The White Horse;

Zed Bar;

How to get there By bus:

G10 Gold Bus
from Glasgow to Inverness

Stagecoach No.35
from Inverness to Elgin

Peterhead

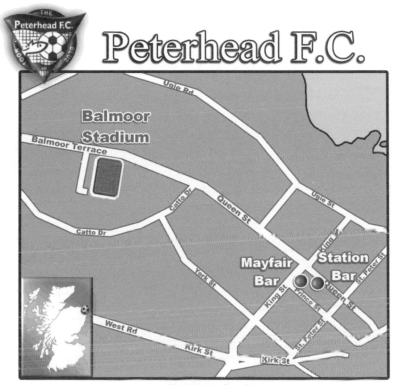

Balmoor Stadium
Ground opened - 1997

John: We were up early in the morning and after a full breakfast we were on our way from Inverurie to Peterhead. I had planned the route, which involved three buses. Craig had no faith in us ever getting to Peterhead, but we did, and as planned.

It was simple, the 493 to Ellon, the 450 to Newburgh, then the 63 to Peterhead. And the sun was still shining.

Their nickname 'The Blue Toon' is not great. A better attempt would be 'The Blue Warders', after the jail in the town.

The walk to the ground was a long one for us, and it was almost all uphill. Craig was knackered. Remember, we were still carrying the books in our bags. Somehow we got to the top of the hill and saw the ground which was very nice, but not worth the walk. The number 66 or 69 will take you up to the ground if you are as old as us.

Craig; We have visited Peterhead before on our travels and last time we were not too impressed with the drinking holes we found. This time around we decided to find a football park before we settled down to a bit of recreational drinking.

It may have been the heat, the distance or the incredible weight of the books we were carrying, but I was knackered by the time we go up there. I wish I could say it had been worth it but I can't. The one good thing was that the two pubs we were due to visit and the bus station were all downhill.

John; Again our time was very short and we were keen to find the bars nearest the grounds. There are two which are about the same distance from the ground and just round the corner from each other. The first one we went into was 'The Mayfair' on King Street. Our time was very limited but it is a great pub and the barmaid Anne Gillespie was very nice and gave us the history of the bar.

We had to rush, so round the corner we went to Queen Street and into 'The Station Bar'. This is another great bar and Rebecca the barmaid was good company. The people in Peterhead, and up north in general are great and very friendly and helpful. One thing we learned in these two pubs is that the first one was a 'Rangers' bar and the second a 'Celtic' bar. This does not mean that the supporters of these clubs don't go into the other bar, they do, it's just funny to remember that Rangers and Celtic have many more supporters in Peterhead than the local club, and almost every town in Scotland is the same.

All too soon it was time to leave Peterhead and find the bus to take us to our next destination, Aberdeen.

Craig; The Mayfair is the nearest pub to the stadium but only by about twenty yards. It is fairly old-fashioned but good just the same. I would imagine it was last decorated sometime in the early 70s but since that was my favourite time I was quite happy about it. The pub apparently gets a good crowd when Peterhead play at home.

Round the corner at the Station Bar it was pretty much the same thing. We had a couple of drinks there and enjoyed a wee chat with the barmaid Rebecca.

Apparently there are two separate bars in this pub. The first one is the noisy bar where the young guys hang out. Rebecca was just about to say the other one was for old codgers just like us but managed to stop herself just in time to avoid losing any chance of a tip.

We left the Station Bar and made our way down to Main Street to buy a few supplies for the bus to Aberdeen.

Pubs we visited:

The Mayfair Bar;

The Station Bar;

How to get there by bus:

G9 Gold bus
Glasgow to Aberdeen
Stagecoach 60
Aberdeen to Peterhead
66 or 69 bus station to ground

Aberdeen

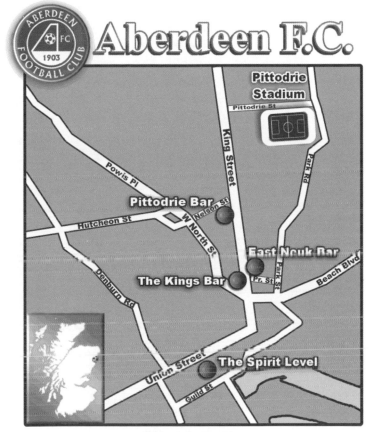

Pittodrie Stadium
Ground opened - 1899

John; Our bus, the number 60 from Peterhead to Aberdeen left on time, the journey passed quickly as we both slept most of the way. Two days on the road is hard work at our age.

It was still glorious as we got off and wandered down the slope to Pittodrie. Aberdeen, 'The Dons', which is an ok nickname, were at home to St. Johnstone, and the supporters were starting to gather as we staggered round the stadium. We were looking for 'The Broadhill Bar' just behind the stadium. We found it no problem. It was shut and looked as if it had been for years. The place looked like a bomb site.

Craig; Even after John's meticulous planning we had no real idea where to get off the bus for Pittodrie but fortunately my smart phone turned out to be smarter than both of us. In no time at all we found ourselves standing outside the stadium and that's as close as we got to getting inside the stadium.

Fortunately John had heard of a pub just outside the stadium; unfortunately he must have heard about it many years ago as not only is the pub shut it looks as if it's about to collapse.

John; We knew there were plenty of bars up on King Street, so up we went and wandered toward the city centre and into 'The Pittodrie Bar'. The bar was, as you can imagine, packed with supporters. It was so busy and noisy that you couldn't hear yourself think, but it is a nice bar, and handy for the ground.

A few yards along the road are two bars across the road from each other. We couldn't make up our minds which to go into, so we went into both. The first, 'The East Neuk' was really old fashioned and a bit run down, but we liked it and the company was good, another bar worth a visit if you're going to a match. Across the road, 'The Kings Bar' was a bit better-finished inside and also worth a visit on match day. Nothing wrong with any of the three bars we visited.

It was getting to about four o'clock, and our Gold Bus back to Glasgow left at the back of five, so we headed up to Union Street and delivered our books, it was great to get the load off our backs. We spent the last hour of our trip in what we both agree is the best bar in Aberdeen, 'The Spirit Level'. We have visited it a few times in the past. The girls who run it are the best in the country.

Craig; There was nothing else for it but to walk back up Pittodrie Street. Actually I was quite a bit less than pleased when I found out that the Pittodrie Bar was nowhere near Pittodrie Street. It's about a mile away along King's Street. To me that is just cheating.

Aberdeen was playing St. Johnstone that day and we had expected to see lots of fans making their way to the game. There were quite a few, but it was far from busy.

After an epic hike along the road we eventually reached the Pittodrie Bar. By the time we got there I didn't expect to be able to get into the place let alone get a pint there. But we were in luck and although the bar was quite busy there was still a fair bit of room left for the weary traveller and they don't come much more weary than me.

This pub reminded me of the Horse Shoe in Glasgow in style with a large round bar and the central serving area. There was absolutely no chance of us getting to talk to anyone in the bar, it was hard enough getting the barman to look in our direction never mind talk to him.

One pint was enough and then we went back out onto King's Street in search of another, hopefully more interesting. pub.

We spotted the tell-tale signs of an open pub as we staggered down the street under the weight of our rucksacks. There were three blokes standing in a doorway smoking. That's a dead giveaway, usually.

The East Neuk Bar is a good old-fashioned pub and we were looking forward to sampling a brew or two in it. A bloke at the door told us that the barman would be back in a minute as he had nipped out for a smoke. We duly waited at the bar and a couple of minutes later the same bloke came in and served us, he was the barman, cheeky bugger.

The bar itself looked like a health and safety nightmare with cables hanging from the ceiling and some dodgy-looking fixtures and fittings. The beer was good though so we didn't mind.

Just down the street I spied another pub. The King's bar at first glance appeared to be shut. In fact it looked a couple of weeks short of becoming derelict but we had a look inside and were surprised to find a great wee pub. It was clean and friendly with a good selection of draught beers, one of which I enjoyed greatly.

Still looking out for likely pubs to review we suddenly found ourselves standing on Union Street. John, who had been forced to listen to me whining on about how heavy my pack was, volunteered to take my books along to Waterstones leaving me free to head round to our favourite Aberdeen pub.

The Spirit Level on Stirling Street is the pub that we always visit when in town. It's a medium-sized pub with good beer and great service. There is a good age range of customers and we have always found it a friendly place to visit. It was good to end our latest adventure there. Apart that is from a swift couple in the Horse Shoe in Glasgow.

267

We had a great time on this longer than usual trip and I have to say John did a splendid job of planning it all. I wouldn't usually be caught congratulating him for anything but as he never actually reads anything I write I think that I'll get away with it this time.

John; The Gold Bus home was a new Double Decker and very luxurious. Craig did nothing but complain about not getting a cup of tea. How can you complain about not getting something that's free. What a man. We did manage a quick one in 'The Horseshoe' in Glasgow before getting the train back to EK. The train home was a nightmare; about 50 girls of about 14 or 15 years old were on their way back from Glasgow after a party of some kind. Modern day kids, as I've said before, are the loudest things on the planet, they just never shut up.

If you divide how much I spent by four, as we visited four grounds, it doesn't sound so bad. Without the cost of the digs I had little change out of a hundred quid. Mind you, we did have a chicken supper on Friday night and a couple of snacks in Aberdeen.

Pubs we visited:

The Pittodrie;

The East Neuk;

The Kings Bar;

The Spirit Level;

How to get there by bus:

The G9 Gold Bus
from Glasgow to Aberdeen

East Fife

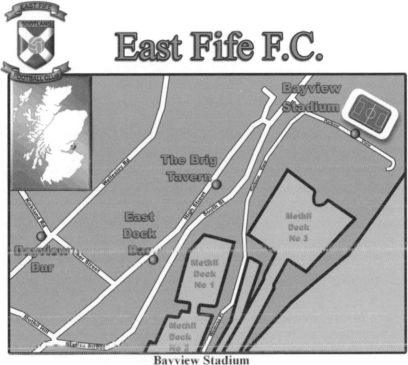

Bayview Stadium
Ground opened - 1998

John: Today we were doing one of our multi club visits. These are never easy and full of potential disasters, mainly me getting the bus times or numbers wrong. I had printed out all the journey details and was as confident as I could be that nothing could go wrong. Can you believe that? Of course something will go wrong, and it will be my fault!

It was an early start. Our bus from Glasgow left at 8.50am, so I picked Craig up at 7.20am to give us plenty of time to get into Glasgow and walk up the hill to Buchanan Street Bus Station. Only point of interest on the journey into Glasgow was that the No. 18 bus driver decided to go a different way through Glasgow. We were almost at the King's Theatre when we all got off the bus. Everyone was mad, but we all thanked the driver. What are Glasgow people like?

After a minor slip up on my part of trying to get on the wrong bus, we had a great run over to Kirkcaldy, where again I managed to get on the wrong bus. In my defence it is very complicated. There are hundreds of buses with lots of numbers. The driver told us the bus we wanted was next to his and was leaving right away, so we dashed over and on to it. After having a laugh at us, our next driver, a very helpful young girl, drove us up the coast to Methil. We sat upstairs at the front. Craig was mad as I bagged to be the driver.

Our lovely driver dropped us off right across the road from the ground. East Coast drivers are definitely very friendly, unlike others I could mention.

Craig; Visiting three football grounds in one day requires a lot of planning and more than a little good fortune. John certainly supplied the first of these elements but from the outset the second one looked to be in short supply.

It all began with a less than magical mystery tour. Our bus into Glasgow took off in an unexpected direction once it reached the city centre. Apparently bus drivers are not required to inform passengers that their bus route has been changed and now goes nowhere near their stated destination. I suppose we should be grateful that our bus actually arrived in Glasgow and not some other Scottish city. Luckily we had caught an earlier bus than planned and therefore had enough time for the forced march to the bus station.

John; Methil, unlike most Fife seaside towns in the area is an industrial sort of town, and even today there is a fair bit of industry down at the waterfront. The new industry is building these huge wind turbines. At least they are giving some people in the area employment.

Bayview was bathed in sunshine as we wandered over. It's a nice wee park and we had read that there was a bar in the ground. It was only the back of eleven so it was not open yet, but that didn't stop the Chairman Lee Murray and the Vice Chairman Davie Hamilton welcoming us warmly and showing us round. We had a great time.

East Fife's nickname is the 'The Fifers'. I would suggest the 'Methil Magyars', but people would say I was copying the Thistle, so I won't.

Jemma, Debbie, Anna, Charlie and Kelly
The girls from Bayview Stadium

Craig; *Once in Methil we made straight for East Fife's stadium. It looked really good in the brilliant sunshine that day but I wonder what it is like in deep midwinter with the howling gale blowing in from the North Sea*

Although it was too early for a beer, or so they claimed, we had a good look around the Main Stand. The first person we met was Dave Hamilton the club's vice chairman. He showed us around the hospitality area and introduced us to the girls who make the place work.

Debbie and the rest of the girls eventually agreed to pose for a photo but I still think I would have preferred a pint. I would have liked to come back to Bayview Stadium later in the day as I think it would be a really good place to have a beer. But we had to move on.

Fay and the 'Dockers'

John; Anyway, back to our business of visiting pubs. The first one, and the one closest to the ground was 'The Brig Tavern', so in we went. It is a great wee pub and the barman Dave Mitchell was great company and a really friendly bloke. Well worth a visit next time you are going to watch 'The Fifers. He even bought us a round before we had to leave. Our next pub was called 'The East Dock Bar'. This was a bigger bar and was brilliantly decorated, all dead authentic. The first thing I clocked was that the place was full of old clocks, and about five or so old blokes who, along with a great barmaid called Fay kept us going with their patter. This is another great bar and a must to visit.

The only problem we had was that the instructions they gave us to get to our bus stop were wrong, or more likely we went the wrong way. Anyway, we missed the bus and had an hour to kill. Fortunately, there was a bar across the road called 'The Bayview Bar'. It looked like a prison from the outside and the décor inside was not much better. But, as always, it's the people who matter, and the girl behind the bar, Lorraine was great company and we enjoyed our time there. She even bought us a round. Methil is some place.

We had to go, so after hearing our tale of missing the last bus, Lorraine took us outside and gave us detailed instructions on how to get to the right bus stop. She even counted out the lamp posts we had to pass. So we said our goodbyes to Methil and waited for our bus to our next port of call.

Craig; *Not far from the park we found a great pub where we enjoyed our first drink of the day. The Brig Tavern is a fairly old building but inside it has been modernised.*

Our barman came straight over to talk to us as soon as we entered; we liked that. He seemed to know quite a bit about using the bus pass and we asked him why. It turns out that he has one of his own. We couldn't believe he was old enough. There must be something in the air over on the east coast.

After a couple of drinks and a few swapped bus trip stories we made our way along the street to the East Dock Bar. This bar is worth a visit just for the atmosphere alone. The decor is unique with many of the interior fixtures having been reclaimed from other buildings.

The wood panelling which covers all four walls was once part of an old Edinburgh cinema. While the tables were formally Singer sewing machine stands I was particularly impressed with the huge wooden gantry behind the bar.

Even better, the barmaid and customers were a great laugh. Kay the barmaid was in good form and between serving drinks and keeping her customers in order, told us all about the pub. Apparently the East Dock gets a good crowd when the football team plays a home game. It also gets a good turn from local golfers.

One customer told us that the pubs in Methil had once always been busy. In fact back when the towns docks were at their peak there were people from all parts of the world visiting the local boozers. Indeed the building just across the street had once been part of the German embassy.

After hearing that, we marched swiftly up the road to catch our next bus, which we missed. Not because we had spent too much time in the last pub but because we were standing at the wrong bus stop. These things happen even to seasoned travellers.

However I was amazed to find that the bus stop had a name on it. The sign said Bayview Bar stop. What a great idea. Maybe all bus stops should have the name of the nearest pub displayed on them, with direction if necessary. Personally I do most of my navigation using pub locations.

Since we had missed our bus we decided to go into the nearby Bayview Bar even though it looked like the sort of place best avoided. Bricked up windows tend to send out a message. Where I come from it is usually a brick through the window that sends out a message, but that's another story. Despite being a wee bit feart I'm glad that John's desperate need for alcohol meant we had to enter this pub.

Lorraine sees us right at The Bayview Bar

I am not quite sure how to describe the inside of the pub let's just say it was very different; a wee bit more modern and brighter than I had expected to be honest. I didn't really like it at first but as they say you shouldn't go on first impressions.

Lorraine - the owner and barmaid - changed our minds about the place. She was a great laugh and made our visit an enjoyable experience. We said our goodbyes to Methil and got our bus to our next stop, Cowdenbeath.

Pubs we visited:

Bar in ground (closed at time);

The Brig Tavern;

The East Dock Bar;

The Bayview Bar;

How to get there by bus:
X26 Glasgow to Kirkcaldy
No.8 Kirkcaldy to Lower Methil

Cowdenbeath

Central Park
Ground opened - 1917

John; Our bus from Methil to Cowdenbeath dropped us off at the corner of the High Street outside 'The Dunvagen Arms', so in we went. It is a busy pub but the lady behind the bar, June Ross, was very friendly and helpful. She has owned the bar for three years and is working very hard to make a success of it. It is not easy to make money

275

running bars in today's economic climate, so good luck to her. The bar is nice and well worth a visit.

Leaving the bar, we wandered along the High Street in the sunshine and round the corner to the ground, home of the 'Blue Brazil'. Now that's a good nickname. A nice boy on the door of the fence round the ground allowed us in and told us we could watch the match if we wanted. We were there anyway and couldn't help but see the game. Today they were playing Falkirk. Just thought I'd tell you that. The nickname, 'Blue Brazil' sums up the team. They play in Blue, well anyway, half the nickname sums them up.

We go stravagin into The Dunvagan to meet June

We went in a door and up the stairs to see where the bar was. As the game was started the bar was shut. We were told by the three policemen who were watching the game to ensure the three supporters didn't get out of hand that the bar only opens when the speedway is on.

After hearing that interesting piece of information, we left the game behind and went into the bar on the corner called 'Partners'. The best thing we could say about the bar is that it is very handy for the ground. We had one drink and wandered across the road to catch the first of three buses we would need to get us to our next ground. Craig was not confident.

Craig; *We arrived in Cowdenbeath and managed to get off the bus just across the road from the Dunvegan Bar. John claimed* *that he had planned it that way all along. I couldn't be bothered reminding him that not only had he taken us to the wrong bus stop but to the wrong bus stop on the wrong street while attempting to get us here.*

Inside the Dunvegan we found that it was a very nice pub run by a very nice lady. June, the owner, chatted to us as she pulled the pints. She told us that her pub gets a good number of supporters in for a drink on match days. I told her that had one of us not made an arse of our transport arrangements we may have arrived in time to see some of them.

After a good pint and some great patter we strolled round to the football park. I can't really say too much about the bar in the stadium as the fact that it was shut prevented us from doing any kind of assessment. Too late again John!

The nearest pub to the ground is called Partners and to be honest its position is about all it has going for it. After a quick pint, about 15 minutes being the average, we left for the bus to Alloa, our final port of call for the day.,

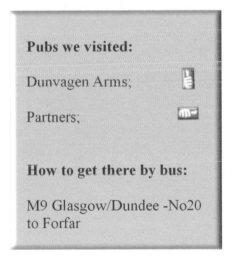

Pubs we visited:

Dunvagen Arms;

Partners;

How to get there by bus:

M9 Glasgow/Dundee -No20
to Forfar

Alloa

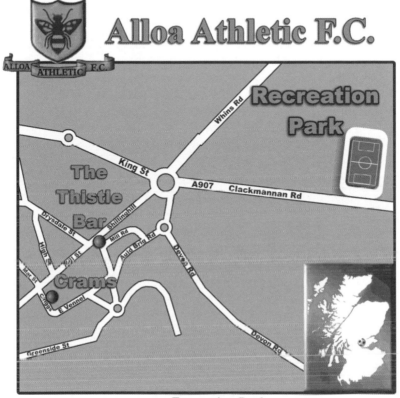

Recreation Park
Ground opened - 1895

John: Because of my brilliant planning and a bit of luck, three buses after leaving Cowdenbeath, we were in Alloa. We passed the ground on the way into the town and it looked very nice. That's as close as we got. The club nickname is 'The Wasps', as they play in Gold and Black. I can see where the nickname came from, it's not too bad.

Our first pub was only a short walk down the road from the bus stop, so in we went. 'The Thistle Bar' is another great place. The East side of Scotland or East-ish in Alloa's case has a lot of really good bars.

We don't say a bar is great if it's not. The barman Brian Parkhouse, along with Alex and George, a couple of local worthies, were great company and kept us going with patter. Can't remember any of it as the bevy was starting to kick in by then. We had at least a couple there before saying goodbye, following their instructions to the next pub and getting lost. Craig had his web phone out to Google where the next pub was, but by the time he had service, or whatever you call it, I had asked a local who showed us where to go. The phone went back in the pocket. I sometimes wonder if that, in the future, people will live their lives without actually speaking to each other face to face.

Anyway, who cares? We wandered into our last pub in Alloa, 'Crams'. I'm not kidding when I say that this was another great wee bar. The manager Marion was great company and we had a good time talking to her and a nice couple next to us. The lady was called Alison Wallace and her partner, a bloke who was as pissed as us had the nickname 'Cabbage'. Alison never told us how he came by that nickname, but she didn't need to. Ten minutes later he emptied the place. I think he had been eating cabbage all day. It was ages before we could get back into the pub and finish our drinks. Time was getting on and it was with great sadness that we said our goodbyes to everybody and told Cabbage to put a cork in it.

Craig; *We reached Alloa after a short stopover in Kincardine and made straight for the Thistle Bar. It was the nearest bar to Alloa Athletic's football park, as far as we know.*

Whether it was because it was a Saturday afternoon or perhaps because we had started drinking at the same time of day as the rest of the guys in the bar we found that we fitted right in with the clientele.

The barman, Brian, and his customers seemed tuned into our particular wavelength, that is to say we were all slurring from the same hymn sheet. It all made perfect sense to us but I would imagine that a sober bystander would have been more than a little puzzled with our patter. Only men of a certain age who have dedicated their lives to consuming the produce of their local grog shop can make sense of pub speak. John and I are both fluent in this particular language.

Just for a bit of balance we decided to visit one more pub in Alloa. The guys in the bar, George and Alec, provided as with detailed directions to a pub they thought we would like. Despite their best efforts we actually found the pub fairly quickly.

Crams is a great wee pub with only one drawback as far as I can remember. You really would have to have a serious medical condition, not to mention a really strange sense of humour, to manufacture an odour like that produced by one of the pub's patrons. That kind of smell should only be produced under licensed laboratory conditions. The appropriately named Cabbage is a man you might wish to avoid if you are a bit of a sensitive soul.

Apart from that we thoroughly enjoyed our short stay in Crams and I would recommend it to anyone looking for a friendly pub to relax in. Just take your gas mask!

John; We got our bus, the No. 62 to Stirling and had time to rush about to find a bar to get a quick one before catching our bus to Glasgow, the M8. We slept all the way back to Glasgow. By the way, Stirling Bus Station is a bit of a nightmare when the shopping centre above is closed. There are no toilets or anything else for that matter. Take note Stirling Council.

We had one drink in an Irish Bar in St. Vincent Street. Craig might mention why it was only one, before getting the train back to EK. Irene picked us up at 'The Monty' after another quick one.

It was an expensive day, as you could probably guess from the number of pubs we have been in today. Not much change out of £40. People say you only live once. At this rate the end is coming quickly.

Pubs we visited:

The Thistle Bar;

Crams;

How to get there by bus:

X26 Glasgow to St. Andrews
(get off in Kincardine)

No,78 to Alloa

Ayr

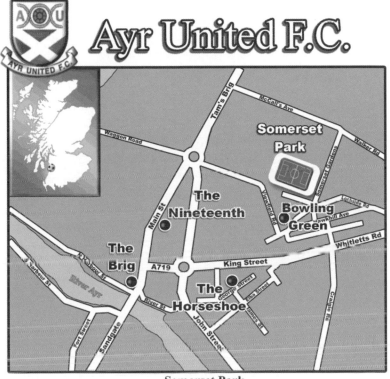

Ayr United F.C.

Somerset Park
Ground opened 1896

John; Ayr United. 'The Honest Men'. It's a great nickname for a team, and Craig and I were hoping that we would find that the barmen were just as honest, and friendly. We travel in hope. That would be a great saying for Craig and me. I'm going to use this phrase from now on, *'We travel in hope'.*

Ayr is also one of the easiest places to get to from East Kilbride. The old X16 takes us from the town centre right to Ayr. Magic.

This was our second attempt at going to Ayr. The last time the game was called off on the morning of the game because the park was frozen after a frosty night. This was in January for goodness sake. What do you expect. I thought all grounds had underfloor heating, or whatever you call it. So this was our second attempt, *'We travel in hope'*.

I had been in Rothesay for a couple of days and only got home on the Saturday morning. I caught the 8.00am ferry. The things I do for this book. Even leaving Rothesay. Now that's saying something.

Kate had my pieces all ready when I got home. All I had to do was pack my stuff for the day and head down to pick up Craig at 10.45am as we planned to get the 11.01am X16 to Ayr. It was the day of the Ayr Gold Cup so we were a tad worried that the bus to Ayr might be full of punters. Craig reckoned it was even money we wouldn't get on the bus. We did no bother - you canny beat the bookies!

Craig; It was second time lucky for us on this latest trip. We had tried before to get down to Ayr to check out the pubs near Somerset Park, home of Ayr United FC. That time things had ended in farce. We had made all the preparations even managing to wangle an invite into hospitality courtesy of a friend and member of the committee down there, Douglas McKenzie. It seemed too good to be true: it was.

Our careful plans went out of the window as a cold front moved in from the north. The playing surface was frozen solid: game off.

This time around there was no chance of that happening as it was a fairly pleasant day when we boarded the X 16 at East Kilbride bus station.

John; Craig knows Ayr well as he is an Ayrshire man, so I left it to him to organize which pubs we would visit. His first choice was called 'The Drouthy Bar'. It was shut - what can you say! Craig's excuse is always the same, 'Google Earth Street View can't tell if a pub is shut'. This was no problem as there are hundreds of pubs in Ayr. A short walk along the same street and we were outside a wee pub called 'The 19th'. It said it was a golf theamed bar, and so it was. A minute later we were inside enjoying our first drink of the day in a very unusual, but nice wee bar. There were photos, trophies and other golf memorabilia covering every inch of the walls and shelves.

A thought then came into my head. In Ayrshire there must be more golf courses than anywhere else in the world. You only have to turn a corner and you fall into a bunker. But the funny thing is that I reckon this pub was as far away from a course as you can get in Ayrshire. Check it out if you are as crazy as me.

The barman was called Smudger. This was a nickname. His real name was Davie. I asked him why he is called Smudger, he said he has always been called Smudger. Some great background reporting for you there. We had a great time talking to him and a local called Shaun who was a great football fan - of Celtic! Just like everywhere else in Scotland, most of the locals support one of the old firm clubs. It's just daft. Every club could have a reasonable sized support if the locals supported their team. Is this too simple an idea?

When we asked if there were any pubs near the ground, Spudger gave us directions to a bar called 'The Horseshoe Bar'. There must be dozens of bars with that name in Scotland, and we've been in a good few of them. The directions included going through two underpasses which took us into a housing scheme which, to put not too fine a point on it, looked a bit rough, really rough. I won't mention the name of it in case the locals take offence.

Craig; *I had been boasting to John about my intimate knowledge of all things Ayrshire. One of the pubs I had identified as being closest to Somerset Park was the Drouthy Bar. Actually I had never heard of that place before but I had seen it on Google Earth.*

Looking back on it perhaps it would have been better if I hadn't made such a big deal about how good the place looked. Discovering that it was shut and had been for some time kind of put a dent in my credibility as a pub guide. To say John wasn't impressed would rank as a bit of an understatement. He pointed out a number of my shortcomings for quite a long time after we found out that we wouldn't be sampling any booze in the Drouthy. He was still ranting when we stumbled across the 19th.

The most striking thing about this particular pub is that it doesn't look anything like a pub. I'm glad we didn't let first impressions put us off going in. It was great inside.

285

The decor is unlike any I've ever seen in any pub before. It's quite a small pub with every inch of it covered with golfing memorabilia. I'm not into sport but I really liked this place. You could pass an hour or two just looking around the place checking out all the quirky items hanging on the wall or from the ceiling.

While we were doing just that we got into conversation with one of the customers. Sean told us that not very many supporters visited this pub. John asked him if he was a football supporter himself and if so, was he going to the game.

Sean said yes to both but, unfortunately, his team was not Ayr United and the game he was going to see was a good 30 miles further north of Somerset Park.

He did however tell us about another pub we should visit. This one was much nearer the park and was called The Horseshoe. It was quite a complicated operation just getting there but somehow we managed. I would have to say that The Horseshoe is not in what you might describe as being a great area of the town. However it turned out to be a really good pub.

On the day we were there the Ayr Gold Cup was being run and quite a few of the pub's customers were dressed for the occasion.

It was a bit weird seeing so many guys wearing suits in a wee pub in the middle of a housing scheme. The good thing about that was that it gave me a chance to tell one of my very few memorised jokes.

Q. What do you call a Govan man in a suit?
A. The accused!

The manager of the pub, Jenny, turned out to be our first genuine Ayr supporter. She goes to many of the games and often travels down to England to support her other favourite team. Unfortunately I don't remember which team that was and in the interests of my continued good health I shall refrain from taking a wild stab in the dark at it.

286

I can usually just about bluff my way through a conversation about football. My usual tactic is just to agree with whoever happens to be talking. But Jenny really knows her stuff about the game so I had to admit defeat.

Jenny races to serve her customers in The Horseshoe

John; The locals didn't need to take offence. We found 'The Horseshoe Bar' and in we went. It was a good bar and all the locals were great people. There were even some all dressed up in suits and everything ready for the 'Gold Cup' meeting at the race course just up the road. The manager Jenny was great company and we had a couple of drinks and a great time. Another Ayr bar well worth a visit.

Following Jenny's instructions, we wandered up the road and found Somerset Park. It was nice in a very old fashioned sort of way, the kind of place we like. The man and girl on the main door were very pleasant, but as there was no bar in the ground the best they could do was to give us instructions to Hawkhill Bowling Green which was right next to the ground.

This is a brilliant wee club, very friendly, and the Secretary, Treasurer and Barman Donald McLean was good company and filled us in with all the comings and goings in the club. Ayr were playing Brechin City today and Donald introduced us to their Chairman Ken Ferguson and five directors of their club. They were all really nice people and always visit the bowling green when they play Ayr. We were able to tell them that we had a great time on our visit to Brechin and wished them, and Ayr, good luck for today's match.

We said our farewells and left the green as the bowlers played their closing day match. Closing day in bowling clubs is a sure sign of winters icy finger approaching. A wee bit of Burns-esk patter there.

Craig; The Horseshoe Bar is a good pub and close enough to Somerset Park to make it a reasonable venue for a pre-match tipple. Finding it may be a bit of a problem though. But it is well worth the effort to get there.

Over at Somerset we checked out the stadium although we knew there was no bar there which was open to the general public. We talked to a couple of stewards at the stadium and asked them if they knew another place where we might be able to get a pre-match beer. To be honest we didn't hold out much hope, but once again we were in for a surprise. One of the stewards told us that most of the supporters used the near-by bowling green.

Apparently it was only a couple of minutes' walk away and we hadn't noticed it. We are definitely losing our touch.

Donald trys to remember which of his many jobs he is actually supposed to be doing right now

The Hawkhill Bowling Club is an excellent place to sample a few beers before the game. Donald McLean seems to do just about anything and everything around the club. He has more titles than the Duke of Edinburgh. But the best thing he does however is fill a really good pint of beer. A skill we both appreciate greatly. Right enough he tells some really good stories as well.

It was while we were in the club that we saw our first Ayr United supporter, in fact we also saw a few Brechin fans as well. Donald even introduced as to the entire Brechin City FC committee. Meeting actual Brechin supporters was something we had dismally failed to do when we were in Brechin. So we felt that we could at last tick that box.

It would be hard to top a fine bar like the Hawkhill Bowling Club and of course we didn't. We went to The Brig Bar instead.

It was okay really, especially if you are not too fussy about where you knock back the odd pint or two. Just don't get your hopes up for an evening of convivial chat and witty banter.

We had a final pint in McCabes at the bus station while we waited for the X 16 back up to East Kilbride And it is every bit as good as The Brig Bar, just a bit more modern.

John; On our way to the bus station we dropped into 'The Brig'. It was very busy and it was hard to talk to any of the staff, but it was a nice bar and we had no complaints. We only had a quick one and walked along the road to the bus station. After checking the time of our bus back to EK, we found that we had half an hour to kill, so it was killed in 'McCabes' across the road from the bus station.

A quick one later and we were on the X16 back home, although a couple in 'The Lum' were needed before we finally felt we had to get home or fall down. What a life! Must have spent about £30 today, hope the book sells or it's the poor hoose for me!

Pubs we visited:

The 19th;

The Horseshoe;

Hawkhill B.C.;

The Brig;

McCabes;

How to get there by bus:

X77 Glasgow Ayr

St.Johnstone

McDiarmid Park
Ground opened - 1989

John; Their nickname is 'The Saints', a fairly predictable one if you ask me, which you're not. Never one to slag off anything without coming up with an alternative, how about 'The Perth Pirates', 'The Saint John Dons' or even 'The Tayfairers'. I suppose you're thinking 'The Saints' seems fairly good now.

This trip was originally going to be done as part of a two club visit. Stirling Albion and then St. Johnstone being our original plan. The problem was that we had such a good time in Stirling we never reached Perth. Flexibility is important in any plan.

So today we were more determined than ever to reach Perth. Now since it is the only place we were going to today, not a lot of determination was needed, just a couple of free buses. So off we went.

Just to be on the safe side, I booked us on the buses to and from Perth. Better safe than sorry I hear you say, or maybe not. We left EK on the old No. 18 at about 9.30am, heading into Glasgow to catch the 11.00am M8 to Perth.

One thing we noticed on the bus is the noise that most young people make when talking. I'm sure it's because they spend most of their waking lives in front of a telly or a games machine. In the old days only ex helicopter pilots spoke like that.

Apart from that we had a very nice journey over to Perth. My planning on Traveline had told me that it was an eight minute walk from the Bus Station in Perth to the stop where we would get our local bus to McDiarmid Park, home of St. Johnstone. Craig got out his computer phone as soon as we got to Perth and got a map up to show us the way to walk. To cut a long story short, we walked for about 20 minutes in a circle before the bus we were supposed to be on, the number two, flashed past us. Thankfully, its terminus was just up ahead and it was still there when we arrived, breathless.

Craig; At long last we have managed to visit Perth, home of St Johnstone FC. We had intended to pay McDiarmid Park a visit some time ago but because of a mild case of poisoning we had to cancel. The particular poison in question was alcohol and the sufferer was John. Need I say more?

This time we made it to Perth with little difficulty apart from an overpowering urge to give our very rude bus driver a well merited hard slap about the head.

John had once again been in charge of the transport arrangements and assured me that everything was in order. We would arrive in Perth get off the bus walk for eight minutes to our next bus stop then proceed to McDiarmid Park. No problem no hassle. That would be likely!

About half an hour after arriving at the station we eventually found our next bus stop. Eight minutes always sounded a bit optimistic but to get to the stop any quicker than we did would require the services of a native guide and or a helicopter.

John; The web had told us that the park was out of town and that there were no pubs near it. The web was wrong. As we got near the ground we passed a social club with a Tennents sign outside and then a pub called '208 Public House', which Craig claimed he saw on Google. So our revised plan was to visit them after we had a look at the ground. Today was a Thursday so we knew that there would be no game on, but there's always something happening, so on we went.

McDiarmid Park is very nice and there was a girl on the reception desk called Yvonne who was very pleasant and helpful and even offered to let us see round the ground. St. Johnstone have a great ambassador there. Full marks to her.

Craig; *On the way up to the park we passed a couple of likely looking prospects for a quick drink. After walking around the park only to find there was no bar I'm glad that we did spot them.*

The girl at the reception desk at the park did say that we could come back the next day and we may be able to get a drink. The thought of John waiting 24 hours for a drink was rather amusing but was also highly unrealistic.

I had known about the 208 Public Bar for some time, courtesy of Google. What I didn't know was that it had rather odd opening hours. It didn't open until 4 o'clock. Unfortunately when we tried the door it was only 1 o'clock. I could feel the disappointment in the air. Actually I could also hear some of it. Being from Govan John knows quite a few four letter words and he deployed most of them in my direction when he found out that we were not getting into the pub.

We retreated along the road to the place we had seen from the bus. I was pretty sure that it was also shut. There was no sign of life and no cars in the large car park. There was only one other customer in the very large bar of the Institute. But nothing was going to put us off having a nice cold drink or two. As it turned out we were quite glad it wasn't too busy as it gave us time to talk to a couple of very nice people.

Helen is a bit of an institution in The Institute

We had our long and very amusing chat with Helen, the barmaid and Dave, our fellow drinker, about the fortunes of St Mirren over the last few years, but to be honest most of it was wasted on me.

I think it must have been all the talk about us using free bus travel to visit the football parks but somehow we eventually got onto the subject of retirement. Helen said that her husband had recently been off work for a few weeks due to ill health. Till then they had both been looking forward to a happy retirement together in the not too distant future. After three weeks she had changed her mind about that.

Her exact words were, "There will be blood on the walls if we are stuck in the house together".

The local postie came in, off duty I hasten to add, and joined in the fun we were having. Beaky, a former football player in the junior divisions, had quite a bit to say about the state of the game today. Unfortunately he had also had quite a lot to say about my old hometowns junior team, Auchinleck Talbot. Let's just say not all of it was complimentary.

Helen and Beaky gave us directions to a pub we had not heard of but they did seem a wee bit concerned that it might not entirely suit us. We decided to go anyway.

The bus trip to the pub is not one I would recommend. We were panicking most of the way there. However, despite its setting and perhaps its reputation we really liked The Welcome Inn. The beer was good, the service was excellent and the manager even came round to talk to us. Audrey runs her bar well and tries to keep all of her customers entertained.

They do get away supporters coming in on match days but the pub is just a wee bit off the main trail to benefit too much.

It is a good community pub and well worth a visit, if you can find it.

As planned we caught the same service bus back round to the 208. In fact it was the same driver. What amazed me was the fact that he wasn't in the least bit surprised to see us back on his bus again.

John: After a look around the ground, we walked back up to '208 Public House' and was told by a young lady on here knees painting behind the entrance door that they opened at four o'clock. At least she didn't give us the brush off. As this was only about half one, I said to Craig we should go round the corner and check out the 'Tulloch Institute Social Club'. Craig said it was shut, but after pressing special buttons on the door we were in.

The bar was nearly empty, not unusual at that time of day, and only the barmaid Helen and a local worthy Dave were present. This made no difference, we had a great time and the company was brilliant. We were soon joined by the local postie called Stevie, Steven to his wife and Beaky to everyone else. We had a great time and after the brilliant Helen had bought us a round it was time to leave and search out the next pub.

As it was still only about three o'clock, and Helen gave us instructions to another pub near the ground, only 'two' minutes on the local bus. Nice as they are, locals have no idea of time. The two minute journey seemed like 10, but it dropped us off outside our next port of call, 'The Welcome Inn'. When we got off the bus we were right in the middle of a housing scheme that would have made the good people of Easterhouse feart. There was no bus to escape in, so our only option was the pub, so in we went, trying to look as hard as possible, which isn't easy!

Audrey & Joan say your 'Welcome Inn'

The usual happened, it was a great bar, the locals didn't hit us, and the barmaid Joan and the licensee Audrey were great company and very friendly. I imagine away supporters would find the other two places we visited handier for the ground, but there's nothing wrong with 'The Welcome Inn', if you can find it and you're no feart.

Craig; The 208 Public Bar was open for business and we were determined to give it some. We were in the bar at the back of the pub. The bar at the front is more of a lounge bar and is only open at the weekends.

We then met our second Helen of the day. This one, Helen Doris, turned out to be the owner and she was really friendly and welcoming. We knew straight away that we had once again found a great pub. While we disposed of a couple of beers we chatted to Helen. She told us that the 208 gets quite busy when there is a game on over at McDiarmid Park. Both home and away

296

supporters are made welcome. The bar is only 100 yards or so from the entrance to the stadium car park and would be hard to miss.

One piece of advice might be useful though, get there early as I would imagine that it fills up quickly.

208 is Helen's favourite number

The journey back to Glasgow was uneventful although once there things changed slightly. Suffice it to say the sight of John dancing in the street with 15 would be transvestites will haunt my memory forever. I was half hoping that I was suffering from an alcohol induced hallucination but unfortunately it really did happen. John insisted that it was just a bunch of lads having a laugh while out on a stag party. And that is the story he is sticking to.

John; We retraced out bus steps to the '208 Public House' which was now open as it was exactly four o'clock. The wee woman with the brush who was painting turned out to be the lovely owner of the pub, Helen Doris. Helen made us very welcome and gave us the history of the pub and we had a great time, even met her daughter and her daughter's wee boy. Her daughter just came in and helped herself to a drink. What a great mum to have. This is a pub very handy for the ground and a great one as well.

So after thinking we would have to go into the centre of Perth to find a pub, we found three good ones within spitting distance of the ground.

After a pantomime of both of us nearly getting knocked down running back and forth across the road trying to get one of two buses that arrived at the same time – going in opposite directions - one of the drivers took pity on us and waited till we got our breath back and onto his bus for the short journey back to the town centre.

We both slept almost the whole way back to Glasgow and after a walk down West Nile Street through a tunnel of about 50 boys dressed up as girls, a stag night we hoped, we went into 'The Horse Shoe' for a nightcap. The train back to EK and a run home from Craig's Irene ended our day out in Perth.

I said to Craig on the way home that this had been our cheapest ever day out. I think the £20 we each put into the kitty covered the day, and that included a bag of chips from 'The Blue Lagoon' outside The Central Station. Got to mention that they are starting to put real vinegar on the chips, not the watered down stuff I'm sure they used to use.

Pubs we visited:

Tulloch Inst. S.C.;

208 Public House;

The Welcome Inn;

How to get there by bus:

M8 Megabus Glasgow-Dundee. get off in Perth
No.2 Circular from Miller
Street to Ground

Hearts

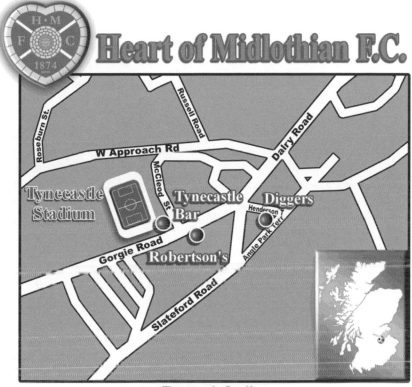

Tynecastle Stadium
Ground Opened - 1886

John; Hearts, 'The Jam Tarts'. One of the great nicknames in Scottish Football. Recently Hearts, like a lot of teams have been in financial difficulties, only there's been worse than some, but not all. As you know today is not about the state of the clubs themselves, either football of financial. Today is about the state of the pubs around the Stadium.

East Kilbride to Edinburgh by bus would be reasonably easy. There is a bus every 15 minutes from Buchanan Street, and very nice they are. The problem starts when you get into Edinburgh. Traffic is a nightmare. I believe the council thought that building tramlines would be a good idea. It seems about 50 years ago they had that thought. That's the time it seems to have taken, and as I write this there are still roadworks all over the place. Edinburgh is a crap city to get through anyway. But it is a good looking city. I've got to give it that.

The day started with a pleasant surprise. Our No. 18 bus passed us before we got to the stop, but the driver saw that we wanted on and waited for us. We thanked him getting on and off the bus, not just the traditional getting off bit.

There was a big queue of oldies (like me) waiting to get the 900 to Edinburgh. I'm beginning to think there are thousands of us oldies who just move about the country and don't actually live anywhere.

As we passed Edinburgh Airport we saw the huge Tram depot. There seems to be thousands of trams. I wonder if the council have forgotten to reduce the number of trams to match the huge reduction in the distance they will be travelling. It looks to me as if you could just fill the track with trams and the passengers could get in the back one, walk through them all and get out the front one. Or am I just being silly?

We got off at Haymarket, wandered through the road works, passed all the workmen doing nothing and got a number 25 bus the short distance to the ground. Tynecastle is an old fashioned and very atmospheric stadium build right up against tenements. It looks great.

Craig; In the past I have not been very complimentary when talking about Edinburgh but recently I think I may have changed my mind. Our latest wee travelling adventure saw us arrive in Edinburgh on a day when Hearts were playing Dundee United.

We got off the bus at Haymarket and tripped over all the nice shiny unused tram rails on our way round to Dalry Road.

John, the expedition leader, insisted he knew the way down to Tynecastle. He did but what he didn't know was the bus stop we were standing at was no longer in commission. I think the large red letters painted across the shelter proclaiming 'Bus stop not in use' could have confused the best of us. Eventually we found a bus willing to take us down to Gorgy Road.

We got off the bus just at Tynecastle Stadium and I'm amazed to tell you that the bus driver waved us across the street before driving on. Glasgow bus drivers take note! That is a thing called courtesy and people appreciate it.

John; Another great thing about a ground being in amongst tenements is that there are plenty of pubs round the ground. 'The Tynecastle' was the first we went into. This is a traditional bar full of supporters and has a great atmosphere. The service was good but because it was so busy we could not get to talk to the staff. We spoke to an old worthy, John Gaughan, who is 77 and still gets about and has a pint most days. I asked him if he was on his own and he told me that he was married only once, and only for five months. I said that I didn't want to pry but he said it was no bother. 'She ran away with my best man'. He didn't seem too bothered! He insisted on telling me that he used to live in Leith but that he didn't like the people there. To quote old John, 'you can tell a Leith man, but you canny tell him much'. I felt really sorry leaving old John, but he understood we had work to do.

Kathlleen & Colin before Robertson's got Jammed

We crossed the road and wandered into 'Robertsons'. The bar was almost empty and really Spartan looking. Although it looked pretty crap, it was a great bar and as it filled up we had a good time in it. The bar staff Kathelene and Colin were very good and great company. We were sorry when we had to leave. A good thing about this pub is that there were no big screens or jukeboxes blaring. We like pubs like that.

Craig; *The Tynecastle Bar was busier than we expected but we got served quickly. And most importantly it was a fairly decent pint of lager sold at a reasonable price.*

The place was too noisy to talk to any of the bar staff but they seemed to be coping very well with the crowds of thirsty football fans.

There were quite a few suits standing around the bar and from experience we knew that they were just biding their time until the hospitality suite opened round at the stadium.

John got talking to an old guy, also called John, who had a seemingly endless supply of equally old jokes. Given that the bar was so busy we decided to limit ourselves to only one pint of beer before making our way to our next pub.

Robertson's is only a hundred yards away from The Tynecastle Bar and we had heard that it tended to get very busy on match days.

Irene's cousin, Annabelle, an Edinburgh resident and staunch Hearts supporter, had phoned to say that Robertson's might be a wee bit rough for two old delicate souls like us. Govan? Auchinleck? Delicate?

To be honest hearing that it might be a wee bit rowdy just made Robertson's all the more interesting for us. Expecting a bit of a bear pit we slipped into the bar like a couple of arthritic ninjas.

It was practically empty but we both really liked it. The fact that whoever owned the place had spent practically nothing on its decor in the last 20 years only adds to its charm. Who doesn't appreciate a nice bit of vintage Formica? With all of the matt white painted wood panelling it looked like a licensed scout hut. The bar stools seemed to be made of wrought-iron, or something equally heavy, and would need a couple of hefty blokes just to shift. We reckoned that that was to stop, or at least slow down, the bar fighting. Anyone trying to use one of those things as a weapon is more likely to do himself some serious damage than any opponent.

The bar staff were first rate I would have to say. Kathleen chatted away with us and made us feel really welcome. I got the distinct impression that she wouldn't be long sorting out any rowdy fan daft enough to start getting stroppy in her bar.

We had just finished telling Kathleen how much we liked the spartan look of the place when she dropped a bombshell. Unfortunately it would seem that the pub is soon to be renovated and all of the character of the place will be dumped into a skip; sacrilege I say!

The pub started filling up with supporters and we decided to have another beer just to soak up the atmosphere.

I had been told about another bar close by which might be worth visiting. Its official name is the Athletic Arms but everyone just calls it Diggers.

When I asked her about Diggers she didn't seem too keen on it but it turned out that it was our apparent state of health that she was more concerned about. Without actually coming out and saying it she let us know that the pub was on a hill so steep that two old slightly sozzled authors might not make it to the top.

Just to be on the safe side we stopped for our sandwiches just before we began the ascent. Fortunately we survived the climb up Henderson Street and entered the pub. The noise was amazing. There must have been over 100 people in the place and all of them seemed to be shouting, but in a friendly fashion.

John; A friend of ours called Ian, one of the great editors of our time, had told Craig about a great bar just round the corner and up the hill from Tynecastle. It is called 'The Athletic Arms', although nobody calls it that. It's the 'Diggers' bar. And so it should be, for obvious reasons!

The bar was packed with Hearts fans and the atmosphere was brilliant. Although it was busy we got served right away each time we wanted a drink, which was often. We were really enjoying ourselves. The licensee Kevin McGee and his staff Maria, Sharon, Eric and Nicole were all brilliant and very good at their job.

We got into company with a great crown of young blokes. One of them, Ryan Jack (what a great name) was just back from Navy duty

303

and the drinks were flowing. They insisted on buying us god knows how many Dark Rums and the time just flew in. By the time they left us I was all for taking them up on their offer to take us to the game. Craig was more sensible, or sober, than me and pointed out that by the time the boys were ready to leave us it was almost half time. What a great time we had. Don't know if we should be carrying on like this at our age!

John and some big Diggers

Craig; *The Diggers has to be one of the best pubs I've ever been in. Everything about it was great apart from that hill of course. It's what a city pub should look like. Better still we met a great bunch of young guys who kept us laughing for ages.*

One of the lads was just back from a long deployment abroad in the navy. Being a traditionalist he insisted that his mates, and for some reason we were included in that group, all drink his health in dark rum. John, being a patriot, joined in enthusiastically. While I spent a lot of my time hiding glasses of rum behind one of the bar pillars. I have my suspicions that John found my hiding place as he got a fair bit more jolly than usual.

In our many visits to pubs during the writing of our books we have had our fair share of surprises but watching a group of football fans marching out of the pub doors while chanting our names really takes the biscuit. John became so emotional that he needed a large glass of black rum to calm himself down.

With the boys away to the match we turned our attention to the bar staff. Even when the place was packed the staff managed to keep things running smoothly. At no point did we have to wait more than a couple of minutes to be served. They also made time to chat to their customers.

The staff of The Diggers undertake to be the best

The beer was great and, considering where we were, was reasonably priced. I've no idea what the rum was like but certain persons couldn't get enough of it.

It is probably just as well that we didn't start our investigation into football pubs with a visit to Diggers. I think we would have been a bit disappointed to find that they were not all up to this standard.

The journey back to Glasgow passed in a flash as we both fell asleep. I had after all been doing a lot more walking than usual and John had rediscovered his love of black rum.

John; It was time to make our way home, and after thanking the great bar staff we staggered back down the hill singing sea shanties till our bus arrived to take us home. Slept all the way.

Now you would think that we would have had enough, but it was a Saturday evening and the sun was shining, so we had one in 'The Horse Shoe' in Glasgow before getting the train back to EK, walking into the village and having another couple in 'The Monty'. There's no stopping us. I had started the day with £25 in my pocked and ended up having to go to the hole in the wall, so about £35 was done in. When you think that it was all on drink and we got a few rounds bought for us by the British Navy, it was a hell of a day.

Pubs we visited:

Tynecastle Arms;

Robertson's;

Diggers;
(Athletic Arms)

How to get there by bus:

900 Glasgow/Edinburgh

Dundee United

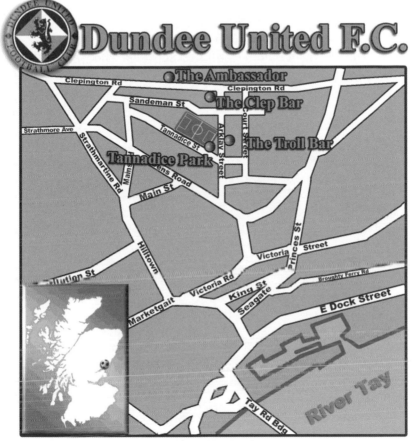

Tannadice Park
Ground opened - 1909

John; 'The Arabs', I like nicknames that are not obvious. I believe this one is something to do with the ground being covered in sand in the old days. If that's wrong, write to Craig.

Dundee is one of our favourite towns to visit, mainly because of 'The Bush Bar' near the bus station. I'm sure we will end up there today at some time.

This was our last of the 41 clubs we had set ourselves the Herculean task of visiting. I was very emotional as I walked down the path to collect Craig for the last time in this masterpiece.

I don't normally, or ever, shit myself after knocking on Craig's door. Today my knock was met with a noise like the hounds from hell being let loose. Irene and Craig were dog sitting for some crazy dog owned by one of Irene's kids. People should know better than to get a boxer. In I went to be set upon by some crazy hound. This was early morning for any favour. It's usually later in the evening before my bowels start getting the better, or worse, of me!

A great Glasgow word is 'sleber', and that sums up boxers. If you don't know what I'm talking about you have never been sleberred on; enough said.

Our usual trip on the number 18 into Glasgow was uneventful until we reached Glasgow Cross, when we heard the driver, or some official shouting from downstairs (we were upstairs) that there was a detour and if you wanted to go to Marks & Spencers in Argyle Street to get off here. No mention of anyone who wanted to go to Tannadice to get pissed. We stayed on the bus as it wandered along the Clyde and eventually abandoned ship at the bottom end of St. Enoch's Square. Who knows where the bus was going after that.

A ten to fifteen minute trek up Buchanan Street got us to the Bus Station just in time to get on the end of a huge queue already boarding the M9 Glasgow to Aberdeen bus that would take us to Dundee. Does that make any sense? Thankfully, it was one of these huge double deckers and we got seats no bother.

Craig; *The day of our final trip around Scotland's senior football grounds had arrived at last. To celebrate and start the day off with a laugh I set the dog on John when he arrived at my door bang on 9.05. Strangely only one of us thought that that was hilarious. Molly the largest boxer that I have ever seen played her part to perfection. John was covered in dog drool.*

We are getting used to the bus in the morning into Glasgow going in every direction but the one that it is supposed to. Today

308

there was no exception to that annoying trend. In a voice which couldn't carry much more than 10 feet the driver announced something about Marks and Spencer's. Half the passengers got up and left the bus. We assumed that yet again the bus would be taking a bit of a detour. When it eventually turned into a road barely wide enough for a wheelbarrow we decided it was time to take to our feet.

On the way up to the bus station we discovered the reason for our latest bus misadventure. The Great Scottish Fun Run was taking place in the city centre. We didn't think it was particularly funny. The bus up to Dundee was a bit of a nightmare. It was one of the new double deckers which seem to be built for very short people. There is more cabin space aboard a Ryanair plane. We were also treated to some improvised humour courtesy of a group of moronic mid 20 year old guys who behaved like spoiled foul mouthed schoolboys. You just can't beat public transport.

John; A shock awaited us when we got off the bus and walked the two minutes into our favourite watering hole in Dundee, 'The 'Bush Bar'. Harry, the owner, had leased the place to some woman. Nothing, and everything, had changed; a bit of drama there. We had a quick pint and left, with sadness. Would Dundee ever be the same? Time, and a few pints, would tell.

We wandered, heavy footed, along the road and got the number 22 up to Tannadice, at least that's where I asked the driver to take us, and he said ok. We got off the bus 10 minutes later miles away from the ground. We had, as usual snipped a map from Google and could work out where the ground was. The sun was shining and it was a lovely day as we wandered along some road looking for some bar Craig had seen on 'Street View' called 'The Centuary'. He took me up back streets and everything before I had a staggering non Google idea of asking a local. This done we found the pub, which we had passed twice already. It had changed its name to 'The Ambassador'.

It was a nice enough pub and the barmaid Kirsty, although rushed off her feet, was very nice and helpful. The bar is ok and handy for the ground.

Kirsty is less than impressed by John's patter

Craig; *When we arrived in Dundee we couldn't help but notice that there were an awful lot of police officers wandering around the streets. There was even a helicopter circling the city centre. I thought this was a bit over the top for the visit of a couple of hundred Killie supporters but John pointed out that they were from Ayrshire and therefore took a bit of watching.*

It turned out that there were two groups of people marching in Dundee that day. The Scottish Defence League and the Anti-Facist League, or whatever they call themselves, were planning a friendly exchange of views on the streets of the city.

Happily we managed to avoid both groups and we didn't waste any precious time waiting for them to jackboot their way along our bus route.

After a slight misunderstanding worthy of a Glaswegian bus driver we found the way to our first football pub of the day. The Ambassador, which really should have been the Centenary, on Cleppington Road may well have had a makeover on the outside but inside I doubt much has changed in the last 30 years. It's a wee bit grim but the barmaid, Kirsty, fair brightens the place up.

She was on her own behind the bar but managed to keep all of the thirsty patrons well stocked with beer.

I don't really think she believed us when we told her that we were writing a book. In fact I'm pretty sure she thought that John was just a bit of an old perv. It was an easy mistake to make.

The bar was gradually filling up with supporters, both Dundee United and Kilmarnock, but Kirsty still found time to talk to us. She told us that as far as she knew there wasn't a bar at the club which was open to the public, but she couldn't be sure as she didn't follow United.

That was enough to get John excited and so after a single pint we decided it might be a good idea to check out the stadium before it got too busy.

Adi's job looks secure

John; Customers in 'The Ambassador' had told us there was no bar inside the ground, but we felt we had to check it out as it was match day. Kilmarnock was the opposition today. After walking right round the ground we found the main entrance and came up against a giant of a security man. The two Vodkas I had already had made me decide to try and get into the ground, past this giant.

As usual my fears were unfounded. The giant was called Adi, a lovely big bloke who pointed us in the direction of the reception where Susan, another lovely person contacted Spencer Wallace, one of the guys

311

in charge of the place who was kind enough to give us his time. He passed us on to the Internal Events Manager Bill Wallace who took us into the bar and looked after us; a great guy. The people we met in Tannadice are a credit to the club.

Craig; The only indication that there might be something worth investigating at the park was the presence of a couple of large security blokes at a side gate. Actually only one of them was large, the other one was enormous.

I suppose when you are as big as Adi you don't have to try to be menacing. He was actually very nice and instead of telling us to move on he sent us in to plead our case with Susan the receptionist. She listened patiently as I stuttered out my explanation of what two old geezers with no apparent interest in football were doing trying to bluff their way into Dundee United's Supporters Club.

We get a good reception from Susan

Meanwhile John had wandered off to see if he could just sneak in. He was caught and escorted back to reception by a friendly official. The chap was probably used to taking care of elderly befuddled supporters.

Thanks mainly to Susan we were eventually allowed in to the club. Apparently it had been full but two people came out while we were standing at the desk.

312

The club itself was fairly standard. It was big, noisy and very busy. There was a whole team of servers behind the bar keeping the long queue moving.

The beer was good and the manager Bill Wallace's patter was very interesting. He has been involved in the bar trade for over 40 years and has therefor seen it all.

The time fairly flashed past and before we were ready for it last orders were called. That was our cue to find another bar where time was on our side.

John; Kick off time was approaching so the bar had to close and we had to visit another couple of pubs near the ground, so we said our goodbyes and wandered round the corner into the 'Troll Bar'. No idea how they got the name, it's not under a bridge or anything, although there were some ugly people leaving as we went in! Only kidding.

The 'Troll' is a really great bar and the owner Chris Airlie and the girls behind the bar Lisa Stewart and Tracy Beattie were great. We had planned to have a quick one but ended up staying for a good few and were sorry to leave. This bar was so good it could replace 'The Bush', a must to visit if you're in the UK.

Our last official bar we, or Craig to be honest, wanted to visit was called 'The Clep'. Dundee has some funny named pubs. The girls in the 'Troll' told us the 'Clep' was just up the road and along to the right, or was it left. Craig, against his better judgment followed my instructions and we walked right for 10 minutes before turning back, retracing our steps and finding the pub about 20 yards to the left of where we had been. If Craig had any breath left he would have turned the air blue.

In we went. Our first impression was of a slightly dark and old fashioned place, but what a brilliant bar it turned out to be. The owners Jim and Joyce Ferrie welcome supporters of both the Dundee clubs and made us feel very welcome. This is a family run bar and their nephew Matthew was behind the bar as well.

The place was full of great characters. Dick McTaggart's brother Henry, who is his double, was in the bar and is a great bloke. Another great local Tam even supplied us with the best Clootie Dumpling I have ever tasted, and I've had a few. This dumpling is made by Bruce Brimer in Brechin. The information you get in this book is staggering.

The 'Troll' and the 'Clep' are two of the best pubs we have visited and a must if you are going to support your team.

Craig; *The Troll Inn really doesn't look that great from the outside but it was within spitting distance of the football ground. So in we went.*

I knew immediately that we were going to like this bar. It may well look as if it is in need of a major makeover but with any luck that will never happen. There is no point tampering with perfection!

According to John the only thing that could be added to make it better would be coat hooks on the bar. The serious beer drinker will always take his jacket off before getting stuck into several pints of the frothy stuff.

John decided that the owner of The Troll, Chris Airlie, needed to be told about the benefits of coat hooks and launched into a ten minute lecture on the subject.

Lisa, Chris & Tracy

In an act of desperation Chris bought us both a drink, obviously hoping that John might stop talking long enough to finish it.

The beer was good, especially the free one, and the service was excellent. The girls behind the bar were a great laugh and made our stay very enjoyable. In fact I could quite easily have finished our last journey right there.

But I just had to find out what the Clep Bar was like. I had found it on the internet and liked the look of it. Besides, it was on our bus route.

John totally arsed up the detailed directions we had been given by the girls in The Troll. As you can imagine he was severely verbally abused for his duff navigating efforts.

Once I took over directional control things got much better. We wandered into The Clep a few minutes later. What a great pub. It was clean, tidy and friendly. Added to that, the beer was pretty good as well.

Jim, Joyce and Matthew run a great family bar

Jim Ferrie, the owner, told me that his pub often had some very famous customers dropping in. One of my favourite actors Brian Cox has been known to knock back the occasional gin and tonic, or whatever Hollywood legends are drinking these days.

He wasn't there that day so he missed out on getting a slice of the best clootie dumpling I have ever tasted. All the more for us then!

We managed a couple more drinks and many more laughs with Jim, his wife Joyce and of course the pub regulars before it was time to wind up our last trip of the year.

Just to round off a near perfect day I had a great journey back to Glasgow. John had knocked back just enough of his sleepy medicine to keep him quiet all the way home.

John; The journey home was the quickest on record. I slept the whole way. Craig had to waken me as we came into Buchanan Street Bus Station.

The sleep refreshed me and after the Train journey back to EK, we had a drink in the 'Monty' before going home for the last time in this epic encyclopedic journal.

On a more mundane note, I only spent about £25. No idea how I ended up so drunk, I think people were buying rounds for us. It's a life and somebody's got to do it. Goodbye.

Pubs we visited:

The Ambassador;

Dundee Utd. Club;

Troll Inn;

The Clep Bar;

How to get there by bus:

M9 Glasgow to Dundee
No 22 from Commercial St.
to Ground

Livingston

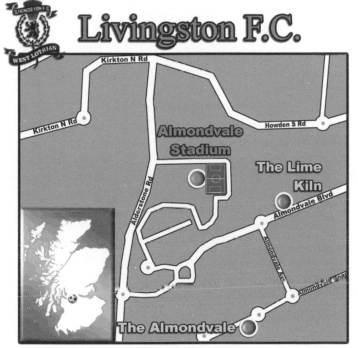

Almondvale Stadium
Ground opened - 1995

Craig; Livingston FC play their football at Almondvale Stadium and although it was the close season I had the opportunity to check out their stadium in early June.

For reasons which will become apparent I did not manage to check out the town's other pubs. The transport arrangements for today's trip were a bit unusual as well. Come to think about it everything about this trip was different. For a start there was no John to annoy me with his daft jokes or even dafter songs. And of course there was no bus travel, free or otherwise. The main reason for my visit to Almondvale Stadium was to watch the mighty Auchinleck Talbot take on Linlithgow Rose in the final of the Scottish Junior cup.

John had managed, yet again, to avoid coming to watch Talbot play in the final. I actually think that he is feart some of 'the boys'

317

remember that he said some nasty things about Auchinleck in our first book.

The day started off in traditional fashion. Irene drove me down to Glasgow where I had a few bottles of beer and a couple of hot pies at my pal Tam's place. We were joined, as usual, by Eugene, another pal and former resident of my old home town. I say traditional because, as anyone who has even a passing interest in Junior football will know, 'The Bot' are a bit of a permanent fixture at cup finals.

After our refreshments Deirdre, Tam's wife, kindly drove us all to Livingston. Despite only having three quarters of an hour before kick-off we managed to circle around the stadium until we found the bar.

Showing a fine flair for names this little pub has been called 'The Stadium Bar'. Let's hope they didn't pay their P.R. consultants too much to come up with that clever piece of wordage.

The bar itself is really quite good. It even looks like a real pub. I was surprised to find that the beer was also quite passable. The one drawback to drinking in the Stadium Bar was their use of plastic glasses. I really hate them. Try picking them up too quickly and half your pint suddenly slops down the front of your shirt.

We were served in good time and the young girl who did the serving did it very pleasantly. Price wise the bar was fairly reasonable, charging about the same as a regular pub.

We were told that the bar would shut quite suddenly and so we made sure we finished our drinks a good fifteen minutes before kick-off. I managed to ask a local about other bars nearby. The guy said there were a couple within walking distance but he wasn't too impressed by either.

As a footnote I feel I should point out that the result of the football match was as predicted. We crushed Linlithgow by one goal to nil.

How to get there by bus:

900 City Link Glasgow/Edinburgh
change at Harthill services
walk to Main St Harthill
No.701 Blue Bus to Livingston

318

Craig: *Readers might have noticed that one team seems to be missing from our list of senior Scottish League teams.*

Berwick Rangers has been missed out for one very good reason. John refused to go down to Berwick-upon-Tweed.

He claims that because Shielfield Park is in England we cannot be expected to cross the border to check it out.

However I happen to know the real reason. It is quite simple really. John was more than a little put out last year when he found out that his bus pass doesn't work in England.

So it is apologies to all of 'The Borderers' and of course the publicans of Berwick-upon-Tweed.